Law, Morality,
and the Relations of States

Law, Morality, *and the* Relations of States

Terry Nardin

Princeton University Press
Princeton, New Jersey

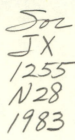

Copyright © 1983 by Princeton University Press
Published by Princeton University Press,
41 William Street, Princeton, New Jersey 08540
In the United Kingdom: Princeton University Press,
Guildford, Surrey

All Rights Reserved
Library of Congress Cataloging in Publication Data
will be found on the last printed page of this book
This book has been composed in Linotron Caledonia

ISBN 0-691-07663-4 (cloth)
10155-8 (limited paperback edition)

Clothbound editions of Princeton University Press books
are printed on acid-free paper, and binding materials
are chosen for strength and durability
Paperbacks, although satisfactory for personal collections,
are not usually suitable for library rebinding

Printed in the United States of America by
Princeton University Press
Princeton, New Jersey

i

For Jane

Contents

Preface

MY AIM in this book is to consider the ideas of law, morality, and society as they pertain to the relations of states. These ideas are central and not, as many hold, peripheral to the study of international relations. I want to defend the view that the practices of international law and international morality constitute the indispensable foundation of all durable international association. To the extent that the relations of states achieve a significant degree of permanence, rising above the level of mere episodes in the separate histories of isolated political communities, they must be understood as taking place on the basis of common, authoritative practices and rules. And this, I shall argue, means that they must be understood as occurring within a world of legal and moral ideas.

Two topics often treated by theorists of international relations are also considered here. One is whether legal and moral order can exist at all in an international system lacking centralized institutions for making and applying law and characterized by deep cultural and ideological differences. The other is the tension between what might be labeled "state-centric" and "cosmopolitan" conceptions of international society, law, and morality—an old topic recently revived in controversies over human rights and international distributive justice. But my main concern is with an argument that has not been adequately considered in connection with international relations, and this is that morality and law are best understood as authoritative practices constraining the pursuit of different purposes rather than as instruments for the joint pursuit of shared purposes. International morality and international law are authoritative practices that have evolved in the course of

ix

relations among separate political communities, practices by which international conduct is to be guided and judged. It is in terms of these practices that those who have different values, interests, and beliefs, and who may be engaged in the pursuit of different and sometimes incompatible purposes, can coexist with one another. It seems to me that the distinction between what I have chosen to identify as the "practical" and "purposive" conceptions of international society is at least as illuminating and important as any of the more familiar distinctions that have occupied the attention of theorists of international relations. This book is largely an exploration of that distinction and its implications.

The main distinction is developed in the introductory chapter. Part One is concerned with the idea of international society, and in particular with the gradual emergence of the idea of the society of states as a kind of practical association. It considers how the view that international law is an institution specific to the society of states developed from an earlier understanding of the law of nations as a branch of natural law, and explores the historical fortunes of the practical conception of international law in the unfolding of nineteenth- and twentieth-century international politics. Part Two contains an analysis of the authoritative common practices and rules of international society, where these are understood as comprising a system of positive law. And Part Three examines these practices and rules in their moral aspect, that is, as a set of ideas handed down within an independent moral tradition or traditions. I also attempt to trace some of the implications of the practice/purpose distinction for the topics of international justice, human rights, and the just war. The question whether the view of international law and international morality I defend has any relevance to an ideologically and culturally diverse world is considered in the concluding chapter.

The approach adopted here differs from that of many works of international relations theory. It is perhaps best described as philosophical, in the sense of an examination of the as-

sumptions underlying particular ways of speaking and thinking. This is not a work of science—of "empirical theory," to
use a common if misleading expression. But neither is it a
work of "normative theory," if by that is meant an inquiry
aimed at justifying or recommending conduct. I don't want
to deny the possibility or significance of either scientific or
normative inquiries in the field of international relations. My
own engagement, however, is with a mode of inquiry that
would appear to be excluded by the current empirical/norm-
ative dichotomy. To theorize about morality and law, I would
argue, is above all to be concerned with understanding the
character and presuppositions of moral and legal conduct and
argument. It is to engage in an activity distinct from the making of moral or legal judgments. The concerns of the theorist
are not to be confused with those of the moralist, lawyer,
citizen, or statesman. This is not to say that theory and action
are unrelated, for they are indeed related in many ways. Nor
is it to claim that the theorist can avoid making normative
judgments. It is simply to hold that the job of the theorist,
qua theorist, is not to prescribe but to interpret and explain.
The present study is intended largely as a work of theory in
this sense.

All who are familiar with the work of Michael Oakeshott
will recognize the extent to which I have relied upon his ideas,
especially those developed in *On Human Conduct*. Reading
this book upon its publication in 1975 was the catalyst that
transformed my reflections on the law of nations into an argument by confirming a pattern that I vaguely discerned, but
could not articulate, in the materials with which I was working. From Oakeshott I have also learned much about what it
means to engage in political theorizing. I am equally indebted
to my colleague and friend Richard B. Friedman, who helped
me often with this project and from whose intellectual guidance I have benefited for many years.

For their early help and encouragement I want to thank
Michael Walzer, Richard A. Falk, David A. Hollinger, and
the late Richard R. Baxter. I owe thanks as well to many

others for their criticism and suggestions: to Hatem El-Gabri, Gunnar Pálsson, and Gehad Auda, who read some of the chapters in Part One; to Virginia A. Leary, who commented on an early draft of the central chapters on international law; to Charles R. Beitz and Harold Guetzkow, who criticized some of the material on justice; to John Charvet, Barrie Paskins, Michael Donelan, and other members of the 1981-82 seminar on international relations theory at the London School of Economics and Political Science, who heard and responded to a presentation of my main argument; and to Joseph V. Guerinot, who was kind enough to read and comment on the penultimate draft. I am especially grateful to Jerome Slater for the criticism, advice, and companionship he provided throughout the course of my work on this book. The final version owes much to the suggestions of Michael Barkun, R. J. Vincent, and Richard H. Ullman, who read the manuscript for Princeton University Press.

A Humanities Fellowship from the Rockefeller Foundation made it possible for me to write most of the book during the 1978-79 academic year. Additional support came from the State University of New York through its University Awards Program. I am also indebted to the University of Wisconsin in Milwaukee for making the resources of its library, particularly its interlibrary loan department, available to me during the course of my research, and to my own university in Buffalo for granting several indispensable leaves of absence. For preparing the manuscript with unusual care I want to thank Shirley Dement. Tania Modleski, Karin Benson, and my daughter Rachel were generous in helping me through various difficulties during the last stages of my work on the manuscript.

My greatest debt is to my wife, to whom I dedicate this work with gratitude and affection.

Law, Morality
and the Relations of States

CHAPTER 1

Introduction: Two Modes of International Association

BECAUSE IT IS generally acknowledged that international relations are shaped by the pursuit of common as well as conflicting interests, it strikes us as a mere truism to be told that
"there is cooperation in international affairs as well as conflict," and therefore that there exists an international society
which, like any society, is constituted by "a number of individuals joined in a system of relationships for certain common
purposes."[1] What we have here, however, is not a truism at
all but a particular theory of international association. According to this theory the basis of international association is the
joint pursuit of shared ends, and an international society can
be said to exist only to the extent that there is cooperation in
this pursuit. Because it understands all association among states
to be association for shared purposes, it will be convenient to
refer to this conception of international association as "the
purposive conception."

As this brief characterization implies, the purposive conception constitutes a theory of all human association and not
only of relations among states. It is also a theory so deeply
embedded in how we think about human affairs that we often
find it difficult to think in other than purposive terms. So we
should look more closely at the purposive conception in general before attempting to consider either its application to
international relations or the existence of alternatives.

The purposive conception is closely tied to common sense.
When we wish to know what some unidentified thing is, we

---

[1] Wight, *Power Politics*, p. 105.

3

often inquire into its use or purpose. Or we may give an account of an organization or institution in terms of what we take to be its aims, even though we recognize that our account simplifies a more complex reality. Thus, the character of a seminary is best explained by referring to its primary purpose, which is to train future members of the clergy; a political party exists to secure the election of its candidates to office; a library is an organization that provides books for its subscribers. It is clear that many people (including some distinguished political theorists) have understood the state in something like these terms: that is, as an enterprise whose purpose is the promotion of the common interests of its members. It is shared aims, however defined, that provide the rationale for the existence of the organization and justify whatever rules it may impose on those associated with it. To have identified an organization in terms of its purposes is thus to have said a good deal about it.

The tendency to think in purposive terms disposes us to see human arrangements and institutions as springing from transactions grounded in shared values and aims. Some of these transactions are ephemeral, mere bargains struck between individuals who then proceed along their separate paths. Others result in the foundation of more lasting relationships, in the establishment of families, corporations, universities, or churches. In each case, however, the key to the relationship is to be found in the benefits anticipated from exchange or from more enduring cooperative endeavor. To understand human beings as related on the basis of shared purposes is to see them as united above all else by an interest in what association can provide: by wants satisfied, values realized, beliefs reaffirmed, interests protected, goals achieved. What might be called "purposive association" consists of relations among those who get together to further particular ends and who, if they adopt rules, adopt them as instruments of that pursuit.[2]

[2] Michael Oakeshott refers to relationship in terms of common purposes as "enterprise association" (*On Human Conduct*, pp. 114-118, 157-158, 315-

Interpreted according to the purposive conception, international society appears to be an association of states—or, where international society is understood in cosmopolitan terms, of individuals linked across national boundaries by shared beliefs, values, or interests—joined in a cooperative venture to promote common ends. Many relations among states and their inhabitants do indeed exist for the sake of furthering certain shared purposes: to encourage trade, promote economic development, or propagate particular religious or political doctrines. And many kinds of organizations are established to further such ends. But it would be a mistake to regard all international relations as defined and governed by the pursuit of shared purposes. I want to argue that there is another mode of relationship that is more fundamental because it exists among those pursuing divergent as well as shared purposes. Durable relations among adversaries presuppose a framework of common practices and rules capable of providing some unifying bond where shared purposes are lacking. Such practices are embedded in the usages of diplomacy, in customary international law, and in certain moral traditions. These practices are extremely important for international relations of any regular, enduring sort for they not only regulate such relations but define and facilitate them. Specifically, by prescribing restraint, toleration, and mutual accommodation according to authoritative common standards of international conduct, they make it possible for states pursuing different ends to coexist. And they provide procedures on the basis of which particular transactions and purposive cooperation can be arranged.

---

317) and once (on p. 313) as "purposive association." The implications of understanding the state itself as an association of this kind are explored by Oakeshott in an extended discussion of the idea of the modern European state (pp. 185-326). The main distinction on which the following discussion relies—between "purposive" and "practical" association—derives from and is most closely related to Oakeshott's distinction between "enterprise" and "civil" association. (*On Human Conduct*, pp. 112-122.) The reader should be warned, however, that there are significant differences between Oakeshott's distinction and my own version of it. The precise relationship between the two will be indicated as the discussion proceeds.

Because it regards all association as purposive association, the purposive conception of international society is essentially an incoherent one. We can understand this better by considering why the purposive conception is deficient as an independent account of any form of association, although in the case of organizations that exist to pursue shared purposes this deficiency is not immediately apparent.

In focusing on the transactions that people undertake in order to realize their joint and separate purposes we sometimes forget that such transactions presuppose other more enduring relationships, some of which are themselves neither transactions nor the outcome of transactions but constitute the circumstances within which transactions take place and provide the rules on the basis of which they can be carried on. It is these relationships and rules that we most often have in mind when we speak of "practices." The ritual of shaking hands through which many of us customarily confirm our mutual acceptance of the terms of a bargain, and the more elaborate procedures through which international treaties are solemnized, are practices in this sense. So are languages, ceremonies, games, judicial procedures, military regulations, and diplomatic protocol. All human association presupposes practices in terms of which those involved are related to one another. We must therefore look more closely at the idea of a practice.

As ordinarily used the word "practice" is ambiguous, referring in some contexts to conduct and in others to standards of conduct. In the present context, it is the latter sense that is intended. A practice is a set of considerations to be taken into account in deciding and acting, and in evaluating decisions and actions. Practices therefore always reflect an ideal conception of the activities out of which they grow and of the agents engaged in them: the virtuoso performance, the just war, the responsible parent, the "perfect ambassador."[3]

[3] On the last, see Mattingly, *Renaissance Diplomacy*, ch. 22. The argument that "rules need not be practiced in order to be rules" and that "the word 'rule' does not mean 'a practice' " (Raz, *Practical Reasons and Norms*, pp. 53, 55) presupposes that to speak of "practices" is to generalize about

Practices can be made, that is, deliberately devised and instituted, like the rules of a newly invented game, or they may emerge from habit and usage, like the principles of a cuisine handed down from one generation of cooks to the next. Every practice, however, has a history, because every practice is continuously modified and reconstituted in the actions of those who interpret and apply the usages, procedures, instructions, and rules of which it is composed. All practices are therefore more or less liable to change, those newly instituted as much as those that have acquired the character of a tradition. Some practices, like gardening or storytelling, are relatively open, allowing their practitioners considerable latitude with respect to the manner in which they participate in them. Others, like the practices of legislating, playing tournament chess, or performing a mass, may be quite rigorously defined and institutionalized. Participation in such practices ordinarily requires conformity to an elaborate set of rules presided over by appointed or self-appointed referees, judges, critics, and custodians. And because particular actions always fall within the jurisdiction of more than one practice, they can be described in a number of different ways.

As the examples of practices I have given suggest, a practice does not prescribe particular purposes to be pursued by those whose conduct it governs, but it may guide or limit their pursuit. A practice is not itself a source of goals but rather a set of directions for or constraints on the pursuit of goals already chosen. Like the hedges to which Hobbes likened the laws,[4] practices keep travelers on the roads but do not prescribe their destinations. The practice of making treaties, for example, specifies the forms and procedures to be

---

conduct. Similarly, when international lawyers speak of "state practice" they mean the actual conduct of the states and not that which is believed to be lawful. It is, on the other hand, the idea of a standard of conduct that underlies Oakeshott's definition of a practice as "a set of considerations, manners, uses, observances, customs, standards, canons, maxims, principles, rules, and offices specifying useful procedures or denoting obligations or duties. . . ." (*On Human Conduct*, p. 55.)

[4] *Leviathan*, ch. 30.

observed in reaching international agreements and in handling the problems of interpretation and application that may arise with respect to them. But it does not impose upon states any duty to make or avoid making treaties, nor does it specify, except indirectly, anything concerning the purposes for which treaties should be made. If there are purposes served by the practice of making treaties itself, they are of a very different character from those for which states may conclude particular treaties. I shall say more about this in a moment. The main point to be noticed at this stage, however, is that the essence of any practice is to be found in the conditions it recommends or imposes on the conduct of agents pursuing self-chosen purposes.

Practices may be distinguished according to whether the conditions they prescribe are those useful for achieving a given end or those proper to be observed in acting, regardless of one's end. Practices of the first sort are prudential or instrumental: they consist of rules, maxims, precepts, and procedures whose rationale is to be found in the contribution their observance makes to the pursuit of a particular goal. Practices of the second sort are formal or authoritative, and consist of rules, principles, ceremonies, manners, and procedures that all who fall within their jurisdiction are supposed to observe, regardless of whether such observance is favorable or unfavorable to the pursuit of particular ends. While instrumental practices can be thought of as providing directions to facilitate the pursuit of particular purposes, authoritative practices are more properly regarded as limiting or constraining that pursuit.[5]

[5] Although this account of "practices" draws heavily on that provided by Oakeshott in *On Human Conduct*, pp. 55-58, I have preferred to speak of authoritative practices, at least, as imposing "limits" or "constraints" on conduct to his milder characterization of practices as adverbially qualifying the manner in which actions are performed. For a discussion of certain alleged difficulties in Oakeshott's formulation, see Flathman, *Practice of Political Authority*, pp. 53-61. There are many different kinds of authoritative practice, but in this book I am concerned primarily with the practices of morality and of law and with the different kinds of practical association they define.

8

The distinction between "instrumental" and "authoritative" practices is of fundamental importance, and one must be very careful to distinguish association governed by the requirements of an instrumental practice from association in terms of the considerations embodied in an authoritative practice. Those who are associated in a cooperative enterprise to promote shared values, beliefs, or interests are united by their convergent desires for the realization of a certain outcome that constitutes the good they have come together to obtain. Association of this kind is what earlier I identified as "purposive association." The label is appropriate because even though practices are involved in purposive association, it is the shared purposes for the sake of which the associates are joined, and not the practices they may have adopted for the promotion of those shared purposes, that account for the relationship. Those who come together for the sake of promoting a candidate for office or producing a play may give themselves rules. But it is the goal of winning the election or putting on a successful performance, and not the rules through which they seek to implement that goal, that provides the reason for their association.

Association on the basis of an authoritative practice, on the other hand, is appropriately called "practical association," because in this case the associates are related in terms of constraints that all are expected to observe whatever their individual purposes may be. Often there is no shared purpose uniting those whose conduct is governed by an authoritative practice such as a morality or a system of laws, and in such cases there is no basis of association other than these common constraints. Practical association is a relationship among those who are engaged in the pursuit of different and possibly incompatible purposes, and who are associated with one another, if at all, only in respecting certain restrictions on how each may pursue his own purposes. It is not a common goal but the authority of the common constraints embodied in the election laws and in the ethics of political competition that govern the relationship between those backing different candidates for office.[6]

Purposive and practical association can therefore be distinguished according to the different kinds of authority characteristic of each. In purposive association the authority of the rules governing the relations among the associates is derived from the shared purposes that the association exists to promote. It is the pursuit of these shared purposes that provides the rationale for the rules through which the associates seek to promote the common end. Rules that are not a means to this end are at best pointless and at worst an obstacle to be overcome. The purposive conception of authority is thus an instrumentalist one, for the rules of purposive association are justified only insofar as they serve the ends that are the real basis of association. They are recognized as having authority because they are instrumental to the realization of these ends, which is to say that if they can be shown to be irrelevant or counterproductive their claim to be acknowledged as authoritative is undermined. It follows that the obligation to defer to the rules depends, ultimately, on their utility in the common pursuit. And when the rules need to be revised, the

---

[6] In this book the word "practical" means participation in or subscription to an authoritative practice. It should be noticed that this usage differs both from that favored by Oakeshott, who defines "practical" as meaning participation in or subscription to instrumental as well as to authoritative practices (*On Human Conduct*, p. 57), and ordinary usage, which tends to make "practical" a synonym for "useful" or "instrumental." The purposive/practical distinction should not be confused with others that superficially resemble it, such as Bertrand de Jouvenel's distinction between the two forms of human association he calls "the Act-together" and "the Live-together" ("Pure Politics Revisited," pp. 427-428; see also *Sovereignty*, pp. 33-34 and 40-41), or F. A. Hayek's distinction between artifical and spontaneous social orders (*Law, Liberty, and Legislation*, vol. 1, ch. 2). People "act together" or organize to create and sustain systems of mutual constraint as well as to pursue shared purposes, and they must "live together" or settle disputes in the pursuit of shared purposes as well as in the clash of conflicting purposes. And they may be associated both in the pursuit of shared purposes and in terms of respect for common practices either spontaneously or by agreement.

relevant considerations will concern the proper relation between these rules and the purposes they are thought to serve.

In purposive association it is the existence of shared purposes that provides the reason for particular acts, but practical association presupposes no such shared purposes. In practical association the reasons for acting are derived from the
standards of excellence or the rules of duty that constitute a
practice. The reasons for action provided by an authoritative
practice are therefore of a different order from those derived
from individual or collective goals. Where conduct in a particular situation is governed by authoritative rules, other considerations are ordinarily excluded as reasons for acting contrary to the rule. Authoritative rules, in other words, provide
"exclusionary reasons" for acting—reasons to refrain from acting for other, nonauthoritative, reasons.[7] The considerations
embodied in authoritative practices override other sorts of
considerations. This is what is meant by calling them "authoritative."[8]

In practical association, then, the authority of the standards
or rules governing relations among the associates is independent of the particular ends sought by each. Indeed, there
is no reason to assume that those who are related through
participation in an authoritative practice such as a language,
a morality, or a body of laws either have or ought to have any
shared purpose to be pursued through their relationship. While
in purposive association the authority of the common rules is
secondary and derivative, in practical association it is primary
and constitutes the basis of association.

[7] Raz, *Practical Reason and Norms*, p. 39.

[8] For the sake of simplicity I have confined the discussion of authority in
the text to authority over conduct, excluding any explicit mention of authority over belief. But authoritative practices can provide reasons for judging
and believing, as well as for deciding and acting. Thus we can speak of the
authority of standards of judgment or taste as well as of conduct. On the
distinction between authority in the realms of belief and action, see Friedman, "On the Concept of Authority in Political Philosophy," pp. 122-124 and
139-146. The argument that authoritative practices are possible only where
there exist authoritative shared beliefs is considered in Chapter 12, below.

Nothing that I have said so far should be construed as implying that purposive and practical association are mutually exclusive. Those who are associated in the pursuit of some shared purpose may find that their conduct falls under the jurisdiction of certain authoritative rules constraining that pursuit, as well as of rules instrumental to it. And practical association always involves the pursuit of purposes by those whose conduct it governs. All action involves the pursuit of some end and not merely respect for the constraints of a practice. One can act lawfully or morally only in doing particular things, on particular occasions, for particular ends.

At this point it may be objected that the attempt to distinguish purposive and practical association fails, because to act in a manner prescribed by an authoritative practice—for example, to act lawfully or morally—is necessarily to seek or to promote the goods of legality or morality. According to this objection, justice, civil liberty, individual rights, and other essentially legal or moral values are themselves substantive ends to be secured, like any other end, by setting up rules instrumental to their pursuit and realization. Therefore so-called practical association is merely a kind of purposive association.

The purposes of practical association, however, are of an altogether different order from those served by purposive association. There exists a fundamental distinction between the values internal to the moral life and the rule of law and those served by cooperation aimed at securing ends such as wealth, status, power, or the propagation of particular religious or ideological values and beliefs. The latter are ends that can be pursued by a variety of methods. Their pursuit is not intrinsically linked to any particular set of practices. The values of practical association, in contrast, are those appropriate to the relations among persons who are not necessarily engaged in any common pursuit but who nevertheless have to get along with one another. They are the very essence of a way of life based on mutual restraint and toleration of diversity.

Values such as legality, morality, and justice are therefore best regarded not as ends to be produced as an outcome of collective action but as values embodied in the constraints governing all action, values that can only be realized by acting within those constraints. A just person, strictly speaking, is not one who acts to promote "good ends," but rather one who respects certain limits defined by morality and law in pursuing particular ends. Similarly, civil rights exist only insofar as certain fundamental constraints—such as those guaranteeing freedom of association or prohibiting arbitrary arrest—are recognized and respected. Even peace is better regarded as a constraint than as a purpose, for to respect the value of peace is not to achieve as an end the avoidance of all uses of force. It is rather to act on the principle that force is to be used only in authorized ways—to defend threatened rights, for example, or to uphold the law—and to do so in a manner that will restore regular and amicable relations afterward.[9]

[9] This interpretation of the ideas of justice, rights, and peace is defended at length in Chapters 10 and 11, below. The distinction between two categorically distinct kinds of end or *telos* goes back at least as far as the Greek distinction between *praxis* and *poiesis*. See Aristotle, *Nichomachean Ethics*, VI, 4-5. A number of sociologists have used the distinction between substantive goods and immanent values to define different types of human action and association; the most familiar of these typologies, however, correspond only roughly to the distinction between purposive and practical association. Tönnies, for example, distinguishes between action motivated by what he calls *Wesenwille* or "essential will," which involves the affirmation of a practice or association for its own sake, and action motivated by *Kürwille* or "arbitrary will," which involves the affirmation of an activity or association because of an end or purpose extraneous to it. (*On Sociology*, p. 65; see also *Community and Society*, p. 247.) Tönnies then uses this distinction to define two distinct modes of association: *Gemeinschaft*, which is based upon a consensus of essential wills and is typically expressed in folkways, mores, and traditional religion; and *Gesellschaft*, a mode of association based on self-conscious agreement among those pursuing their own private ends, hence a product of arbitrary will, and expressed in contract, legislation, and public opinion. (*Community and Society*, p. 223.) *Gemeinschaft* is characteristic of traditional society and of traditional forms such as the family, *Gesellschaft* of modern or individualist society and of modern institutions such as the corporation or voluntary association. Max Weber, following Tönnies, distin-

To summarize: purposive and practical association can be distinguished both according to the authority of their rules and the kinds of end or good they make possible. Purposive association is a relationship among those who cooperate for the purpose of securing certain shared beliefs, values, and interests, who adopt certain practices as a means to that end, and who regard such practices as worthy of respect only to the extent that they are useful instruments of the common purpose. Practical association, in contrast, unites those engaged in the pursuit of different and sometimes incompatible ends through their recognition of the worth of those ways of life constituted by the authoritative practices that apply to them as moral agents or as members of a political community. The classic maxim "Let justice be done though the heavens fall" is simply a hyperbolic way of expressing the outlook embodied in the conception of morality and law as essentially constraint-oriented (practical) rather than end-oriented (purposive).

I suggested earlier that international society could not be regarded as a kind of purposive association. The preceding account of practices helps us to see why this is so. The pursuit of shared purposes presupposes the availability of procedures according to which the agreement to cooperate in a common pursuit can be made. This can be seen clearly in the case of contracts, which could not be concluded were it not for the prior existence of a more basic set of rules defining their char-

---

guishes between *wertrational* or "value rational" and *zweckrational* or "instrumentally rational" social action (*Economy and Society*, pp. 24-26), and between "communal" relationships, which are based on a subjective feeling of belonging together, and "associative" relationships derived from rationally motivated agreement and the adjustment of interests (pp. 40-41). For Weber as well as Tönnies, "associative" relationships are both instrumental and conventional (that is, deliberately instituted), whereas "communal" relationships are typically noninstrumental and based on shared beliefs and values. There is no reason to assume, however, that all deliberately instituted arrangements must be instrumental, or that participation in the authoritative common practices of morality and law is only possible where there is unity of beliefs and values.

acter and prescribing the procedures for making them. More complex forms of agreement, such as those setting up organizations with various kinds of powers likewise presuppose the prior existence of practices and procedures within which the creation of the organization can proceed. Legislation presupposes the existence of constitutional rules specifying the identity and scope of the legislative body and conferring on it the power to legislate. And the making of treaties and setting up of international organizations presupposes the existence of rules and procedures not all of which can themselves be the product of treaties or collective decisions. Who shall be recognized as having the power to represent each of the parties in an international transaction, and how is their acceptance of its outcome to be authoritatively indicated? How shall disputes over the terms of an agreement expressed in language that is inevitably ambiguous be resolved? These are questions that arise with respect to any international transaction and that must be resolved by reference to existing practices as these are embodied in the customs and usages of international law and diplomacy.[10]

Where international society is identified as an association of states in terms of authoritative common practices, we may speak of "the practical conception" of international society. It is possible to identify different versions of this conception, but all share the premise that it is common practices and not shared purposes that provide the terms of international association. International society, according to the practical conception, is constituted by the forms and procedures that states are obligated to observe in their transactions with one an-

---

[10] The concept of an authoritative practice can be seen as including what H.L.A. Hart has called "secondary rules" providing for the identification, alteration, and application of other, or "primary," rules within a legal system. (*Concept of Law,* ch. 5.) It does not follow, however, that all authoritative practices are "secondary" in Hart's sense, or that the rules of purposive association are "primary." The reader who equates Oakeshott's distinction with Hart's will go badly astray. Hart's ideas and their signficance for the present inquiry are discussed in Chapter 7, below.

other. To understand international society as an association of states in terms of common rules is not to deny that states often cooperate to promote shared purposes or that their desire to realize these purposes is an important factor in motivating them to observe existing forms and usages. It is simply to notice that, when states do cooperate, they do so within an existing framework of practices and procedures, at least some of which have not been deliberately instituted. International society is thus something more than the sum of the transactions of its members; it cannot be defined apart from the practices that states use (and misuse) in their dealings with one another and that limit or constrain those dealings.

The practical conception of international society is the result of an attempt, coextensive with the evolution of the modern states system, to interpret the relations of states according to an analogy with the relations of persons in civil society. This is possible only where the civil relationship is itself understood in practical rather than purposive terms. The practical conception of the modern state, as it has been explored by thinkers such as Hobbes, Hegel, Kelsen, and Oakeshott, understands it to be a union of citizens under a common law. The identity of the state is located in that union and not in the particular substantive values, desires, interests, or purposes that its members may happen to share. This conception of the state has often been overshadowed by other ideas, such as the notion that a political community is a family presided over by a patriarch to whom his "children" owe filial obedience, or that it is a scheme of social cooperation whose participants have a right to a fair share of the benefits it is able to procure. From the standpoint of the practical conception, however, the state is a "commonwealth" or "civil society" understood as an association of individuals united, despite all other differences, in being subject to the same body of laws.[11]

[11] If Oakeshott is correct, something like the distinction with which we are both concerned can be identified in the political thought of Aristotle, Hobbes, and Hegel, among others. (*On Human Conduct*, pp. 109-110, 251-263.) The

16

One of the critical insights of this understanding of political society has been the perception that association on the basis of common laws is most important where there exists little agreement on ends and therefore few shared purposes through which individuals might be united. In such circumstances the basis of association must be found in the rules and procedures observed by individuals pursuing different purposes. The relationship of citizens to one another, where this understanding prevails, is thus ultimately formal rather than substantive, procedural rather than purposive. The idea of the state as a form of practical association is that of citizens living together according to recognized rules constraining the pursuit of individual and collective ends.

It is sometimes said that a state or political community is an association that exists to promote a certain end, variously identified as "the common good," "the public interest," or "the general welfare." Consequently it might be argued that the state must be regarded as a form of purposive association whose laws are justified to the extent that they do in fact promote this end. But there is no reason to suppose that the members of a political community are necessarily united by any such shared purpose. Where, however, the political community is understood as an association of individuals united by a common law, that is, as a kind of practical association, the common good is recognized not as a set of aims to be achieved through cooperation among those moved by a common wish to achieve them but as a set of values defined by common laws. The precise content of the common good, thus defined, depends upon the circumstances of particular communities and is a matter for the statesman and the citizen to determine. But it can be specified roughly as having to do

---

terminology of these writers is not always consistent, however. Hobbes speaks of the "commonwealth" and Oakeshott of "civil association" in discussing the idea of the state as an association in terms of common rules. For Hegel, however, the expressions "state" and "civil society" stand for radically distinct ideas; the former is the realm of practical, the latter of purposive, association. (*Philosophy of Right*, sect. 258.)

above all with peace, justice, protected liberty and guaranteed rights, authority clearly defined and circumscribed by law, and perhaps also with provisions for the education of the members of the community and for certain minimum standards of well-being, not as ends in themselves but as conditions for the public order of the community. The common good, however specified, consists of ends that are immanent in the idea of the political community as an association of citizens united not in the joint pursuit of particular purposes but because they fall under the authority of a common body of laws.[12]

Some international associations are purposive; they exist for the sake of pursuing various shared purposes; the rules they adopt and the ethic they foster are instrumental to the achievement of the purposes for which they were created; and the relation of the association to the purposes it is supposed to serve determines its claim to be respected—that is, its authority. But international society as such—that inclusive society of states, or community of communities, within which

[12] The idea of the common good as a set of values internal to practical association can be found within both the tradition of civil association and the tradition of natural law; compare Oakeshott, *On Human Conduct*, pp. 61-62, 118-119, 152-154, and 315, and Finnis, *Natural Law and Natural Rights*, pp. 154-156, 160, 168, 210-218, and 303-305. The latter defines the common good, in its most important sense, as "a set of conditions which enables the members of a community to attain for themselves reasonable objectives . . ." (p. 155). This definition, argues Finnis, "neither asserts nor entails that the members of a community must all have the same values or objectives; . . . it implies only that there be some set . . . of conditions which needs to obtain if each of its members is to obtain his own objectives" (p. 156). The conception of a political community as a framework within which individuals can pursue their own self-chosen ends does not rule out the inculcation by the community of moral virtue in its citizens, as critics of "liberalism" often assert. On the contrary, it has often been recognized by liberals as well as others that the common good of an association of free individuals may require that the associates be educated not only in respect for the laws but also in honesty, tolerance, self-knowledge, fraternity, and other moral virtues. Emphasis on the importance of such virtues is characteristic of plural societies in which individuals committed to different ways of life and pursuing diverse ends are able to coexist with one another.

all international association takes place—is not a purposive association constituted by a joint wish on the part of all states to pursue certain ends in concert. It is, rather, an association of independent and diverse political communities, each devoted to its own ends and its own conception of the good, often related to one another by nothing more than the fragile ties of a common tradition of diplomacy. The common good of this inclusive community resides not in the ends that some, or at times even most, of its members may wish collectively to pursue but in the values of justice, peace, security, and coexistence, which can only be enjoyed through participation in a common body of authoritative practices.

The precise character of this international society is of course a matter of controversy, and some of this controversy will be considered in the following pages. Among the issues that have been prominent for several centuries are whether there exists any international society at all; whether this international society is a society of states or a universal society of individual human beings; whether the common good of international society, however defined, is limited to respect for the authoritative practices of international law and morality or includes the pursuit of substantive ends such as the economic and social well-being of political communities and their inhabitants; and, finally, whether international morality and law are better understood as instruments of purposive cooperation or as authoritative and noninstrumental constraints on such cooperation.

Because these issues have arisen in the context of particular historical controversies, they should be considered historically as well as analytically. The first part of this book explores certain aspects of the historical emergence of the idea of international society as an association of states in terms of certain common authoritative practices and rules. It was during the latter part of the eighteenth century that the society of states was most clearly and consistently understood to be a practical association, and international law to embody the authoritative rules of such an association. These rules were con-

19

cerned largely with such matters as territorial titles and boundaries, diplomtic immunities, jurisdiction over persons, and the conduct of warfare. They were premised on the formal recognition of states as independent members of a society of states, on the juridical equality of these members regardless of their size or power, and on their freedom to pursue external and internal policies subject only to the minimal constraints imposed by international law. And international law, despite uncertainties as to whether it adequately reflected the conditions required by the civil analogy (both in being an association of states rather than of individuals, and in consisting of rules of uncertain identity, application, and effectiveness) was understood as being concerned with the terms of association among sovereign states, and as being occupied almost exclusively with securing such terms as would permit them to preserve their independence. International law was understood as part of the structure of coexistence: a set of regular procedures within which states might survive and according to which they could pursue their own purposes, excluding only those activities that threatened to undermine the system itself.

The resulting conception of international society was one in which that society was regarded as a sort of meta-state: an association of political communities united through the authority of common rules governing their relations but lacking the institutions through which the laws of political communities are ordinarily created and applied. Instead of legislation, for example, international society has had to depend for its rules on the often haphazard development of customary law, augmented (and sometimes undermined) by additional rules created through formal agreement. Instead of relying on an apparatus of government to interpret and apply the common rules, international society has had to accommodate itself to the fact that its rules are for the most part interpreted and applied by the very parties whose conduct they are supposed to regulate. Because the institutions with which we identify political society within the state exist in such attenuated form in international society, discussion of the latter has always been dominated by debates concerning not only its identity but its very existence.

Because the state possesses an apparatus of political rule, it is at least superficially plausible to regard it as an organization and to ascribe to this organization purposes in terms of which the rules it makes and the policies it pursues may be justified, as if it were an enterprise analogous to a club, church, or corporation. The lack of such apparatus at the international level has meant that there has been less temptation to interpret the states system as a purposive association. Instead, the states system has been viewed either as a decentralized version of the civil order of the state, or as an anarchy in the extreme sense of a system lacking either government or rules. While many regarded the latter condition as inevitable, others (like Montesquieu, Vattel, Burke, and Gentz) saw in the former the possibility of a mode of international relations that might be governed by rules even in the absence of governing institutions. Furthermore, they regarded this mode of association as a source of freedom, for they believed that the states system, despite its wars and its persistent tendency toward lawlessness, provided a guarantee against a universal despotism that, were it to develop, would extinguish the liberties of individuals along with those of states. They regarded the practices and institutions of the European states system not as constituting a primitive stage in the evolution of a European superstate but as displaying a degree of organization appropriate to the circumstances of a continent inhabited by a diversity of peoples, and therefore as constituting a political order in which Europeans might properly take pride. Many of the proposals advanced during the eighteenth and nineteenth centuries for reforming the inevitable inefficiency and uncertainty of this order demonstrated an attachment to its premises by exploring how the authority of its rules might be strengthened without abolishing the principle of multiplicity and submitting to a single sovereign power. Some thinkers investigated the possibilities implicit in existing practices, such as the balance of power and great power diplomacy. Others, like Bentham, Kant, and the many publicists and reformers who were inspired by their ideas, explored various modifications of these practices that would be involved in the slightly more centralized order represented by a confederation or alliance of independent states, an arrangement that might reduce the uncertainty of the common rules of international society while preserving the diversity of a system of independent states. The practical conception of international society, then as now, reflected a willingness to tolerate a considerable degree of disorder as the price of preserving the independence, and thus the distinct identity, of its associates.

The alternative conception of international society as a purposive association also had its theoreticians and advocates. The purposive conception is evident in the programs of religious parties to secure the propagation of their faith that characterized the revolutionary period of the Protestant Reformation and Catholic Counterreformation. Such a conception is clearly intimated in the attempts to reorganize international society to match the successive ideals that accompanied the French, Bolshevik, and National Socialist revolutions. But it may also be seen in the programs of those who began by thinking of themselves as preserving the international system against revolutionary transformation, and therefore as committed to making only those reforms that were necessary to keep it from destroying itself, yet who in the end were unable to resist attempting to impose a purposive character on it. A purposive understanding of international society can be detected in the idea of the Concert of Europe, for although at times it was understood as no more than an effort to perpetuate the states system, the Concert was also often understood in purposive terms as an enterprise of the great powers to promote their privileged status within the international order. In the more extreme versions of the Concert idea reflected in the Quadruple and Holy Alliances, an attempt was made to ensure that the members of the society of states would continue to display the Christian and legitimist character that appeared to be threatened by the French Revolution and the spread of liberal nationalism in Europe.

It is in the present century, however, that the purposive conception of international society has become the leading doctrine of world order. The League of Nations can still be seen as reflecting the traditional conception of international society as an association of states within a common framework of rules and procedures, combined with a new determination to institutionalize in a quasi-sovereign body the practices of rule creation, interpretation, and enforcement that had previously existed in the decentralized and uncertain forms of custom and treaty. But the United Nations introduces a new element to the extent that it is understood as the institutionalized embodiment of an international society united by a determination not only to fend off disruptions of international peace and to preserve the security and independence of its associates, but also to promote the realization of the social and economic welfare of its constituent societies—to do this not merely as a means to international peace and security but as an end in itself. Outside the United Nations others have argued the need for international society to be reconstituted through a "global transformation" toward a new world order in which certain postulated values might be more fully realized.[13]

If the argument sketched in this book is correct, such views mistake the basis of international association, the character of international law, and the meaning of moral conduct in world affairs. In identifying the basis of international society with agreement to pursue certain shared goals and interests, they

---

[13] A purposive conception of international society is particularly evident in the proposals of the less developed countries for a "new international economic order" (see Chapter 10, below). Some representative "world order" works are Mendlovitz, *On the Creation of a Just World Order*, and Beres and Targ, *Constructing Alternative World Futures*. The premises of this approach are examined and criticized by Bull, *Anarchical Society*, pp. 282-296, 302-305.

forget that any international agreement presupposes commonly acknowledged rules and procedures according to which agreements can be made. Most versions of the purposive conception also fail to offer any account of how the unity they postulate is to be reconciled with the actual diversity of ends that characterizes our world. They therefore neglect to consider the implications, for their own proposals, of the fact that international society is distinguished from a state of extreme conflict not so much by the degree to which its members are moved to cooperate in the pursuit of common interests as by the degree to which they understand themselves to be members of a society defined by common rules, moved sometimes by common and sometimes by divergent interests. It is not only because it avoids the logical incompleteness of the purposive conception but also because it is capable of providing a satisfactory positive account of international association that the practical conception, despite certain difficulties and obscurities that need to be resolved, is entitled to stand as the most adequate and illuminating of any of the conceptions of international society, morality, and law in terms of which the attempt to understand world affairs has been made.

PART ONE

International Society and Its Law

CHAPTER 2

International Relations and International Society

NINETEENTH-CENTURY TREATISES on international law often began by positing a necessary connection between international law and international society. Their authors liked to repeat the maxim *ubi societas ibi ius*, "where there is society there is law," taking comfort in the observation that if law is an inevitable aspect of society it must have a place in the society of states. To say that states form a society, suggested one interpreter of international law, is simply another way of saying that its members "claim from each other the observance of certain lines of conduct, capable of being expressed in general terms as rules. . . ."[1] It is, he argued, generally accepted that there exist rights and wrongs in international relations, and that an injured state is entitled to redress when wronged and to approval and support by other states in seeking this redress; and there is agreement about where the rules defining those rights and wrongs are to be looked for.[2] As late as 1928 the author of one of the most frequently consulted manuals of international law in the English language still spoke in these terms, arguing both that "law can only exist in a society" and that "there can be no society without a system of law."[3] This manner of speaking reflects a tradition of thought and expression going back many centuries. Once a commonplace of writings on international relations, it has now been eclipsed by an altogether different style of discourse.[4]

[1] Westlake, *Collected Papers*, p. 2.
[2] Ibid., p. 60.
[3] Brierly, *Law of Nations*, p. 41.
[4] Britain provides an exception to the assertion that the expression "inter-

27

Why has the expression "international society" gone out of fashion? The decline of natural-law thinking doubtless had something to do with it, although there is in fact no necessary connection between the idea of international society and any doctrine of natural law. The nineteenth-century writers who employed the term were mostly legal positivists skeptical of the idea of natural law. Another factor may have been the identification of the idea of international society with the notion of an exclusively European Family of Nations, a notion that began to lose its hold with the retreat of European colonialism. But, more importantly, the expression "international society" and the style of thought that accompanied its use died out because it did not fit in with the increasingly realist and scientific temper of twentieth-century writing on international relations. The last considerable body of writers to use the expression were the defenders of the League of Nations in the 1920s, and, when their idealism was discredited as naive and even hypocritical by the realist critics of the 1930s and 40s, the idea that international relations might be understood as taking place within a society governed by legal and moral rules lost all credibility. At the same time a scientific style of writing about international relations was beginning to come into vogue. Gradually the ordinary idea of "society" was driven out by the more abstract concept of "system." In place of a familiar world in which people deliberated, made decisions, and acted on the basis of reasons and with reference to rules, there appeared a new world of phenomena and processes to be accounted for in terms of forces, variables, correlations, and causal laws. Theorists turned from the inter-

national society" has fallen out of favor. Among more recent British writers on international relations who have relied on it are Wight, *Power Politics*, chs. 10 and 24; Butterfield and Wight, *Diplomatic Investigations*, chs. 2, 3, and 7; Manning, *Nature of International Society*; Midgley, *Natural Law Tradition*; Luard, *Types of International Society*; Bull, *Anarchical Society*; and Mayall, "International Society and International Theory." In the United States the expression "international society" has been used by a few writers on international law, for example, Corbett, *Law and Society in the Relations of States*, and Levi, *Law and Politics in the International Society*.

pretation of "conduct" to the explanation of "behavior." It was not merely the idea of international society that had become discredited, but a whole way of looking at international relations.

This state of affairs is unsatisfactory, whatever one's opinion of the possibility and worth of a science of international relations. For even if, as is likely, there is room for such a science side by side with older and more familiar ways of speaking of world affairs, it cannot replace them. In many respects rejection of the old idea of international society, as a notion at once parochial, moralizing, and productive of dangerous illusions, is amply justified. But, despite the distortions that have been imposed upon it, the idea suggests a concern for international law and international morality that is inadequately served by the vocabulary of the realist and scientific perspectives. The terms "international society" and "international association" deserve to be renewed because they stand for a manner of thought and expression that is indispensable for understanding the legal and moral dimensions of world affairs. International relations theory, as it is cultivated today, lacks an adequate conceptual vocabulary for moral and legal inquiry. It would be surprising if the ideas of an age that took such inquiry more seriously had nothing to contribute to its revival.

The Idea of International Society

It is, of course, not the term "international society" that is important, but rather the idea it represents. The term "society" has a place in scientific as well as in moral discourse, just as the term "system" may be employed without implying any particular explanatory theory of the activities and arrangements it is used to name. (The expression "states system" has long been used simply as a descriptive term without any particular theoretical connotation to refer to the coexistence within Europe of independent political communities.) Despite these and other ambiguities, there is some support for preferring the term "society" where we are concerned with understand-

ing human activities and arrangements as the work of thinking agents acting and responding to the acts of others. Although there are exceptions, "society" suggests the internal
perspective of a participant in the activities and arrangements
we wish to understand, while "system" suggests the perspective of an external observer employing theoretical concepts
rather than the ordinary notions of those whose conduct is
being observed.[5] From the perspective of the participant,
conduct is understood in terms of intentions, reasons, choices,
and responses. But the scientific observer characteristically
approaches the task of understanding human activity as if it
were a part of nature. If the human is subsumed in the natural, then the terms in which it can be explained do not differ
in kind from those suitable for explaining natural phenomena.

The attempt to understand international relations in terms
of the concepts of natural science is well illustrated by the
efforts of certain eighteenth-century thinkers to explain the
pattern of European international relations as the outcome of
an automatic balance of power. For these theorists of international relations the idea of balance stood for a process through
which the threat of hegemony by one state was checked by
the natural tendency of other states to form a coalition to
oppose it. The balance of power was understood as a kind of
mechanism producing both order and change within the international system. Rousseau, for example, described the operation of the balance as "the work of nature" rather than of
human artifice, able to maintain itself "in perpetual oscillation
without overturning itself altogether."[6] Equilibrium is the result of a process, not the outcome of choice; it appears not
because statesmen seek it but rather as the unintended consequence of what they do seek, which is power and security.

[5] To adopt the perspective of the participant is to understand human conduct in terms of choices and actions but not necessarily to accept the substantive content of any participant's beliefs about their own or others' conduct. On the relationship between the perspectives of participant and observer
in the study of law, see Hart, *Concept of Law*, pp. 55-56, 86-88, and 99.

[6] *Oeuvres complètes*, 3:570.

The expression "balance of power" refers to a process that arranges, as if by a hidden hand, the activities of statesmen in such a way that the European system of independent states is preserved and perpetuated.

Understood in terms of the concepts of human choice and conduct, on the other hand, the balance of power appears as a condition of international society that must be consciously pursued in order to be enjoyed. From the internal perspective of the participant in international society, to balance the potential preponderance of one state through the formation of an opposing coalition requires diplomatic effort. The balance of power is understood as a policy, not a description and explanation of a process, and a theory of the balance of power consists of a set of precepts, not descriptive generalizations or causal laws: those who would preserve the balance must be sensitive to shifts in the relative power of states, ready to encourage or discourage particular alliances, and careful to avoid destroying any major power whose loss might make adaptation to shifts in the distribution of power more difficult. Although such an understanding may draw upon a scientific view of international relations, the perspective it suggests is not that of the external observer but the participant statesman. Its concepts are not those required for a naturalistic explanation of the operation of the international system, but those of international society itself.

There is no need, here, to take sides in the controversy over whether human activity is better understood as "behavior" or as "conduct," whether the study of human activity is or is not distinct from the study of natural phenomena, or whether the concepts and methods of the natural sciences are useful or even relevant to the understanding of human activity. Instead, I will simply assume that each perspective is a possible mode of understanding human activity possessing its own distinctive concepts and methods, reflecting its own criteria of descriptive and explanatory adequacy, and guiding its practitioners along different but not necessarily opposite paths toward distinct but not necessarily incompatible conclusions.

In using the expression "international society," therefore, I wish to be understood not as rejecting the scientific perspective but rather as trying both to revive and refine a vocabulary appropriate for inquiry into international relations as an activity of thinking agents (the quality of whose thought may be excellent or poor) responding to an understood (or misunderstood) situation, in accordance with (or in violation of) various practices, rules, or maxims of conduct. My concern is thus not with international relations understood as a system of causally or functionally related variables but with the arrangements of an international society constituted by the actions of thinking agents who must take each other into account in making decisions, whose decisions are accounted for in terms of intentions and reasons rather than dispositions and causes, and whose acts are understood as being shaped and guided by rules of conduct rather than laws of behavior.[7]

It will perhaps help to avoid misunderstanding to emphasize that in reconsidering the ideas of an earlier era our intention need not be to reclaim its conclusions regarding international law and its place in the relations of states, but rather to profit from its experience in considering this topic. Furthermore, it is important to be clear that, in exploring the idea of international society, one is engaged in a particular kind of inquiry whose character must be clearly grasped if one is to avoid becoming confused. It is a kind of inquiry that is essential to the work of the theorist, although it is by no means the only sort of inquiry in which the theorist may engage. Its distinguishing characteristic is that it aims to specify the criteria by which an idea is defined and instances of that idea recognized. The theorist's concern here is with the essential features of a class—with the characteristics in terms of which members of a class can be distinguished from other kinds of things. The aim of this sort of inquiry, in other words, is to specify the defining or distinguishing marks of a class of

---

[7] This formulation of the idea of "conduct" owes much to Oakeshott, *On Human Conduct*, pp. 31-55.

particulars from the merely accidental features that some of the particulars subsumed under it may happen to display. In seeking to distinguish defining from accidental features, we are in effect specifying the boundaries of an idea. We are looking for criteria according to which things identified by this idea can be distinguished from other things that may resemble them in various ways. And we are engaged in exploring the presuppositions and implications of the idea thus identified. The exploration of the ideas of international society, law, and morality to which the present study is devoted illustrates each of these aspects of this first kind of inquiry.

This concern with ideas must not be confused with the attempt to describe the particular features of actual, historic events or situations. The two forms of inquiry are distinct. The latter is concerned with accidental as well as defining features, and thus with achieving descriptive accuracy and richness rather than conceptual consistency. It is concerned to portray accurately the activities and arrangements of particular times and places in terms of whatever features they may happen to display, and not to distinguish the distinct ideas that may be combined in them. To put it differently, this kind of inquiry seeks not to define ideal types but to describe complex phenomena that constitute mixed types. Approached in terms of a concern with description, the thing identified and described displays a combination of features some of which are definitive and others accidental. Thus, the task of exploring the identity and presuppositions of an idea is not to be confused with the quite distinct task of describing this or that conjunction of historical events and of determining the extent to which a given abstract idea constitutes an adequate description of it. The tasks are related and are often carried on simultaneously, but it does not follow that they cannot be analytically distinguished. Therefore, to explore the idea of international society is not to describe the actual features of, let us say, the states system of eighteenth-century Europe. The idea of international society is an abstraction that may or may not be discernible in a particular states system during any given period, and a particular system may reflect the impress of more than one organizing idea.[8]

Both kinds of inquiry are sometimes confused with a third, one concerned neither with defining nor with describing, but rather with discovering the circumstances required for something to exist or occur. The essential or defining features of a thing and the empirical conditions of its existence are particularly likely to be confused, perhaps because both are sometimes said to be "necessary," although in the one case the necessity is logical and in the other causal. The failure to resolve this ambiguity leaves the character of the inquiry in doubt. For example, inquiry into the nature and existence of international law often founders because of confusion over the question of whether the existence of centralized institutions for making and applying rules is a defining characteristic of legal order, an empirical condition for its existence, or merely one of its accidental features. The history of the ideas of international society and international law is in part a history of how the essential criteria and presuppositions of these ideas were gradually distinguished from the contingent features and conditions of modern European international relations.

Society or Anarchy?

The expression "international society" as it is understood by many writers on international relations refers to the idea of states related to one another in terms of common practices, customs, and rules. Such rules provide the basis for making judgments of just and unjust international conduct, for advancing claims concerning respect for rights and the performances of duties, and for seeking vindication and redress when

[8] Like all ideas, the idea of international society is, in Oakeshott's terminology, an "ideal character"—that is, an arrangement or composition of selected characteristics detached from their contingent circumstances. (*On Human Conduct*, p. 4.) On the related notion of an "ideal" or "pure" type, see Weber, *Methodology of the Social Sciences*, pp. 89-110, and *Economy and Society*, pp. 20-22, 57-58.

rules are violated, rights infringed, and duties ignored. Yet the reality of this whole way of speaking and thinking about international relations is often questioned. It is a commonplace of talk about international relations that the idea of international society, so understood, stands for a wish rather than an actuality. There are no common rules governing the relations of states, it is suggested—or, if such rules exist, they are not a significant factor in international relations because they give way as soon as vital interests appear to be threatened, and therefore govern only activities of marginal importance in the pursuit of security and power. There is, therefore, a marked contrast between international society, to the extent that it exists at all, and domestic society. Hence the tendency to make "power politics" a synonym for "international politics."

Denial of the reality of international society is often expressed in a preference for speaking of "international anarchy" instead of "international society." But the word "anarchy" is an ambiguous one, and careless use of it has done much to obscure what it means to speak of international relations as governed by rules. The standard definition of "anarchy" is "absence of rule."[9] But the latter can mean "absence of *government*"; it can mean "absence of *law*" or of other kinds of rules; or it can mean "absence of *order*." The three are not equivalent. Strictly speaking, the first is the original and basic sense of the term, which derives from *an-* (without) and *archos* (a ruler or superior). Although it may often be the case that where there is no government or rule by a superior there is lawlessness or disorder, it does not follow that the absence of government must always, as a matter of contingent fact, have these consequences.

The characterization of international relations as taking place in a condition of "international anarchy" is seldom intended to suggest complete disorder or chaos. The expression is more often used to suggest either the unreliability of common rules

[9] *Oxford English Dictionary*.

of international conduct or the absence of international government. Let us consider each of these meanings in turn. When anarchy is understood as a kind of rulelessness, "international anarchy" refers to the coexistence of independent states within a shared environment but without the benefit of common rules. The international system is not to any appreciable extent a society united by common rules, but simply an aggregate of separate societies each pursuing its own purposes, and linked with one another in ways that are essentially *ad hoc*, unstable, and transitory. The conduct of each state may in fact be rule-governed, in the sense that each observes rules of its own choosing. But because the decisions of each are governed by different rules, the separate states cannot be said to be members of a single society of states united by common rules of conduct—rules whose authority is acknowledged by all states. A collection of individual agents, each of which makes decisions according to its own private rules, does not constitute a society but exists instead in what, following Hobbes, has been understood as a state of nature. It constitutes an assemblage of solitary agents with little in common save the predicament of being alone and insecure in a world lacking dependable order, exposed continually to the invasions of others. So it is with states, for the civil amenities of international society—the institutions of international law, of justice, and of recognized rights against other states—presuppose common rules, and these are—by hypothesis—absent.

The way in which this view of international relations is usually defended tends, however, to undermine the premises upon which it rests. It is commonly argued that the relatively small number of states, their relative self-sufficiency, and the perpetual inadequacy of the available alternatives to self-help create an environment hostile both to relations on the basis of regular and impartial principles and to the expansion of common interests that might provide a motive conducive to a more effective system of common rules. Therefore the area of international life subject to normative regulation is necessarily limited; the most important concerns of the state, those pertaining to what used to be called its "dignity and honor" and more recently its "vital interests," are excluded from the jurisdiction of a common international law. These are concerns that fall within the "domestic jurisdiction" or "reserved domain" of the state and that are sometimes identified as matters of "fundamental right" with which international law is neither authorized nor strong enough to interfere. The trouble with this argument is that it presupposes the very framework of common rules whose impossibility it purports to demonstrate. Dignity and honor, as Martin Wight points out, need not imply independence from all common standards of conduct but can also mean fidelity to such standards.[10] Even honor as consciousness of and pride in status presupposes a common standard according to which gradations of status are measured. Similarly, to insist that a matter falls within the domestic jurisdiction of a state is to advance a claim within an existing framework of law. It is true that the larger such claims and the more readily they are recognized, the narrower the scope and significance of international law. Nevertheless, logically speaking, the claim to exclude something from legal regulation assumes the existence of a body of law whose inapplicability is being claimed. The notion of fundamental rights, if urged as something distinct from and superior to the positive law of nations, still presupposes a common moral order and thus has no place in an international anarchy in the sense of an aggregate of collectivities whose relations with one another are regulated by no common principles whatsoever. Even the idea of vital interests—which is not, like the others, defined in terms of common standards—implies the existence of a body of international law regulating the pursuit of interests that are not vital, as well as providing some criterion for distinguishing between vital and nonvital interests.

The other meaning of "international anarchy" to be considered is the absence, in the system of states, of any superior power or government able to make and enforce rules govern-

[10] *Power Politics*, pp. 96-97.

ing state conduct. If anarchy is the absence of governing institutions, then a states system is anarchical by definition; it is "a multiplicity of powers without a government."[11] Such a multiplicity might in fact be governed by a body of common rules, although many theorists of international relations appear to regard the existence of such rules as contingently unlikely in the absence of a common government. It is the absence of common government in the system of states that is thought to explain one of the most striking features of that system, its perpetual tendency toward war. Since the seventeenth century the implicit point of departure for discussions of order in the system of states has been the analysis of war made by Thomas Hobbes in the thirteenth chapter of *Leviathan*. Sovereigns, wrote Hobbes, are perpetually "in the state and posture of gladiators," which is "a posture of war." This condition of war "consists not in actual fighting but in the known disposition thereto during all the time there is no assurance to the contrary," and lasts as long as sovereigns are without a common power "to keep them all in awe." The persistent theme of the countless discussions of the causes of war inspired by this analysis is that, whatever may be the circumstances of the outbreak of particular wars, "the fundamental cause is the absence of international government; in other words, the anarchy of sovereign states."[12] Anarchy is a condition of war because of the fertile ground it offers for the germination of mutual fear. Each power, unable to count on the amity of others, must take steps to protect its own security. It must seek power. But in doing so it necessarily threatens the security of others. The consequence is perpetuation of what has come to be labeled "Hobbesian fear" or, more commonly, the "security dilemma," a predicament so exasperating as to invite resort to desperate measures to escape it.[13]

[11] Ibid., p. 101.
[12] Ibid.
[13] Butterfield, *History and Human Relations*, p. 21; Herz, *Nation-State*, pp. 72-73.

Yet it does not follow that common rules cannot exist in the absence of common government. The idea of the security dilemma can be understood as implying not that in the absence of government there can be no society, but rather that where government is lacking such society as exists is apt to be rudimentary or unstable. In the agreement of individuals to abstain from aggression against one another there is the beginning of an order based on common rules. Where these individuals are sovereigns there exists a potential international order based on common rules. But this order is a fragile one because the temptation to defect from the agreement on which it rests is so great. For one thing, each party may be tempted to take advantage of compliance by others in order to advance his own power, security, and well-being. But even those who wish to respect the agreement may be tempted to break it through mistrust. The motive for such preemptive defection might be said to be "defensive" rather than "aggressive," although in this situation of mutual insecurity the two are hard to distinguish. In either case the agreement is likely to break down.

Common rules must be understood as limiting or constraining the struggle for power. But conformity with their provisions can ensure the security of each member of the society that common rules bring into being only if everyone respects the limits they impose. To keep faith when the faith of others cannot be relied upon is to expose oneself to the risk of being taken advantage of; it is to render oneself vulnerable to the depredations of others, whatever their motive, and to make one's own well-being dependent on their will. Agreements to observe limits on conduct are therefore liable to be undermined as soon as they are made. The rationale of government, on this analysis, is to prevent this from happening. A superior power is required not only to deter and punish those who would exploit for their own advanatage the trust of others but to provide assurance to those entering into agreements, and who rightly fear such exploitation, that the terms of their agreements will be enforced and the performance of others guaranteed.

There would appear, then, to be two levels of rule-governed order in human affairs. The first is the possibly unstable and unreliable order that appears where individuals or groups are associated in terms of common rules but do not enjoy the benefits of a government to secure observance of them. The other is the presumably more stable order in which rules and government are united. Thus, between the extremes of anarchy as a situation lacking either government or rules and the order of the state, there exists the possibility of life according to common rules ("society") even in the absence of common government ("anarchy"). International society, understood as an association of states in terms of common rules but without a common government, is thus at least a logically possible form of international order, however unstable or otherwise unsatisfactory it may turn out to be. Many have gone further than this, arguing not only that society is possible in the absence of government but that the system of states does in fact constitute a society based on common rules: an "anarchical society," as it has been called, in which independent states are reliably related on the basis of common rules derived from custom and agreement, despite the lack of any superior rule-making and rule-applying power or "government."[14] Perhaps because the consequences of anarchy are less devastating for states and their inhabitants than for individuals in a postulated state of nature, the former are not

[14] The modern states system has been characterized as "the anarchical society" by Hedley Bull in his book by that title. But in defining "society" Bull does not consistently distinguish association on the basis of common rules from association for the promotion of shared ends or interests, a very different matter (see Chapter 1, above). Bull is one of a long line of writers on international relations to argue that anarchy (in the sense of absence of government) is not only compatible with the existence of international society but constitutes the form of organization most appropriate to it. The original eighteenth-century versions of this argument are discussed in Chapter 3, below. A specifically Oakeshottian interpretation of the modern European states system is provided by Keens-Soper, "Practice of a States-System."

compelled to resolve the problem of the instability of their arrangements by forming an inclusive political community through submission to a sovereign world power. Indeed, it is not at all clear whether it is the dangers of international anarchy or those of submission to such a power that are more to be feared.

The value of the Hobbesian analysis for the understanding of international law and morality is thus to be found not only in its denial of the possibility of international society but also in an affirmation of that possibility that can be extrapolated from it.[15] It set the stage for subsequent exploration of the character and conditions of "society" in the relations of states: of how, in the absence of a common superior, states might nevertheless manage to carry on their relations with one another within a framework of common rules. If the states system of Europe was not to be a unity under a single sovereign power, what was the character of such unity as it did possess, according to which it might be distinguished from a ruleless anarchy? How can anarchy in the sense of absence of common government be reconciled with society in the sense of association on the basis of common rules? It is the attempt to explore these questions that has given rise to a body of thought about international society which, as I have already suggested, is indispensable for the analysis of international law and international morality.

If discussion of the idea of international society is today still pervaded by a sense of paradox, how much more must this

---

[15] Hobbes is usually interpreted as denying the possibility of international society. The most influential exposition of this view, so far as the history of international relations theory is concerned, appeared in 1672 in Pufendorf's *Law of Nature and of Nations*, book 2, ch. 2. A more recent version is that of Bull, *Anarchical Society*, pp. 24-25, and 46-47. This interpretation has recently been challenged by Forsyth, "Thomas Hobbes and the External Relations of States," who argues that, although for Hobbes sovereigns are not subject to the authority of any earthly superior, they *are* governed by the law of nature: they are, for example, to seek peace and hence to observe the constraints concerning the treatment of ambassadors, the conduct of war, and so forth, which follow from that injunction.

have been the case in the early modern period of European history when the idea of the modern states system was just emerging from a set of very different ideas. Although there is evidence in the sixteenth and seventeenth centuries of the existence in Europe of a system of states, its character was more often interpreted in terms of the kind of unity provided by a higher sovereignty, one that was embodied either in the ideal of a unified Christendom or in the ideal of a universal secular empire or monarchy. It is only in the eighteenth century that the idea of a states system whose unity is provided by its own distinctive institutions—those of diplomacy, the balance of power, and international law—really emerges as an independent and fully articulated conception of the character of European international society. Yet even during this period there were many who found this conception an unsatisfactory one and who were concerned to explore the idea of international society in terms of more centralized forms of organization.

The idea of international society as a system of independent sovereignties within a common framework of rules is, then, one that has long appeared to rest on contradiction and to stand for a form of human association that many observers continue to regard as anomalous. The logic of international society appears to point toward the poles of complete disorder on the one hand and a world state on the other. The realization that a decentralized association of sovereign states might perpetuate itself without reaching either of these extremes, and the attempt to think through the character of such an association, is one of the remarkable achievements of modern European international relations theory.

The Society of States and World Society

The idea of international society, as so far explored, excludes the notion of a mere assemblage of solitary agents whose acts may have consequences for one another but who are not associated within a common framework of rules. The idea of international society may, however, be further elucidated by attempting to specify the character of the units composing it. In the international society that began to emerge in Europe during the sixteenth and seventeenth centuries, these units were slowly coming to be understood as "states": that is, as territorially defined and independent political communities. The idea of a society of states was derived by analogy from civil society. First the prince, and later on the state itself understood as a corporate entity, replaced the individual person as a member of the greater society beyond the local realm and as a subject of its laws. International society was understood to be a society of states.

The expression "international society" is thus, strictly speaking, a misnomer. It is not "nations" in the sense of ethnic communities that are associated within it, but states. Yet the notion that nations are the proper units of international society is one that tends to merge with a state-centric conception because statehood has in the past proved to be the only reliable vehicle for participation in world affairs. The principle of national self-determination, which could be taken to mean that each ethnic community or nation should be free to decide its own form of association, has more often been expressed as the claim that each nation should be free to organize itself into an independent state and to participate equally with other states as a member of the society of states. So close indeed is this notional link between "state" and "nation" that the English language now scarcely distinguishes them in many contexts. It allows us to speak of the "nation-state," "international relations," and the "United Nations," even though it is almost always states rather than nations that are being talked about.

The chief alternative to this state-centric conception of international society is one in which the individual person is regarded as the real member of international society and the proper subject of its laws. "International society" here becomes the name for that transnational and potentially universal society in which states have become merely one of a num-

43

ber of intermediate levels of political organization: a synonym for "world society." It is based on a conception of human unity that has been part of the Western tradition at least since the time of the Stoics. The postulated unity is a moral one that is believed to exist in principle even if at times it seems only inadequately reflected in practice. According to this conception the world is morally and therefore potentially a single universal society or cosmopolis. In this society divisions of class and nationality are arbitrary and without ultimate validity. The existence of such divisions and therefore of different laws governing different groups of people is not denied, but the arrangements defined by local custom and by the laws of the state are thought to be qualified by a higher law based on the premise of the equality of all persons. This is the law of nature, a law based on reason rather than local custom and therefore universally applicable: "one eternal and unchangeable law . . . valid for all nations."[16] Therefore, the universal community of mankind is morally prior to the society of states. The latter is simply the particular form that the organization of the human community has taken in modern times, but it is not the only possible form that this community might assume. Its true character would be most fully realized in a single universal legal order.[17]

Both the idea of a society of states and that of a world society of individuals are abstractions according to which the complex and mutable reality of world affairs has been interpreted. Neither offers a completely accurate description of world order, although at different historical moments one has seemed more plausible than the other. The idea of interna-

[16] Cicero, *De Republica*, III, xxii, 33.

[17] For a recent exposition and defense of a cosmopolitan view of international society and morality, see Charles R. Beitz, *Political Theory and International Relations*. Beitz is careful to distinguish the moral principles of the world society he postulates from the legal and political institutions through which such principles might be implemented, arguing that moral cosmopolitanism in no way commits one to accepting the desirability of a world state (pp. 181-183).

tional society as an association of independent states within a framework of common rules corresponds best to the conditions prevailing in Europe during the eighteenth and nineteenth centuries. It was during this period that the idea of a European society of states achieved its clearest expression in international thought and in the practice of international law. After 1800 the expression "the law of nations"—always an ambiguous one, for it could be taken to refer to the rules found within each nation for regulating the conduct of its own members as well as to those pertaining to the relations among nations—began to be replaced by the more explicit expression "international law." It was also during this period that the idea of an international law based on the actual customs and agreements of states began to drive out the older conception of the law of nations as natural law applied to the conduct of sovereign princes.

In seeking to understand the premises of the idea of international society as a society of states, it is useful to compare the periods preceding and following the flourishing of the European states system. If we go back to the sixteenth century, the idea of a society of states seems to have little application. There are, to be sure, elements of this idea as it later developed. But the differences are more striking. There is first of all the great number and diversity of the often overlapping political entities within the European realm—dukedoms, republics, bishoprics, free cities, estates, principalities, kingdoms, the Papacy, and the Holy Roman Empire. There is the persistence of the idea of a universal society that made it difficult to imagine a unified Europe as anything other than a single Christian community or a universal monarchy. Most important is the lack in sixteenth-century thought of any clear conception of the associates in an international society as entities all essentially of the same kind: collections of individuals within a particular territory, subject to common laws, ruled by a common superior, and independent of the authority of any other such entity. The idea sought—that of a *state*—was one that was only beginning to be articulated.[18] Such articulation was difficult where political arrangements were as complex and diverse as those of Renaissance Europe. What, for example, was one to make of an entity such as Castile in the second quarter of the sixteenth century, whose king, Charles V, was also ruler of Aragon and of the Burgundian Netherlands, Holy Roman Emperor (and thus the nominal ruler of a diverse assemblage of principalities, estates, and cities in cental Europe), and the ruler of vast new domains in the Americas that were of unquestionable novelty so far as existing political forms went? Europe had at this time no clear conception of the identity of the units that composed it. Lacking any clear notion of these units as entities of essentially the same kind, it lacked any clear idea of itself as a society of such entities—that is, as a society of states.

If we turn to the present century, it seems that the firmness of the idea of international society as a society of states is once again in doubt. Numerous observers representing many points of view have called attention to the apparent breakdown of the institutions of positive international law as a consequence of the expansion of the states system beyond its European and Christian base.[19] A new cosmopolitanism is intimated in the revival of natural-law thinking represented by such developments as the Nuremberg trials and subsequent efforts to give international protection to human rights. There is also renewed confusion concerning the identity of the associates in international society, a confusion reflected in the preoccupation of much current writing on world affairs with the place of such entities as multinational corporations, rev-

[18] Late medieval and early modern political thinkers did possess the idea, derived from Aristotle (*Politics*, I, 1-2) and Aquinas (*Summa Theologica*, I-II, q. 90, art. 2. and *On Kingship*, book I, ch. 1, para. 14), of a "complete" or "perfect" community, but these expressions embraced a very wide range of political forms.

[19] See, for example, Röling, *International Law in an Expanded World*; Hoffmann, *State of War*, ch. 4; and Bozeman, *Future of Law in a Multicultural World*. Some of their arguments are considered in Chapter 12, below.

olutionary movements, and international organizations. For many the term "international" has come to be seen as begging some of the most basic questions concerning the character of those activities and arrangements that transcend the boundaries of states.

These judgments have led some observers to challenge the premise of state autonomy underlying the classical order of international law and to question the continued relevance of this order in a world characterized by the growth of transnational relations and interdependence and by a corresponding decline in the importance and legitimacy of the state. It is suggested that international law as we have known it in the past is gradually being replaced by a new transnational legal order directly governing the conduct of individual corporations, international organizations, and other non-state entities, as well as the conduct of states. Such arguments, however, appear both to underestimate the importance of transnational relations in the past and to exaggerate their present significance. There is little evidence that the states system is on the verge of disappearing or that any major change has occurred in the manner in which international law is created and applied. As in the past international law continues to be created primarily through custom and treaties, and to be applied in a variety of national and international forums. Although entities other than states increasingly have certain rights and duties under international law, this law is still one that is created and applied by states.

To reject some of the more extreme claims that have been made about the demise of the states system is not, however, to deny the significance of transnational relations and of cosmopolitan legal and moral ideas. Clearly there is a need to explore the idea of a single world society and its implications for morality and law. But it is also important to continue the effort to understand the idea of the society of states as that idea appears to have flourished within the modern states system that originated in Europe and has since come to include the entire world. We must ask whether the understanding of international society that was explored and refined in the course of several centuries of experience with this system is indeed no longer appropriate, even in a revised form, to the predicament of humanity in the last half of the twentieth century.

CHAPTER 3

The Modern States System as an International Society

WHEN RANKE described the states system of Renaissance Italy as a "diversity in ideal unity,"[1] he expressed a view shared by many others who had reflected on the character of modern European civilization. The diversity of this civilization was apparent in the plurality of its tongues, faiths, and local customs and in its division into a number of independent political communities each governed according to its own laws and traditions. But the basis of European unity was harder to discern. The idea of the modern states system as a number of independent states united through their participation in a common body of authoritative practices—in other words, as a kind of "practical association"—can be understood as an outcome of attempts to specify the character of this unity.

The idea of a society of states is derived from two others. The first of these is the very ancient idea of a universal society of mankind: a great community more inclusive than the particular communities into which mankind is divided and governed by a law of nature superior to the particular laws of these more restricted communities. The second is the idea of a system of states, understood as a multiplicity of independent political communities coexisting within a certain geographical area. First articulated to account for the political organization of the Italian peninsula and then of the German empire, the idea of the states system came to be identified with the arrangements of an ever increasing portion of the globe. But it was only gradually, and in spite of distractions

[1] *History of the Latin and Teutonic Nations*, p. 38.

arising from the exploration of many irrelevant byways, that the two ideas were explicitly combined in a conception of the world as an association of independent states united by their participation in a common law of nations, understood not (as it once was) as the law of nature applied to sovereigns but as a body of law specific to the society of states and rooted in its own unique usages and traditions. The idea of the society of states emerged when the universal society postulated by the theorists of natural law came to be interpreted as an association of independent political communities and when the "system" constituted by the states of Europe began to be understood as a particular kind of system—a "society" whose members were tied to one another by a single body of international law.

According to this idea what unites the separate states in a larger society is not any similarity of language, religion, or government. Nor is their unity to be found in geographical proximity, in their transactions with one another, or in any interests they may happen to share. It is, rather, the formal unity of an association of independent political communities each pursuing its own way of life within certain acknowledged limits: that is, according to generally recognized rules through which cultural individuality and communal liberty are guaranteed, subject only to the constraints of mutual toleration and mutual accommodation.[2] The genesis of this insight and the working out of its various implications was the fruit of an extended intellectual effort in which the essential was only slowly distinguished from the incidental.

MULTIPLICITY AND DIVERSITY

The modern states system reflects not only the division of the world into separate states but into states of the most diverse character. That we refer to these entities as "states" creates a

[2] The extent to which international law and morality require respect for liberty and pluralism within as well as between states is considered in Chapters 9 and 10, below.

superficial impression of similarity that is belied by the fact that they constitute an extemely heterogeneous collection. The states system that was emerging between the fifteenth and eighteenth centuries was composed only in part of those national monarchies that best fit our present notion of the early modern state.[3] Sweden is a good example, as is France if we discount the latter's recurrent imperial ambitions. Less easily accommodated to the modern picture are those personal unions, often transient, created and extinguished by royal marriages and hereditary succession, such as those of the Hapsburgs or a Great Britain and Hanover between 1714 and 1837. After the Peace of Westphalia, the European system was augmented by hundreds of principalities and estates, some very ancient, that were now all but nominally independent of the Holy Roman Empire: duchies and electorates, landgraviates and margraviates, counties and free cities. There were also ecclesiastical territories such as the Papal States or the Bishoprics and Archbishoprics of the Empire, as well as city states like Venice and Geneva and confederations like those of the Dutch and the Swiss. And then there was the Empire itself, a mysterious entity, "neither holy, nor Roman, nor an empire,"[4] which Pufendorf is said to have described as "an irregular body, similar to a monster, if measured by the rules of civil science."[5] Some of these entities had acquired extensive possessions abroad: Victoria was Empress of India as well as Queen of England. The abandonment of dynasticism, the consolidation of many of the smaller entities into larger states, and the growing acceptance in the nineteenth and twentieth centuries of national self-determination as the proper foun-

[3] It is not until the sixteenth century that one begins to encounter "the distinctively modern idea of the State as a form of public power separate from both the ruler and the ruled, and constituting the supreme political authority within a certain defined territory." (Skinner, *Foundations of Modern Political Thought*, 2:353.) From the perspective of international relations, a state is an independent political community: a people organized within a territory under the jurisdiction of such a power.

[4] Voltaire, *Essai sur les moeurs*, ch. 70.

[5] Wight, *Systems of States*, p. 21.

dation of statehood all tended to make for a more uniform system, although this was offset by the addition to international society of a host of new non-European states as a result of the breakup of the colonial empires. Compared with the European past, the diversity of languages, religions, and laws has probably increased rather than diminished. All this suggests the continued heterogeneity of the modern states system.

And yet the idea of a society of states, like that of the state itself, presupposes a certain formal similarity among the entities designated as states regardless of the degree to which they differ from one another in religion and culture, in the size and wealth of their populations, or in their internal political arrangements. From the point of view of diplomacy, to be able to identify the political entities to which it was proper to ascribe the quality of statehood was of more than theoretical importance. Only a state—an independent political community entitled to look after its own affairs—could be a member of the society of states and occupy a position of equality with other members. Implicit in the idea of membership in international society is the idea of speaking with a separate voice, of being an autonomous agent able to order its own internal affairs and engage in transactions with other entities of similar character. It is this idea that underlies the various attempts that have been made, in political thought and in international law, to define the quality of statehood: the idea of the "perfect community" explored by the scholastics, one "complete in itself, that is, which is not part of another community, but has its own laws and its own council and its own magistrates";[6] the notion of "sovereignty" applied to a political community not subject to superior authority and thus free both to alter its own laws and to determine its own relations with other such communities; or the "independent political community" of nineteenth-century international law, identi-

---

[6] Vitoria, *De Indis*, p. 169.

fied by marks such as a defined territory, self-government, and recognition of its independent status by other states.

The idea of a society of sovereign or independent states has a number of important corollaries. One is that each state enjoys a certain right to be immune from the scrutiny and intervention of other states in its internal affairs. The idea of state sovereignty means that an independent political community is free to make and amend its own laws and to enjoy its own religious and cultural life, subject only to those limitations that are necessary to reconcile the liberty of one community with that of others. State sovereignty is therefore compatible with the absence of individual liberty within the state. Self-government can take many forms, and is not limited to constitutional or democratic rule. It is not, in other words, a necessary feature of international law that it include provisions protecting the liberty of individuals within each state. The view that the liberty of states has nothing to do with individual liberty received its most extreme formulation in nineteenth-century writings on international law. According to the leading English treatise of this period, for example, a state "may place itself under any form of government that it wishes, and may frame its social institutions upon any model. . . . A state has a right to live its life in its own way, so long as it keeps itself rigidly to itself, and refrains from interfering with the equal right of other states to live their life in the manner which commends itself to them. . . ."[7] From such an extreme view of state sovereignty, nineteenth-century writers tended to deduce a strong principle of nonintervention, for the greater the range of matters that are thought to fall within the exclusive jurisdiction of the state, the greater the range of state activities protected by the principle of nonintervention. As I shall try to show later on, nothing in the idea of state sovereignty precludes the existence of moral and juridical constraints protecting individual freedom from the exercise of government power. But it is also true that such con-

[7] Hall, *Treatise on International Law*, pp. 43-44.

straints are not required by the idea of the state as a "free" (that is, sovereign) community unless further assumptions are made concerning the moral foundations of state sovereignty.

The idea of the sovereign or independent state also has as a corollary the idea of the formal equality of states. In the seventeenth and eighteenth centuries the view that states were formal equals regardless of other differences was explained in terms of an analogy with individuals in a "state of nature," who were presumed to be equally at liberty to pursue their own security. According to this analogy the natural condition of nations is one in which claims to superiority or precedence are unfounded. Although princes may differ in wealth or in the size of their dominions, suggests Pufendorf, "their power is of the same nature."[8] The same idea is repeated seventy-five years later by Christian Wolff. "By nature," writes Wolff, "all nations are equal the one to the other. For nations are considered as individual free persons living in a state of nature. Since by nature all men are equal, all nations too are equal." And he goes on to illustrate the distinction between incidental and essential features of the state, arguing that "as the tallest man is no more a man than the dwarf, so also a nation, however small, is no less a nation than the greatest nation."[9] The independence of states thus gives rise to a kind of *formal* equality, for the claim of a state to be "sovereign," that is, independent of any superior, is one that all states are equally entitled to make simply by virtue of their status as states. But, as Wolff's metaphor suggests, the idea of state equality does not entail any *substantive* equality. On the contrary, the formal equality of states is compatible with extreme differences in territorial extent, population, wealth, religion, and government.

Thus the formal similarity and equality contained in the idea of a society of states does not necessarily imply political, religious, or cultural uniformity. On the contrary, that idea

---

[8] *Law of Nature and of Nations*, 8:4.
[9] *Law of Nations*, Prolegomena, sect. 16.

reflects a series of compromises through which the inhabitants of Europe accommodated themselves to the inescapable fact of their own diversity, a diversity that some of them not only tolerated but came to value. Where some insisted that international law must allow each state to enjoy its liberty as a matter of natural right, others emphasized the advantages of this liberty. Gibbon, for example, saw in the division of Europe into separate states an antidote to the oppressive despotism and cultural stagnation to which the Roman Empire had succumbed as a consequence of its uncontested dominion over the civilized world, a decline which he feared would be the probable consequence of the unification of Europe under a single sovereign.[10] The gradual inclusion, from the middle of the nineteenth century, of non-Christian and non-European societies only augmented the diversity of the modern states system. It is one of the great achievements of European international law that it acknowledged the claims of pluralism. It reflected an appreciation of the fact that the most likely consequence of attempts to shape international society according to some particular ideal conception of religious truth, political legitimacy, or human good would be perpetual war or a universal tyranny. It therefore rejected the notion that international society should display not merely the formal similarity of its member states but also whatever substantive similarity—a devotion to Calvinism, for example, or monarchy, or communism—that some might try to impose on all. For states, as well as for individuals, it is association in terms of principles to be observed in the pursuit of self-chosen purposes, and not in terms of a devotion to any shared purpose, that "corresponds to and accommodates the dominant moral disposition of the inhabitants of modern Europe: the historic disposition to be 'distinct.' "[11]

---

[10] *Decline and Fall of the Roman Empire*, ch. 38. Arguments concerning the advantages of multiplicity are also made by Montesquieu, *Considérations sur les causes de la grandeur des Romains et de leur décadence*, ch. 9, and Machiavelli, *Art of War*, book 2, pp. 622-623.

[11] Oakeshott, *On Human Conduct*, p. 251.

THE IMPORTANCE OF INTERNATIONAL LAW

It was not until the end of the eighteenth century that deference to the authority of a common body of international law was clearly recognized to be the essential basis of association among the states of Europe, rather than such contingent features or conditions of their association as geographical propinquity, cultural similarity, religious or ideological agreement, or common interests. This discovery was, however, the culmination of explorations of the idea of international society begun many years before.[12] The experience of the century ending in 1648 seemed to prove that the states of Europe could not agree to subject themselves to a universal monarch or to a single religious faith, and thus that neither political nor religious uniformity could form the basis of their relationship. On what basis, then, could they be related? Their common struggle against the Turks, together with religious stalemate within Europe, supported the notion that they had at least their Christianity in common, even if this faith was no longer that of the united Christendom of an imagined past. Later on, as we shall see, other sorts of substantive unity were discerned, urged, and from time to time even momentarily accepted. But all such forms of substantive unity have proved ephemeral; what has persisted is the formal unity of

[12] The history of the idea of a society of states is not to be confused with the history of the European states system itself, although the two are certainly connected. For two different views on the question of origins, compare Wight, *Systems of States*, pp. 129-152, with Hinsley, *Power and the Pursuit of Peace*, pp. 153-185, and *Nationalism and the International System*, pp. 67-84. Wight, who argues for an earlier date, is in fact more concerned with the states system, Hinsley with *idea* of the states system. A related controversy concerns the origins of international law, much of it taken up with a tendentious effort of transfer the honors of originality from the Protestant Grotius to the earlier Catholic writers Vitoria and Suarez. The various arguments are summarized by Nussbaum, *Concise History of the Law of Nations*, pp. 296-306. For reasons given in the text, I think that it was not well into the eighteenth century that the idea of international society as a society of states governed by a body of law arising from the relations of such states, as opposed to natural law, was clearly articulated and widely understood.

an association of states based on mutual restraint and accommodation. It is the sort of unity enjoyed by those who, having failed to get others to adopt their own ideas and institutions, have little choice but to tolerate the existence of differences they are unable to eradicate.

The Peace of Westphalia,[13] concluded in 1648, has been thought by successive generations of commentators to be of great signficance because it reflected an understanding that the states of Europe were to be united on the basis of certain formal principles of mutual toleration and coexistence, and were agreed (if only for tactical reasons) in rejecting political or religious union. Although the significance of the peace may have been exaggerated by the desire to find a constitutional foundation for the states system as well as to have a means of marking the origin of this system, it is nevertheless true the treaties signed at Münster and Osnabrück reflected principles that were later to become thoroughly embedded in European thought and practice and to distinguish the modern international system from the crumbling arrangements of medieval Europe. The impact of the peace can be summarized as follows:

First, the Peace of Westphalia seems to have paved the way for frank acceptance of the idea of Europe as a multiplicity of independent states by requiring from its numerous constituents no more than nominal deference to the interests of the Holy Roman Empire. Thus, the right of the princes, bishops, and cities as independent powers free to pursue their own foreign policies, conclude treaties, exchange diplomatic representatives, and make war was recognized. At the same time the claims of the emperor to the status of ruler of all Europe, long moribund to be sure, were at last explicitly and generally rejected.

Second, the peace also constituted a rejection of religious orthodoxy, although this rejection was implied by the proceedings rather than explicitly incorporated into the texts of

[13] Parry, *Consolidated Treaty Series, 1648-1918*, vol. 1.

the peace treaties. The latter contained many restrictions on religious liberty, but the negotiations that produced them were carried on by Protestant as well as Catholic rulers, and this implied mutual recognition and tolerance, however reluctant. The states system after Westphalia was more clearly based on secular principles than had been the case before.

Third, the discussions resulting in the peace occurred at a general conference at which many states were represented and which was conducted on the assumption that matters directly concerning some few of the participants were also indirectly of general concern. Implicit here is the notion of a society whose members might legitimately interest themselves in disputes to which they were not directly a party, the resolution of which might have consequences for the society as a whole.[14]

Finally, the Peace of Westphalia, by reconstituting the Holy Roman Empire as a collection of states at once independent and yet joined under the nominal authority of the emperor, created an anomalous political entity that was to stimulate later thinkers to puzzle over what Pufendorf in 1675 had identified as a "states system": "several states that are so connected as to seem to constitute one body but whose members retain sovereignty."[15] The name as well as the conception was soon to be applied not to the empire but to Europe as a whole.

Although Europe was increasingly taking the form of a system of states, European thought only slowly accommodated itself to this development. When sixteenth- and seventeenth-

---

[14] Westlake, *Collected Papers*, p. 56.

[15] As quoted by Wight, *Systems of States*, p. 21; also see Krieger, *Politics of Discretion*, pp. 153-169. Whether Pufendorf meant by a "state system" what it has since come to mean is thrown into doubt, however, by the definition he gives in *Duty of Man and Citizen* (1682): a number of states "so connected by some special bond, that their several powers can be regarded as substantially the powers of one state" (p. 115). His examples are several kingdoms each separately administered under its own laws by a common king and an association of separate states united by a treaty according to which decisions regarding the common defense are made by unanimous consent.

century writers on the law of nations imagined a society more inclusive than that of the state, they most often had in mind a world society of individuals, a single *humana civiltas* or *civitas maxima*, not a society of states. Similarly, the law of nations (*ius gentium*) was during this period most often identified with a law of nature whose principles, being universal, would be found in the particular laws of each people or state. Only a few writers clearly distinguished a body of rules specific to the relations of states, a *ius inter gentes* or international law proper as contrasted to the *ius gentium*, and these were mostly lawyers primarily interested in the practices and rules of international diplomacy, commerce, and war rather than in their philosophical foundations.[16] The idea of a distinct body of international law derived from the customs and argreements of states appears only fleetingly in the writings of theologians and philosophers of the early modern period. Too often the ambiguity of the expression "the law of nations" has been resolved by reading back into the writings of writers like Vitoria, Suarez, Gentili, Grotius, and Wolff more recent conceptions of international society as a society of states and of international law as a body of law specific to that society.[17]

[16] In a work published in 1650 the Dutch jurist Richard Zouche explicitly distinguished the "law between nations" (*ius inter gentes*) from the 'law of nations" (*ius gentium*), tracing the former back not to the Roman *ius gentium* but to the *ius feciale*, a body of law concerned specifically with relations between Rome and the foreign nations with which it had contact. (*Exposition of Fecial Law*, pp. 1-2.) A similar distinction is made by Rachel, writing in 1676, in *Dissertations on the Law of Nature and of Nations*, pp. 157-158.

[17] Although in the only available English translation of *De Jure Belli* Gentili is made to speak of "international law," it is evident that nothing resembling the modern concept of international law as a set of rules based on international custom and agreement is to be found in this work. For Gentili the *ius gentium* or law of nations is composed of principles common to all known legal systems and discovered by reason. It is therefore identical with natural law: "The law of nations is that which is in use among all the nations of men, which native reason has established among all human beings, and which is equally observed by all mankind. Such a law is a natural law" (p. 8). Suarez distinguishes between two senses of *ius gentium*, that is, between "the law which all the various peoples and nations ought to observe in their

The tendency of these writers to speak of the law of nations as if it were natural law applied to a particular class of persons, sovereign princes, can be seen very clearly in the sorts of evidence mentioned by Grotius in *The Law of War and Peace* to support his interpretations of the law of nations. Grotius appeals to the authority of ancient authors, invoking their superior perception of what the law of nature (which is known through reason) requires of princes, but largely ignoring modern state practice as evidence of the customs and agreements of nations. This is a method very different from that of the positivist treatises of the nineteenth century.

It is to the writings of the eighteenth century that we must look for evidence of the emergence of a clear and consistent conception of the society of states. The understanding of international unity that flourished during the Enlightenment reflected the shift toward such a conception in its preoccupation with the cutural unity of Europe rather than the legal unity of mankind. This is not to deny the cosmopolitanism of the Enlightenment, but merely to notice that the larger society it celebrated was often that of Europe rather than of mankind. European unity appeared to reside, in part, in the homogeneity of European institutions when compared with those of the non-European world. This unity in diversity could be seen, for example, in the languages of Europe, which re-

---

relations with each other" and "laws which individual states or kingdoms observe within their own borders" and are everywhere similar and accepted. (*De Legibus*, II, xix, 8.) But the law of nations in the first sense, though distinguished from natural law, is nevertheless conceived as consisting of principles both universally recognized and virtually immune to change either through unanimous agreement or the universal adoption of a contrary usage. (*De Legibus*, III, xx, 8-9.) According to Gierke, *Natural Law and the Theory of Society*, p. 196, the idea of a "universal society of states" was defended against Pufendorf by a number of writers, including Leibniz and Wolff. But Gierke evidently does not in this passage distinguish the idea of a society of states from that of a world society of individuals. The claim appears to be more justified in the case of Leibniz than Wolff; see the former's *Codex Juris Gentium* (1693), preface, xx, and Schrecker, "Leibniz's Principles of International Justice," p. 492.

sembled one another more than any non-European tongue, and in the increasing reliance on French as the medium of diplomacy and polite society. European unity was also apparent in the religious faith of its member societies, "all having the same foundation for their religion, though divided into several sects," as well as in their manners, so "nearly similar in all this quarter of the globe," by which they were "advantageously distinguished" from the rest of mankind.[18] The states of Europe rested upon "the same basis of general law, with some diversity of provincial customs and local establishment,"[19] a law whose principles were "unknown in other parts of the globe."[20]

European unity, however, was understood to rest not only on *similar* principles but on *common* ones. The latter were to be found in those practices of international relations whose substance is cogently summarized by Voltaire: "that the European nations never make their prisoners slaves; that they respect the ambassadors of their enemies; that they are agreed concerning the preeminence and particular rights of certain princes, such as the emperor, the kings, and other lesser potentates; and that, above all, they are agreed on the wise policy of preserving, as best they can, an equal balance of power among themselves. . . ."[21] It is expected that each state will pursue its own interests and seek to expand its power, but that it will do so within limits prescribed by an inherited body of common principles. Europe, therefore, might almost be thought of as a single society: "a kind of society and general republic," "one Republic," "one great nation composed of several," "a sort of great republic divided into several states," "one great republic whose inhabitants have attained almost the same level of politeness and cultivation," "virtually one

---

[18] Voltarie, *Siècle de Louis XIV*, p. 159; Burke, *Works*, 5:215; Gibbon, *Decline and Fall of the Roman Empire*, ch. 38.

[19] Burke, *Works*, 5:214.

[20] Voltaire, *Siècle de Louis XIV*, p. 159.

[21] Ibid., pp. 159-160.

great state."[22] The shock of the French Revolution only reinforced the insight that European unity, if it were to exist at all, must exist on the basis of recognized rules and procedures governing the relations of states, whatever their purposes. This is evidently what Burke had in mind when he wrote in his "Letters on a Regicide Peace" about the possibility of regular relations between England and the revolutionary regime in France that "before men can transact any affair, they must have a common language to speak, and some common recognized principles on which they can argue; otherwise all is cross-purpose and confusion."[23] It is the common practices and rules of international society that provide the basis for international relations even in the absence of common interests or other ties.

The publication in 1758 of Vattel's readable and influential *Le Droit des gens* made the literate public more aware of the existence of a distinct body of international law rooted as much in the practices of trade, navigation, fisheries, embassies, truces, neutrality, treaty-making, and the like, as in the civil or political laws of each state. Nevertheless, the rules that Vattel presents are said by him to be derived from natural law rather than from treaties and custom. Vattel is interested in stating the *general* rules of international law, those that are binding on all states regardless of the particular agreements into which they have entered or the particular customs they observe.[24] He therefore claims to exclude treaties, which yield only "arbitrary" or "conventional" law, and custom, which binds "only those Nations which by long usage have adopted its principles." The details of treaties and custom, he suggests, "belong rather to history than to a systematic treatise on the Law of Nations."[25]

---

[22] Fénelon, *Examen de conscience*, p. 99; Callières, *On the Manner of Negotiating with Princes*, p. 11; Montesquieu, *Réflexions*, p. 34; Voltaire, *Siècle de Louis XIV*, p. 159; Gibbon, *Decline and Fall of the Roman Empire*, ch. 38; Burke, *Works*, 5:214.

[23] *Works*, 5:215.

[24] *Droit des gens*, pp. 11a, 9.

[25] Ibid., p. 11a.

Thus Vattel, in the tradition of the writers on a universal law of nations, postulates a universal society. But it is a universal society of states, not individuals. The law of nations expounded by Vattel is unequivocally a law for a system of states, and not the law of a transnational community of individuals.[26] And because it is universal it is not limited in intention to states that are Christian, European, or "civilized." But of course the rules that Vattel states mirror closely the practices of Europe, despite these claims to universal application and to the subordinate status of custom and treaties as sources of international law.

Vattel's work was frequently reprinted, in many languages, during the last part of the eighteenth century and the first years of the nineteenth. This period also saw a quickening of international legal activity, as evidenced by the number of treaties concluded, the increased scope of matters covered by these treaties, an explosion of activity in naval prize courts in connection with the Napoleonic wars, the consequent development of a substantial body of case law on the law of prize, and, finally, the proliferation of claims based explicitly on international law. Equally important, from the last decades of the eighteenth century the habit of discussing international affairs in terms of the principles of the law of nations became more common. This law was understood to embody the traditions of Europe and to serve as a way of expressing those traditions as rules guiding the conduct of states.

The main works of the late eighteenth century concerning international law make it clear that European practice was almost completely replacing natural law as the most important source of legal rights and duties. These works, unlike Vattel's, are explicitly offered as compendia of state practice—and it is the states of Europe whose practice is examined for evidence of the law of nations. The twenty volumes published between 1777 and 1780 by J. J. Moser are devoted to compiling what he referred to as "the most recent European law of nations" as embodied in the texts of treaties, dec-

[26] Ibid., pp. 3, 6, 12.

larations, diplomatic practice, and other evidences of the customary practice of European states.[27] This identification of the law of nations with European state practice is made even clearer in the works of Georg Friedrich von Martens. In a series of studies that greatly influenced subsequent legal thought, Martens defended the idea that international law was "positive" law based on usage and precedent, summarized the rules that might be distilled from state practice, and compiled collections of treaties and judicial cases for the use of statesmen and scholars seeking more precise knowledge of international legal practice.[28] These and other works of the period helped to disseminate the idea that the law of nations was exclusively a European institution—an idea that only gradually diminished its hold in European thought when, toward the end of the nineteenth century, non-European powers began to attain positions of international prominence.

The emergence of the idea of a positive law of nations based on the practice of states corresponded to the decline of natural-law thinking concerning the internal law of the state. Of all the diverse forms of law according to which a country might be governed, one form—that posited or laid down by the sovereign power—was increasingly regarded as definitive of law as such.[29] Legal science turned increasingly to the inves-

---

[27] Moser's principal work on international law is his *Versuch des neuesten europäischen völkerrechts in friedens- und kriegszeiten*, published in 10 volumes between 1777 and 1780. The collection of excerpts from this work published in 1959 as *Grundsätze des völkerrechts* is more easily obtained. Moser's conception of international law is discussed by Walker, *Johann Jakob Moser*, pp. 337-342.

[28] Alexandrowicz argues that the international law whose outlines are traced by Martens is not exclusively a European law because his collection of treaties, *Recueil des principaux traités*, includes those contracted between European states and Asian potentates. (*Introduction to the History of the Law of Nations in the East Indies*, pp. 161-162.) But Martens explicitly defines the general positive law of nations as the "aggregate of the rights and obligations established among the nations of *Europe*" through their treaties and customary practice. (*Law of Nations*, p. 5, emphasis added.)

[29] The expressions "positive law" and "legal positivism" are notoriously ambiguous ones. Hart distinguishes five meanings of "positivism" in contem-

tigation of the acts of legislative bodies in its search for the law, while in international law there was a parallel movement toward an increasingly explicit concern with the treaties and other public acts of states as expressions of their sovereign will. And as the source of international law came gradually to be identified with the will of states, as evidenced both by their treaties and their customary practice, the society of states became increasingly identified with that particular group of countries whose conduct was investigated for the purpose of discovering the content of this law. The nineteenth-century compilers and theoreticians of international law turned toward an almost exclusive preoccupation with European state practice to flesh out the structure of what was coming to be understood as "The Public Law of Europe."[30]

The international system that had developed by the early years of the nineteenth century might, in summary, be characterized as displaying the following features. It was understood to be a system of states resembling one another in some ways but in others happily diverse. These states were regarded as constituting a single society governed by a distinc-

---

porary English and American writing about law. (*Concept of Law*, p. 253.) Since the late eighteenth century, "positivism" in international law has been identified above all with two propositions: (1) that "law," properly so called, is a set of rules distinct from "natural law" or "morality," and (2) that the source of all law, so understood, that is binding on the citizens and officials of a state is the will of the sovereign as expressed internally through legislation and externally through explicit agreement (treaties) or tacit agreement (custom) with other states. The first of these propositions is discussed in Chapter 9, the second in Chapter 8.

[30] The expression "droit public de l'Europe" was used at least as early as 1747 in a work, Mably's *Droit public de l'Europe, fondé sur les traités*, that antedates Vattel's *Droit des gens*. The former is not, however, a legal treatise but rather an historical study of European international relations largely as reflected in treaties of peace. These treaties are identified with "the public law of Europe" rather than with "the law of nations." In the nineteenth century the former expression was linked with the view that a few states might create through treaty rules of international law binding on states that were not among the contracting powers. See Gihl, *International Legislation*, pp. 57-64.

tive body of laws, the law of nations. Its rules were understood to have their source in the usages and traditions of European statecraft and to reflect the experience of European statesmen in managing the coexistence of their separate countries. Furthermore, this law of nations was held to apply only to states, that is, to those independent political communities whose sovereigns possessed the authority (but of course not always the effective power) to make treaties, to send and receive diplomatic representatives, to declare war, and freely to decide their external policy within the framework of procedures that constituted the law of nations. Because all enjoyed the same status as members of the society of states and subjects of its law, the states were formal equals despite actual disparities of size, wealth, and might.[31]

Reflection on the law of nations also helped to clarify the internal identity and external boundaries of the society of states. It led to the eventual realization that what *defined* the states of Europe as a society was not their geographical propinquity, frequent transactions, or common cultural heritage, but rather the fact that they were associated within the framework of a single body of international law. Although the other factors might be important as accidental features or empirical conditions of such an association, theorists were beginning to recognize that these factors could not themselves provide the *terms* of international association.

The irrelevance of geographical proximity or frequent transactions as definitive features of the society of states could be seen as soon as it was realized that the idea of common membership in a single system did not rule out the possibility

[31] Coexisting with this ideal of formal equality was the alternative notion of a special status for so-called great powers, a status that may be defined, following Hedley Bull, as pertaining to "powers recognized by others to have, and conceived by their own leaders and peoples to have, certain special rights and duties." (*Anarchical Society*, p. 202.) As Bull points out, the idea of a great power presupposes the idea of an international society united by common rules and institutions in terms of which the special status of the great powers can be defined and through which they seek to "govern" the society of states.

that some of the members might have little to do with one another. This became increasingly apparent as the society of states came, during the course of the nineteenth century, to include countries which, while coming into contact with the great powers, often had little contact with the lesser European powers or with each other. Nor, as the system expanded, could similarity of culture beyond that implied by a willingness to accept the forms of statehood and diplomacy be said to characterize, much less define, the system. Languages, forms of political rule, religion, and the other dimensions of national culture were multiplied, beginning with the acceptance of the Ottoman Empire as a participant in "the public law and concert of Europe."[32] After this step had been taken statesmen ceased to invoke Christianity as the basis of the unity of international society. The inclusion first of states of European culture located outside Europe and then of states both geographically and culturally non-European marked the demise of the conception of the society of states as an exclusively European society.

During the latter half of the nineteenth century the unity of the society of states was commonly asserted by writers on international law to be based on the fact that its members were "civilized." The "Family of Nations" was understood to be an association of nations that had reached a certain level of civilization, as measured by European standards, and among whom a special set of rules prevailed. These rules did not necessarily apply in the relations among savage, barbaric, primitive, or stateless peoples, or in the relations between members of the civilized world and those outside its boundaries.[33] But as the century came to a close the so-called stand-

[32] Article 7 of the Treaty of Paris, 1856.

[33] See, e.g., Wheaton, *Elements of International Law*, p. 16, and Phillimore, *Commentaries upon International Law*, 1:23-24. When J. S. Mill wrote, in "A Few Words on Non-intervention," p. 253, that "to characterize any conduct whatsoever towards a barbarous people as a violation of the law of nations, only shows that he who so speaks has never considered the subject," he expressed a clear understanding of international law as the law of a par-

ard of civilization was exposed to increasing criticism as a rationalization of colonial aggrandizement, and it too began slowly to disintegrate. Clearly neither proximity, nor cultural similarity, nor the intensity of their transactions united Japan and Paraguay, or Denmark and Siam. They were members of the society of states by virtue of their participation in its common practices and by their recognition of the authority of its common laws.

---

ticular society of states. The standards governing relations with or among outsiders could not be the standards of *this* society. Yet it was not thought to follow from the exclusion of non-European or "uncivilized" societies that the inhabitants of such societies were without duties toward outsiders. The most common way of putting the case for such duties was to say that such relations were governed by "the universal rules of morality between man and man" (Mill), even though they were outside the jurisdiction of the law of nations. The only serious resistance to this separation between international law and morality came from within the tradition of natural law, with its postulated "natural society" of nations and of mankind based not on consent but on the idea of natural justice. The duties imposed by the positive law of nations, in contrast, are obligations derived from a system of law founded on the customs and usages of civilized states. On the idea of a "natural society" in relation to international law see Twiss, *Law of Nations*, 1:8; see also, more generally, Lorimer, *Institutes of the Law of Nations*, and Eppstein, *Catholic Tradition of the Law of Nations*.

CHAPTER 4

A Legal Order without a State

A DECISIVE STAGE in the progressive articulation of the idea of international law was reached with the discovery that the European states system might be thought of as a sort of civil society, on the analogy of the civil order of the modern European state, but distinguished from it by the fact that its "citizens" were themselves states rather than individual persons. Intimations of this idea of international law as a body of law peculiar to sovereign states in their relations with one another can be found in earlier writings. But it was only in the course of the eighteenth century that a self-conscious clarity concerning the character of a distinctively international legal order was achieved and the insights of this achievement consolidated and disseminated. The next stage, which involved working out the implications of this idea of a distinctive international legal order, occupied theorists of international law throughout the nineteenth century and the first half of the twentieth. The result was an extended debate in which various deficiencies of the international legal system were pointed out, according to different conceptions of law, and various proposals for its completion in a system of "true" law were advanced.

One recurrent criticism has been that international law is undeserving of the status of law because it hews too closely to the demands of power politics: its principles are too often indistinguishable from those of reason of state. The customs and pacts of the society of states, according to this view, cannot be called law until they are made to correspond more closely to the demands of morality. Rousseau, for example, dismisses the conclusions of writers on international law as

69

little more than the fruit of a misconceived effort to seek moral guidance from a "history of ancient abuses," by a method of reasoning in which "fact" is offered "to establish right."[1] This attack may be compared with another common criticism of the international legal system as defective because of the absence of any sovereign power within it to make and enforce its rules. The argument that international law is, for this reason, not really law was first given prominence in discussions of the law of nations by Pufendorf, although it is now most often identified with John Austin's definition of law as a body of commands issued and enforced by a sovereign.[2] Another version of this argument is made by Kant, who thought it fruitless to search for rules of law in international customs and agreements so long as states continued in a condition in which they "are not subject to a common external constraint."[3]

Between these two poles of doubt may be found a third critical position according to which the defining characteristic of law is thought to lie neither in its correspondence to a rationally determined moral code nor in the creation and enforcement of rules by a single sovereign power but in the availability of some procedure for authoritatively ascertaining what is to count as the law. A legal order exists, according to this view, when there exists some authoritative method for determining, first, whether a particular rule is a rule of "law," and, second, the meaning of a rule in particular situations. For law to exist there must be some procedure for reconciling divergent claims and interpretations. Without such a procedure, it is argued, a system of rules is unlikely to be effective in regulating conduct. The law of nations, lacking any such

[1] *Oeuvres complètes*, 3:353.

[2] Following Hobbes, *Philosophical Rudiments*, XIV, 4, who defined the law of nations as the law of nature applied to states, Pufendorf argued that there is no "positive law of nations which has the force of a law, properly so called, such as binds nations as if it proceeded from a superior." (*Law of Nature and of Nations*, II, iii.) Austin, too, concerned himself with the character of law "properly so called," and identified it with the commands of a superior. (*Province of Jurisprudence Determined*, lecture I.)

[3] *Political Writings*, p. 103.

means for achieving interpretive agreement, appears to be an incomplete and defective expression of the idea of a common law. Yet to seek rectification of its defects in a world state seems neither practicable nor desirable. Perceiving the impossibility of constructing a universal legal order on the centralized model of the modern European state, a number of thinkers were drawn to explore the extent to which the certainty and stability expected from the legal order of the state might be achieved among a multiplicity of states. For those who saw the lack of a reliable procedure for authoritative determination to the critical defect of the international legal system, the apparent solution was to be found in the creation of some form of international adjudication or its functional equivalent. The institution required for the realization of international relations on the basis of a common law was not legislative but judicial.

The development of this position was the work of philosophers rather than of expounders of the law of nations. While the latter attempted to reconstruct a systematic body of international law on the basis of evidence provided by state practice, the philosophers were already discerning what they took to be the futility of such an exercise in the absence of any authoritative way of resolving differences in the interpretation of this evidence. The long line of publicists who built upon the work of Moser and Martens at the end of the eighteenth century recognized the difficulty of relying upon natural law as a source of agreed principles of international law, but they were much slower to grasp the implications of the comparable uncertainty attending the reliance on treaties and custom as sources of law. The extreme conclusion had already been drawn by Hobbes nearly two hundred years before: in the absence of a supreme power to declare it, a law—apart from the law of nature—governing sovereigns could not be said to exist. Hobbes does not argue that in the absence of a supreme power to interpret and apply them the pacts of sovereigns with one another could not qualify as law. His is the more radical and interesting argument that in the absence of authoritative determination such pacts would be uncertain and ephemeral. States, like individuals, are in competition for resources in their pursuit of power and security, and their sovereigns of course capable of appreciating the utility of arrangements through which the severity of this competition might be mitigated. International agreements to observe limits to the pursuit of national aims and national security can be accepted because to do so is prudent. Rational statesmen will seek to render the pursuit of their respective aims less uncertain through such agreements or pacts. But agreements among sovereigns are as likely to be undermined by the pressures of competition as those among private individuals. The dilemma of the treaty is thus little different from that of the private contract: it is an ad hoc device for reducing uncertainty that is itself uncertain because effective means for authoritatively interpreting its terms and securing their enforcement are lacking.

The importance of authoritative determination in abating the uncertainty and unreliability of a common law governing the relations of states is also urged by Locke. A situation in which individuals or sovereigns remain judges in their own cause and rely upon self-help to enforce their judgments is not a political or civil society, because it lacks the defining feature of such a society: an *umpire* impartially to administer common rules in settling disputes.[4] Lacking a supreme judge or umpire, states remain in a state or condition of nature. It is a condition in which there may be found elements of society—agreements, transactions, cooperation on the basis of shared interest—but not "settled standing rules"[5] or "an established, settled, known law,"[6] impartially applied. Unlike the internal affairs of a civil society, which *are* conducted according to "antecedent, standing, positive laws," the conduct of foreign affairs is with few exceptions "left to the prudence and wisdom of those whose hands it is in, to be managed for

[4] *Second Treatise*, pp. 367-368.
[5] Ibid., p. 367.
[6] Ibid., p. 396.

the public good."[7] In short, there is in the absence of some means of adjudicating disputes between states no positive international law to guide the conduct of statesmen.

The skepticism of Hobbes and Locke regarding the possibility of an enduring law among nations had its impact on subsequent thought. It is particularly evident in Rousseau, who directly attacked the claims of an accumulating body of literature devoted to expounding the content and foundations of the law of nations. In spite of its cultural unity, he argued, Europe is in effect without laws: the so-called public law of Europe is "full of contradictory rules which nothing but the right of the strongest can reduce to order: so that, in the absence of any sure guide, in case of doubt reason will always incline in the direction of self-interest. . . ."[8] Because of this uncertainty in the law of nations, the states of Europe are in fact related not by common rules but only by self-interest. International transactions, even cooperation, are possible on this basis, but nothing resembling civil society: that is, association on the basis of a common, known, and authoritative law. Hence Rousseau's characterization (in an unpublished manuscript on war) of the law of nations as "a Chimera, even feebler than the law of nature."[9] The impossibility of international law arises from the lack of any sanction. Like Hobbes, Rousseau does not mean by this that each state must be forced to obey the laws. His point is rather that association in terms of common laws is impossible among either men or nations without the existence of some superior coercive power to "give their common interests and mutual obligations that stability and strength which they could never acquire by themselves."[10] Without a common superior to enforce general rules the selfishness of some and the fear of all would soon, as Hobbes had suggested, undermine the fragile foundation of mutual trust upon which all enduring political association de-

[7] Ibid., pp. 411-412.
[8] *Oeuvres complètes*, 3:568-569.
[9] Ibid., p. 610.
[10] Ibid., p. 569.

pends. An "authoritative umpire"[11] is required, capable both of interpreting and enforcing those principles of international conduct that emerge from the practices and agreements of sovereigns. It is therefore the judicial and executive power, rather than the legislative, that must be centralized if international relations on the basis of a common body of law is to be realized.[12]

These judgments are shared by Kant. In a famous passage he characterizes Grotius, Pufendorf, Vattel, and other expositors of the law of nations as "sorry comforters" whose codes "do not and cannot have the slightest *legal* force, since states as such are not subject to a common external constraint."[13] Like Rousseau, Kant is inclined to dismiss the principles of the so-called law of nations as a mere rationalization of self-interest. Yet neither regards as desirable the establishment of a superior power to make and enforce a body of law binding sovereigns. The creation of such a power would constitute a remedy worse than the disease it is intended to cure. It might, Rousseau fears, "do more harm in an instant than it would guard against for ages."[14] Kant, seconding this judgment, concludes that a union of independent states is preferable to a single world state, which would inevitably degenerate into "a soulless despotism."[15] But unlike Rousseau, who finds himself forced to conclude that confederation is not a viable alternative to international anarchy, Kant explores the possibility of an intermediate form of organization—which he calls "federation"—in which states might succeed in conducting their relations more fully on the basis of common rules while retaining their independence. Such a federation would

[11] Ibid., p. 581.

[12] The passages mentioned in the text are from the "Abstract" and "Judgment of the Abbe de Saint-Pierre's Project for Perpetual Peace," and from some unpublished manuscripts on war. These writings are conveniently assembled in English translation in Forsyth et al., eds., *Theory of International Relations*, pp. 127-180.

[13] *Political Writings*, p. 103.

[14] *Oeuvres complètes*, 3:600.

[15] *Political Writings*, p. 113.

not require states "to submit to public laws and to a coercive power which enforces them," but would instead constitute a league committed to the avoidance of war and to guaranteeing the security of its members.[16] The only possibility for strengthening international law lies in the institution of a sort of nonaggression pact which, if successful in achieving its purpose, would have the effect of reducing reliance upon war as a means of enforcing rights. A pact of this kind would, however, constitute no more than a "negative substitute" for a true international legal order.[17] Such an order, because it cannot be enjoyed apart from submission to a coercive authority, is both impossible and undesirable.

These arguments are an important benchmark in the continuing development and refinement of the idea of international law. At the very least, they reflect a philosophical search for essentials. One might go further and argue that they achieved some success in this enterprise, for (as I shall try to show in the second part of this study) they are certainly correct in regarding the existence of legislative institutions as a mere contingent feature, and not as an essential or defining characteristic, of a legal system. But their treatment of enforcement is puzzling. Is the existence of a superior power to enforce the common rules an essential feature of legal order—that is, part of the very definition of law? Or is it too, like legislation, a feature that is often present in legal systems, but one that is not invariably and necessarily present? The puzzlement arises, at least in part, because when Rousseau and Kant discuss the requirements of international legal order they do not consistently distinguish the authoritative interpretation of the common rules by a superior judge from the enforcement of these authoritatively interpreted rules.

When Kant, for example, speaks of "common external constraint" as a requirement of legal order, he appears to have in mind both authoritative determination and enforcement by

[16] Ibid., p. 104.
[17] Ibid., p. 105.

a common superior. He does not consider the question of whether authoritative determination might be accomplished within a system of rules that lacked any provision for enforcement by a superior coercive power. And while it is clear that he regards such enforcement to be an absolute requirement of legal order, it is not clear whether he understands this requirement to be *logical* (because enforcement is regarded as part of the definition of law) or *contingent* (enforcement being an empirical condition without which legal order would crumble). Rousseau makes the empirical importance of enforcement as a condition of legal order clear. But the weight he gives to certainty and consistency as qualities of law, and to the importance of an umpire or judge for the realization of these qualities within a system of rules, suggests that he has only begun to sketch the relation between enforcement, authoritative interpretation, and the certainty and consistency of a body of common rules. For more thorough investigation of these questions we must therefore look elsewhere.[18]

Toward the end of the eighteenth century a number of writers began to explore the requisites of international legal order on the premise that such an order presupposes, above all, some means for the authoritative interpretation and application of its rules. For many of those who wrote on international law during the course of the nineteenth and early twentieth centuries, this concern increasingly took the form of an investigation of the possibilities and limits of authoritative determination by a single supranational adjudicatory body:

[18] The difficulties encountered by theorists of international law with respect to the question of whether, and how, international law is deficient as law reflects a puzzlement with respect to the character of law in civil society as well. This suggests that the perplexities of international legal theory are those of legal theory itself rather than of the attempt to understand the character and requisites of law in the circumstances of international relations. If this suggestion is correct, then the theoretical study of international law cannot be pursued as an autonomous discipline. In discussing the foundations of international law in the second part of this book, I have accordingly followed the lead of those theorists of international law who have treated their subject as a branch of jurisprudence in general.

a European, and later universal, court or tribunal. Others sought to reconsider—and revive—the ancient practice of arbitration. Unlike those who held that only rules laid down and enforced by a superior power counted as rules of law and who therefore concluded that international law was not "law properly so called,"[19] those who, like Bentham and James Mill, were impressed by the potential of third party determination were led in their writings on international law to define law in a way that did not tie it to legislation and enforcement by a single sovereign power. On the contrary, they concluded that the law of nations could be applied by arbitrators or by an international court regardless of the manner in which it had been created. At the same time, treaties and customary practice were coming to be regarded by international lawyers as the sources of law most appropriate to the decentralized legal order of the system of states. And just as law might be distinguished from legislation, the analysts and advocates of third party determination began to distinguish the authoritative interpretation of a rule in particular situations in which its meaning was in dispute from the enforcement of that rule as authoritatively interpreted by an international court or arbitral tribunal. Centralized enforcement, like legislation, ceased to be regarded as an essential or defining *characteristic* of law, although few denied the importance of enforcement as an empirical *condition* for the fuller realization of legal order in the relations of states. Because enforcement by a single power seemed neither possible nor desirable, nineteenth-century theorists of international law began to look for functional equivalents. These they discovered in the idea of the force of public opinion.

That a true law of nations might depend upon the creation of an international court is explicitly argued by Bentham in an essay written between 1786 and 1789 although not published until 1838.[20] Bentham's remarks on the relationship

---

[19] Austin, *Province of Jurisprudence Determined*, p. 142.

[20] Bentham was not the first to advocate an international court or "Diet" for the settlement of disputes. See Hinsley, *Power and the Pursuit of Peace*,

between adjudication and international law appear in the form of a proposal for peace based on a treaty among the European powers. Its essential provision is that the great powers should agree to "a plan of general and permanent pacification for all Europe" that would include an agreement limiting the number of troops each power would be permitted to maintain. "Such a pacification might be considerably facilitated," he suggests, "by the establishment of a common court of judicature for the decision of difference between the several nations, although such courts were not to be armed with any coercive powers."[21] Bentham refers to this court as a "Congress" or "Diet" because it would be a permanent body composed of representatives of each state, but it is clearly a judicial and not a legislative body. Its powers would be limited to hearing disputes and reporting its judgment and opinion. These would be published and widely disseminated not only in the countries of the litigant governments but in all countries represented on the court, that is, throughout the European society of states. The decision of the court could, but need not, be enforced by superior force; instead, opinion was to be the sanction. Bentham's suggestion that the decision

---

chs. 1 and 2. His originality lies rather in the clarity with which he distinguished the judicial from the legislative and coercive offices of such a body. It is a bit surprising to find Bentham pursuing this line of thought, for he is better known for his theory of law as an expression of sovereign will—a theory that, as elaborated by Austin, purported to prove the impossibility of international law. But Austin's restatement badly distorts the original. In a manner similar to Hobbes, Bentham had defined law not only as the product of "a volition conceived or adopted by the sovereign in a state" (*Of Laws in General*, p. 1) but as something backed by "the *authority* of the sovereign" (p. 3, emphasis added). Austin's mistake in interpreting both Hobbes and Bentham was to confuse the idea of "authority" with "might," to think that the rules made by sovereign authority were nothing but the orders or commands of those who in a given society were able to compel obedience and therefore in these and other ways to substitute an external or behaviorist account of law for the more complex internal conception of law as rules of conduct that Hobbes and Bentham actually held. These issues are considered further in Chapter 6, below.

[21] *Works*, 2:547.

78

and the reasons for it be circulated in order to inform, educate, and secure the support of the subjects of the various states makes this clear.

There is not the slightest suggestion here that the law of nations, although lacking the coercive sanction provided by a superior power, was not law but rather merely (as Austin was later to put it) "positive morality." For Bentham, it is the authority of rules interpreted in a uniform way, and not coercive enforcement by a superior power, that is the *criterion* of law.[22] If the conditions for the realization of such a system of authority can be produced by some other means, such as the united force of public opinion, this is all that is necessary for international law to exist—that is, for states to be associated in terms of law. Bentham did consider the possibility of some further sanction, suggesting that if compliance is not forthcoming after the opinion of the court has been circulated the refractory state should be placed "under the ban of Europe." States might even consider the possibility of supplying armed contingents for the enforcement of the court's judgments. Such a measure might be necessary if states could not agree to guarantee the liberty of the press in each country in order to facilitate the most extensive and unlimited circulation of the court's opinions and decrees. Coercive enforcement and the sanction of public opinion are alternative means for securing compliance with the judgments of the court, and thus of supporting the authority of that body and of the law it is charged to apply.

Bentham's argument, then, rests on the premise that international relations on the basis of law does not require a sovereign power to originate its rules—that is, to legislate—but only a judicial power to interpret and apply rules having their origin in custom and treaties. And although coercive enforcement might under some circumstances be contingently necessary for a working system of international law, authoritative determination through an appropriate method

---

[22] *Of Laws in General*, pp. 1-2, 133.

of adjudication is the more basic requirement—one inseparable from the very idea of law itself. (Bentham does not consider whether alternatives to the particular form of third-party
determination he proposes, such as arbitration, might not serve
equally well to secure the authority of international law.) Association in terms of law is, moreover, the only alternative to
war between states, for wherever there is a difference of
opinion between two states on a matter of right, concession
and the peaceful resolution of the dispute are unlikely. A nation may yield on a point of interest, but not of right, for to
do so would be to invite further violation of right. Where
there is no common tribunal, there can be no agreed method
of determining rights, but as soon as one exists "the necessity
for war no longer follows from difference of opinion. Just or
unjust, the decision of the arbiters will save the credit, the
honour of the contending party."[23] Bentham denied that his
proposal was visionary. "Why should not the European
fraternity subsist, as well as the German diet or the Swiss
league? These latter have no ambitious views."[24] Like Kant,
he sought to understand what would constitute and what would
help to secure the rule of law among states that retained their
independence. Although brief and polemical, Bentham's essay is still of interest because of the skill with which he is
able, in the course of pursuing other concerns, to distinguish
the presuppositions of legal order in the circumstances of the
states system from both the incidental features of that order
and the empirical conditions for its existence.

Bentham's arguments entered the realm of public discourse, thirteen years before the posthumous publication of
his manuscript, in the form of an essay by James Mill on the
law of nations. Writing in 1825, Mill dissociates Bentham's
analysis of the importance of international adjudication for the
realization of international legal order from Bentham's proposal for a European peace treaty, and avoids as incidental

[23] *Works*, 2:552.
[24] Ibid., pp. 522-523.

any discussion of the particular form a judicial tribunal might take. But he is at one with Bentham in thinking that the efficacy of law depends upon its precision and certainty. These qualities, suggests Mill, depend in turn both upon "a strict determination of what the law is" and "a tribunal so constituted as to yield prompt and accurate execution of the law."[25] If by "execution" Mill means enforcement, he nevertheless distinguishes it from "determination" and leaves open the possibility that it might be carried out by means other than reliance on a centralized coercive power. The great defect of the international legal system is that there is no reliable and authoritative procedure for the interpretation of its rules. It is this defect, Mill suggests, as well as the lack of a supreme legislative and coercive power, that accounts for the fact that the law of nations amounts to little more than mere ceremony, to be observed only so long as there is no motive to behave differently. The "grand inquiry" is therefore "*first*, What can be done towards defining the law of nations? and, *secondly*, What can be done towards providing a tribunal for yielding prompt and accurate decisions" in conformity with this law?[26]

The development of a clear body of rules would be greatly advanced, Mill thought, by the negotiation of an international code to be embodied in generally ratified treaties, which the proposed tribunal would be charged to apply. "Nations will be much more likely to conform to the principles of intercourse which are best for all, if they have an accurate set of rules to go by, than if they have not. In the first place, there is less room for mistake; in the next, there is less room for plausible pretexts; and last of all, the approbation and disapprobation of the world is sure to act with tenfold concentration, where a precise rule is broken, familiar to all the civilized world, and venerated by it all."[27] Because the efficacy of the laws embodied in such a code rests upon the sanction

---

[25] *Essays on Government*, p. 9.

[26] Ibid., p. 10.

[27] Ibid., p. 27.

81

of world opinion, they must be publicized and taught, and they must be administered by a tribunal, "by means of which it might be determined when individuals had acted in conformity with them, and when they had not"; and "by which also, when any doubt existed respecting the conduct which in any particular case the law required, such doubt might be authoritatively removed, and one determinate line of action prescribed."[28] It should be noticed that Mill stresses the difficulties of enforcement less than the more fundamental difficulty of securing the authoritative determination of the law, without which world opinion is without a guide and therefore cannot be brought to bear on behalf of the law. The rationale for a tribunal is thus in part the same as that for the code itself: both are means of focusing public opinion. By fixing and concentrating the disapprobation of mankind, such a tribunal would serve as "a great school of political morality."[29] Contemplating the judgments of such a tribunal, we would correct and strengthen our own.

The view that international law could be strengthened by creation of an international tribunal was taken up, explored, and modified during the course of the nineteenth century by Ladd, Cobden, Lorimer, Laurent, Bluntchli, Oppenheim, and other internationalist thinkers, some of whom were active in the peace and arbitration movements that culminated in the Hague Conferences of 1899 and 1907 and in the founding of the League of Nations and the Permanent Court of International Justice.[30] One persistent issue throughout this period concerned the form of such a tribunal, and particularly whether it should take the form of a congress, diet, or league of states.

[28] Ibid., p. 28.

[29] Ibid., p. 32.

[30] Many of these writers are best read as advocates of particular international policies rather than as theorists of international society, although their proposals do depend upon theoretically significant assumptions about the character of that society. Their views are considered by Schiffer, *Legal Community of Mankind*, chs. 7-9; Hinsley, *Power and the Pursuit of Peace*, chs. 6 and 7; and Holbraad, *Concert of Europe*.

While some thought of such an organization in essentially judicial terms, that is, as being concerned primarily with the settlement of international disputes on the basis of international law, others envisioned an organization that would perform something like a legislative function. Those who understood the office of such a tribunal to be purely adjudicative continued, on the whole, to understand international law in practical terms (that is, as a set of authoritative practices governing the relations of states pursuing diverse purposes), while those who favored the creation of an essentially legislative institution often did so because they thought that such an institution would prove to be an effective instrument of enlightened international policy aimed at realizing the natural harmony of interests that was presumed to exist among states. Thus, to the old controversies concerning the character and possibility of law in an anarchical international society were added new controversies over how a less anarchical, more organized international society should be governed. In order fully to understand the issues raised in these new controversies concerning international government, one must go back to the beginning of the nineteenth century and to the impact of the French Revolution on the theory and practice of European international relations.

CHAPTER 5

The Government of International Society

BY CHALLENGING the arrangements of the European system, French policy following the Revolution stimulated a fundamental rethinking of the requirements of international order, and generated controversies that have persisted to the present day. The successive coalitions against the French culminated in a European alliance of great powers—including, within a few years, a rehabilitated France—and initiated a habit of cooperation among the great powers which, though often disrupted, gradually came to be regarded as the norm. A new element was thereby added to the idea of the society of states as an association of independent political communities in terms of common practices and rules: the idea that these relations might be more formally organized and directed by the members of the system acting in concert. The impulse behind what was, in the first instance, little more than a continuation of their wartime cooperation by the states allied against Napoleon did not spring from any theoretical analysis of the requirements of the rule of law in the relations of states. The idea, for example, that international law required some form of third-party determination was an opinion of philosophers, not statesmen, and did not become generally significant until it was taken up by the peace movement in Britain and the United States after the *Alabama Claims* settlement in the 1870s. The first diplomatic congresses reflected rather a perception that international order, which was understood to include, but not to be limited to, the observance of international law, was not something that could safely be left to itself. Order—at least that kind of order reflected in the stable coexistence of independent states—did not simply occur. It had to be created and, once established, to be maintained. International relations on the basis of agreed principles could not be enjoyed without effort; some deliberate direction was required. The system required to be governed.

The history of international relations since 1815 is thus in part a series of experiments in international government. The diverse conceptions of the European Concert, the various proposals for reforming the relations of states, and the many public international organizations that were created with increasing frequency during these years comprise so many explorations of the problem of how international society might best be organized and directed. It was clear that the system lacked the apparatus of political rule through which the modern state was governed, although some hoped that such an apparatus might in time be constructed. But the immediate problem was how the governance of the society of states might be accomplished, given the political division of that society and the need to adapt efforts at more unified governance to this condition. There is in all of this a novel element, even though international government, in the form of universal monarchy, empire, and federation, had been considered in the past. For the actual system was not a corporate body and did not act as one. The new question considered by statesmen and theorists of international relations after the French Revolution, therefore, was this: if the European society of states was to act as a single body, on what principles should it act? How should its executive decisions be taken? What, in short, are the appropriate principles not only of states acting separately as members of an international society, but of states acting in concert as an international government?

For those, like Burke and Gentz, who understand the unity of the system of states to rest on the acceptance of common principles of international conduct, the task of international government is to secure the more adequate observance of those principles. If, on the other hand, international association is understood to rest on the existence of similar religious, political, or socioeconomic institutions within each country and a common interest in the preservation of these institutions, then the task of international government becomes one of protecting the internal order of each state against any alteration that might threaten the stability of the system as a whole. The former reflects a practical and the latter a purposive conception of international government. This distinction serves in fact to define one of the main dimensions along which debates concerning the proper tasks of international government may be located. Equally important is a second dimension of controversy, one defined by the distinction between the cosmopolitan and state-centric conceptions. The idea of a universal society of individuals reemerged in the wake of the revolution in France to influence both liberal and conservative thought throughout the nineteenth century and to provide one of the principal justifications for international government in the twentieth. It continues to provide the grounds for much present criticism of the organization of the states system. Taken together, these two dimensions define the field on which successive battles concerning the organization and government of international society have taken place.

Conflicting Conceptions of the European Concert

The term "Concert of Europe" is commonly used to refer to the practice of periodic consultation among the powers during the century between the end of the Napoleonic wars and 1914. But the absence of a continuing structure, the irregular intervals between meetings, and the continually changing composition of the body of participating states meant that the institution constituted by this tradition of consultation was an extremely diffuse one. Begun in a series of Congresses controlled by the foreign ministers of the major powers, the Concert gradually took on the character of a succession of Conferences among representatives of ambassadorial rank. During the last quarter of the nineteenth century great power rivalry in armaments and colonies together with the participation of an increasing number of non-European states in an enlarged international system gradually destroyed the European family of nations and the Concert system along with it. After 1885 it is a moot point whether the Concert existed at all, although it may perhaps be said to have been reincarnated in the Hague Conferences of 1899 and 1907. The term "Concert of Europe" itself was not much used before the middle of the century, but after it had become common it was applied retrospectively to the early Congresses, and it continued to be invoked in various contexts until the bankruptcy of the Concert was certified by the outbreak of the 1914–1918 war. These uncertainties concerning its identity were accompanied throughout the period by disagreements concerning its character and purpose. Although the Concert was expected by some to serve as a vehicle for the application of cosmopolitan and humanitarian principles, it was more often regarded as a means by which the great powers might coordinate their policies to preserve the balance of power. And where some thought it was the first duty of the Concert to serve as the custodian of the public law of Europe, others hoped to make it into an instrument of domestic counterrevolution or some other substantive interest.[1]

The tension among these various conceptions of international government was present from the very beginning of the system of European great power conferences, begun in 1815 by the four states (Austria, Britain, Prussia, and Russia) allied against France. A year earlier the four, in the course of forging their penultimate victory over the French forces, had agreed, at Chaumont, to continue their collaboration after the conclusion of a peace and, at Paris, to confine France to its boundaries of 1792. The latter settlement was revised, following Napoleon's escape from Elba and final defeat at Wa-

[1] Alternative conceptions of the Concert of Europe at the end of the Napoleonic wars are considered by Thomson, *Europe Since Napoleon*, chs. 5 and 8; Gulick, *Europe's Classical Balance of Power*; and Schenk, *Aftermath of the Napoleonic Wars*. For the remainder of the nineteenth century as well as for the immediate postwar period, Holbraad, *Concert of Europe*, is indispensable.

terloo, by a second Treaty of Paris in November 1815. Meanwhile the states of Europe, in a series of negotiations dominated by the four but attended by representatives of many smaller states and by France, worked out the general settlement embodied in the Treaty of Vienna of June 1815, according to which the boundaries of Europe were considerably and lastingly rearranged and legitimate monarchs restored to power wherever possible. The participation of Talleyrand and the terms of peace imposed upon France reflected not only a determination that that nation should not again become anything more than a great power, but also a realistic acknowledgment of the fact that France could not be regarded as anything less than a great power. In addition, the proceedings firmly established the principle of great power primacy that was to characterize international relations in Europe until the end of the century. The smaller powers, after protesting their effective exclusion from the deliberation of matters of importance, reluctantly acquiesced and thereby conferred on the system of great power rule an authority that was not seriously questioned in Europe until the Latin American states made an issue of it at the second Hague Conference in 1907.[2]

The Congress at Vienna thus initiated the practice of periodic meetings among ministers or representatives of the major powers to settle disputes that threatened to undermine the order of the European society of states. The system of consultation was formally recognized and established shortly afterward in the treaty of the Quadruple Alliance whose signatories, the four allied powers, agreed to cooperate in upholding the European settlement worked out in the negotiations of the preceding year and a half, and to "renew their meetings at fixed periods . . . for the purpose of consulting upon their common interests, and for the consideration of the measures which at each of these periods shall be considered the most salutary for the repose and prosperity of nations and

[2] On the relations between the small and the great powers since 1815, see Klein, *Sovereign Equality among States.*

for the maintenance of the peace of Europe."[3] Another agreement in 1818 included France in a Quintuple Alliance conceived on similar principles.

Although one can discern elements of a purposive conception of international government in these treaties, their practical component proved more durable. One might take the preference of the great powers for legitimate—that is, monarchical—regimes as reflecting a shared commitment to the preservation of such regimes as an end in itself. But one must distinguish those who, like Metternich, saw the system of alliances as a means of restoring the former aristocratic order of European society from others, like his associate Friedrich von Gentz, who were more sympathetic with liberalism, while fearing the incalculable and possibly dangerous consequences of any precipitous movement from legitimate monarchy to republicanism. Those who shared Gentz's view tended to adopt a legitimist position as a means of preserving the European society of states rather than as an end to be desired for its own sake. For Gentz the European alliances were above all a means of preventing the hegemony of a single power such as France, of securing the independence of even the smallest of the European states, and of ensuring that "everywhere the mutual relations of states are dealt with according to traditional principles of international law and in purely diplomatic forms."[4] This meant protecting the rights of states, like the Swiss Republic, that were not monarchies, as well as the rights of those that were. The alliances were thus a means of securing the conception of Europe as an association of states within a common framework of practices, and of strengtening the authority of these practices as the basis of international relations even among states whose interests were opposed. Before the Revolution these aims had been accomplished in an uncoordinated way, but now—in the disrupted condition of postwar

[3] Hurst, *Key Treaties*, 1:123.

[4] *Schriften*, 3:96-97. See, more generally, *On the State of Europe before and after the French Revolution* and *Fragments on the Balance of Power in Europe*.

Europe—they required more deliberate cooperation by the major powers.

The conception of international government that springs from this conception of international society is therefore one in which the task of government is limited to clarifying and strengthening the forms and procedures to be observed by states in their external relations, to determining the requirements of these forms and procedures in particular situations, and to ensuring that the conditions for their observance are not undermined by the policies of any state. International law, which is simply these forms and procedures understood in a certain way, is the indispensable foundation of international association. It is international law understood as a customary body of general rules, found rather than made, to which the conduct of states is expected to conform. That there is much room for disagreement even within this set of assumptions is sharply revealed in disputes concerning the proper grounds for collective intervention by the powers in the affairs of another state. According to the practical conception such intervention is justified only if it is compatible with the limited office of the powers, acting in concert as an international government, as custodians of the common rules. But when does collective action to uphold the common rules and thus to preserve the very structure of the states system itself become an attempt to impose a substantive policy, one that goes beyond the minimum requirements of international legal order? This question touches just one aspect of the more general issue of the limits of international government. To what extent, for example, may the powers alter customary international law through agreement among themselves? To what extent do these agreements possess the force of legislation? First raised in controversies surrounding the post-Napoleonic alliances, these questions continue to generate disagreement concerning the character and limits of international organization.

These debates about international government were even in the early nineteenth century closely bound up with diver-

gent views on what we would now call "transnational" relations. Although the cosmopolitanism of the eighteenth century led by one route to the idea of a European society of
states under a common public law, it also pointed (through
the idea of natural rights) toward a world society of individuals as the ideal around which the political organization of
Europe should be reshaped. The revolutionary version of the
cosmopolitan ideal is illustrated by the conferral of French
citizenship upon foreigners such as Tom Paine and Jeremy
Bentham who were thought to be sympathetic with the Revolution, and by the establishment of Jacobin clubs throughout
Europe to spread its principles. But it was also a cosmopolitan ideal that inspired the counterrevolutionary doctrine linking aristocratic rule in one country to its continued existence
in others. To restore the social structure of Europe's ancien
régime became the object of a transnational movement determined to use the European alliances for this purpose. The
premises of this movement are apparent in the language of
the Act of the Holy Alliance concluded in 1815 among the
rulers of Austria, Prussia, and Russia and eventually accepted
by almost every European sovereign. Those participating in
the Holy Alliance agreed to be guided in the internal administration of their states, as well as in their foreign relations,
solely by "the precepts of that Holy Religion, the precepts of
Justice, Christian Charity, and Peace, which, far from being
applicable only to private concerns, must have an immediate
influence on the councils of Princes, and guide all their steps,
as being the only means of consolidating human institutions
and remedying their imperfections."[5] They were "to consider
themselves all as members of one and the same Christian
nation . . . thus confessing that the Christian world, of which
they and their people form a part, has in reality no other
sovereign but Him to whom power alone really belongs."[6] It
was the true beliefs of the Christian religion, and not the

[5] Hurst, *Key Treaties*, 1:96.
[6] Ibid., p. 97.

customary law of the society of states, that was both to determine and to be served by the political arrangments of Europe. Conspicuous in their aloofness from this enterprise were Britain, the Papacy, and the Ottoman Empire, each of which was for its own reasons unable to share the purposes of the Holy Alliance.

The Holy Alliance is not to be confused with the Quadruple and Quintuple Alliances. But many people, both at the time and afterward, tended to fall into just this confusion, with the result that the entire postwar settlement was soon widely regarded as a counterrevolutionary conspiracy of the absolutist Christian monarchs to impose their own conception of order on the rest of Europe. The idea of international government through the cooperation of the great powers was undermined, not strengthened, by the attempt to make the suppression of any shift toward liberalism the object of this cooperation. Increasingly, great power cooperation meant different things to different people. To the extent that it was identified with a common wish to restore the old internal order of the states of Europe, the Congress system was becoming moribund. The British refusal to support the proposals made by Austria and Russia at the Congress of Verona in 1822 to intervene in the revolutions then occurring in Greece and Spain meant that the European alliance was virtually at an end. The system began to revert to a less centrally directed balance of power. The result was the development of two alternative conceptions of the Concert. According to the first, the Concert stood for the coexistence of the states of Europe within the structure of principles expressed in international law and supported by the balance of power. According to this view, the Concert was not only capable of accommodating a diversity of political regimes among its members (and thus could include states whose regimes were incompatible with the principles of the Holy Alliance) but was even more to be desired where uniformity of institutions and commonality of interest were lacking than where they were present. A second conception of the Concert, on the other hand, continued to link it with the existence of common interests and thus with concerted action on behalf of shared purposes, even though the particular interests and purposes that had animated the postwar alliance were no longer accepted.[7] Thus even after the Concert had shaken off its link with counter-revolution, it continued to be identified with whatever common interests among the great powers seemed uppermost at the moment. This in turn meant that the idea of the Concert as an association of states in terms of common practices and procedures was continually being confused with the idea that it was an association of states for the cooperative pursuit of common interests. And at moments when, in the course of the nineteenth century, it seemed as if the powers had few interests in common, the Concert seemed to many to have come to an end.

The idea that it was their joint pursuit of shared purposes rather than their acknowledgment of the authority of a common body of practices and procedures that constituted the basis of association among states was reinforced by the way in which the notion of a European Family of Nations was often understood. There is nothing inherently purposive in that notion. The idea of a society of states represented (or, rather, misrepresented) by this expression implies both external boundaries and internal unity, but it does not require that these boundaries be drawn or this unity defined beyond the requirement that its members acknowledge the authority of its common rules. But the phrase "Family of Nations," with its connotation of organic rather than formal relationship, contributed to the tendency to conceive the society of states in purposive terms by suggesting the fundamental significance of ties of propinquity, constant contact, mutual dependence, common interest, and cultural similarity arising

[7] For an early interpretation of the Concert of Europe as requiring purposive agreement in order to succeed, see Saint-Simon, "Reorganization of the European Community" (1814). The Holy Alliance is defended in similar terms by Comte, "Considerations on the Spiritual Power" (1826), reprinted as an appendix to *System of Positive Polity*, 4:618-644, at p. 643.

from a common history. Its popularity helped to foster the view that it was these features of the European states system that explained and justified the obligations of Europeans toward one another—obligations which were not expected to apply in their relations with non-Europeans.

This conception of the character of European unity and the basis of the European international order is reflected throughout the nineteenth century in the texts of treaties and in the writings of historians, international lawyers, and journalists. The gradual expansion of the membership of the society of states that resulted in its being transformed from a European to a nearly universal society of states, and the consequent reduction of the status of Europe itself to that of a regional subsystem, itself internally divided, within the larger global system, rendered the idea that cultural similarity and common interests were the defining features of international society much less plausible. Yet the leading English treatise on international law at the beginning of the present century could continue to characterize the society of states as an international community created by the "constant intercourse" and "common interests" of nations, and to present international law as reflecting the outcome of agreements prompted by these contacts and interests, rather than the constraints to be observed in making them.[8]

A purposive conception of the European Concert also gained support from the idea that the terms of association among the members of the society of states are those to which the members have given their consent. This doctrine follows directly from the idea that these members are associated in terms of common interests. If the society of states is constituted by cooperation in pursuit of common interests, the terms of this cooperation must reflect what the states voluntarily engaged in it are willing to accept. Thus—again in Oppenheim's words— it is "the common consent of the States" that constitutes "the

[8] Oppenheim, *International Law*, 1:10-12.

basis of the Law of Nations."[9] In order to explain how this consent is manifested in the body of international law, a number of corollary arguments are required. The law, insofar as it is embodied in treaties, reflects the explicit consent of those states party to them. The consent to customary law, in contrast, is presented as "tacit consent." The problem of the obligations of new members of the society of states to its customary practices and rules is handled by the argument that new states, by accepting the invitation of the existing members to join the club, have in effect consented to the entire body of customary law in force at the time of their admission.[10] It is not merely the Concert of Europe which, according to this view, is based on a voluntary agreement to pursue certain ends. International society itself is understood as a sort of tacit concert that exists as an expression of the will of its members. Such an understanding leaves unexplained how this joint will can be converted into agreed rules in the absence of more basic rules specifying the procedures according to which such agreement can be pursued.[11]

The idea that the society of states is a voluntary association constituted through the consent of its members and devoted to the pursuit of their common interests leads to a view of international law as an instrument of their common will. The law serves rather than limits. Nor is this all, for international law comes to be regarded as a body of rules serving the interests of a particular group of countries, those who recognize each other to be states. Why should not such an association, already a sort of loose league or confederation, organize itself for the more efficient pursuit of its goals? The Concert of Europe, understood as an enterprise intended to foster cooperation in pursuit of common interests, thus points toward its own transcendence in a stronger and more effective organization devoted to this pursuit.

[9] Ibid., p. 10.

[10] Ibid., p. 17.

[11] Certain issues raised by the idea of consent are considered in Chapter 8, below.

95

The frequent reference in discussions of the Concert to the common interests of states is not, however, always a sign that it is being understood in purposive terms. The element of common interest is often mentioned as an empirical condition for cooperation within a common body of law. Many writers understood that international law can only be effective among states which, in the words of one international lawyer of the late nineteenth century, "sufficiently resemble one another, and are closely enough knit together by common interests, to be susceptible to a uniform pressure of public opinion."[12] Although it superficially resembles the views of Oppenheim mentioned earlier, the argument here is quite different. The pursuit of common interests is for Holland neither the basis of international association nor the purpose of international law. It is, rather, a condition for the effective operation of the international legal system, and therefore for the existence of international society understood as association in terms of law.

Two conceptions of the Concert of Europe, then, existed side by side throughout the nineteenth century. If some regarded it as an instrument of the collective interests and will of the powers, others continued to think of it as a way of attempting more effectively to secure the conduct of international relations within the limits of the practices comprising the traditions of European international relations. Although the Concert idea was in continuous flux in response to the ever changing circumstances of foreign affairs, and although it was colored by successive versions of the view that it existed to promote the shared purposes of its members, it never entirely shed its character as a forum for setting limits to the conduct of sovereign powers whose national pride, preoccupation with security, and competitive rivalry stood as evidence of their divergent purposes. By the period of the Hague Conferences the states of Europe, mired in imperial rivalry and mutual suspicion and perceiving themselves to have few interests in common, were almost entirely occupied with de-

---

[12] Holland, *Jurisprudence*, p. 392.

liberating upon the terms of their relationship with one another in case of war. In spite of the almost complete cynicism of many of their representatives at the Hague, the states participating in these last manifestations of the Concert did succeed in promoting the acceptance of some important rules governing armed combat, although they failed to make significant progress in furthering disarmament or the peaceful settlement of disputes through arbitration—ends which despite strong public support were not seriously desired by the negotiators. But these disappointments notwithstanding, Concert diplomacy still meant keeping a conversation going among potential adversaries, and it was this residue of the nineteenth-century experience of international government that survived the complete breakdown of the European system in 1914 to become one element in the new concert of the League of Nations.[13]

The Ambiguity of
Twentieth-Century International Government

The division of Europe into competing alliances and the Great War that was the outcome of this division marked a disruption of the Concert system more prolonged and more devastating than any that had gone before. But when the peacemakers met to design the institutions that would govern the

[13] The conferences and congresses of the second half of the nineteenth century were concerned not only with fixing the terms of peace and the adjustment of boundaries but also with adding to the body of international law and with setting up machinery to administer such international regimes as those governing commerce on international rivers. For example, at the Paris Congress of 1856 the major powers, in addition to settling the immediate issues of the Crimean War, recognized Turkey as a member of the European Family of Nations, thereby extending the geographical scope of international law—still at this period firmly understood as a body of law peculiar to the European system—beyond the boundaries of European civilization. The Congress also created the Danube Commission to regulate navigation on that river, and adopted a number of rules regulating naval warfare. These actions are typical of the later Concert.

society of states in the future, it was little more than a rehabilitated Concert that they were able to set in motion. It is
true that their ambitions reached further than this. They wished
first of all to rectify the lack of formal and permanent structure that had characterized the system of the Concert, a deficiency that they saw as one of the chief obstacles to rational
international governance. The Concert, according to one of
its most distinguished historians who was also a supporter of
the League of Nations, "was so inchoate and so little elaborated that it depended almost entirely on the personal disposition of the statesmen of Europe." Because its proceedings
were secret, its operation was so poorly understood that "the
statesmen themselves were incapable of analyzing or understanding the machinery they were using. . . ."[14] A permanent
body would help to eliminate the inefficiency and opportu-
nities for arbitrary and irresponsible diplomacy that the Concert could not avoid.

A second ambition was to construct a governing organ that
would in certain important ways transcend the division of international society into separate states. This desire, which grew
out of the platforms of the peace and free trade movements
in the United States and Great Britain, received its most
prominent expression in the words and conduct of Woodrow
Wilson. It rested on a belief in the reality of a universal community of individuals united by a shared interest in the flourishing of international commerce and in the peaceful settlement of disputes. According to this view of the world,
governments were often a factor distorting the half-formed
consensus on cosmopolitan principles that might fully emerge
if public opinion were allowed free expression. These arguments, which had already been made by Bentham,[15] led in
the years just before the formation of the League to conclusions not unlike Bentham's concerning the proper conduct of
diplomacy. Secret diplomacy was to be given up not only

[14] Webster, *League of Nations*, pp. 20-21.
[15] *Works*, 2:554-560.

because it was inefficient and irresponsible but because it was an obstacle to the proper influence of public opinion on the conduct of international relations.[16] Public opinion, if allowed to develop itself freely, would become progressively more enlightened and would increasingly force governments to adopt rational foreign policies—that is, policies designed to promote the common interests that unite people across national boundaries. Thus, the new international organization was expected to go beyond the Concert not only by becoming a permanent apparatus of international government but by being more closely tied to the level of the ordinary citizen, whose views—and not merely the official views of governments— were to be represented in it.

Finally, those assembled at Versailles were determined to construct a defense against the possibility of renewed war on the scale of the one just concluded. The means to this end varied according to one's analysis of the causes of the 1914-1918 war. In its last years this war, whose origins no one understood and which seemed to stand for nothing so much as the futility of all human effort, had in many countries acquired meaning as a struggle to defend international society against the atavistic forces of unreasoning militarism epitomized in the German state. For Clemenceau, a secure peace meant a thorough and permanent reduction of German power. Wilson, with more detachment, thought it meant constructing a system through which the force of enlightened public opinion might be brought to bear against any aggression of the kind now retrospectively discerned in German policy before the war, in order to suppress it at an early stage. For those attached to the idea of an international society united by common moral and legal principles, the new situation created by the war meant an opportunity to reformulate positive international law so that violations of the higher moral law would in future be made less likely by being clearly forbidden by the positive law as well. Each of these analyses of the

[16] Schiffer, *Legal Community of Mankind*, pp. 196-201, 206.

causes of the war seemed to call for a reorganization of international society so that acts of aggression might be clearly identified and the force of public opinion focused on deterring or suppressing them. Collective action against aggression presupposes that aggression can be defined in an agreed way and that the collectivity can agree both on the fact that it should be resisted and the method for doing so. The provisions of the League Covenant for what has come to be called "collective security" reflected these assumptions by making expulsion of a state that breaks the Covenant, and the mobilization of economic and ultimately military sanctions against it, an expression of the united condemnation of the international community. Without general agreement, collective action was impossible.[17]

The steps from planning for a permanent, universal, and united international government to the Covenant itself, and from the Covenant to the actual practice of the League, represent successive stages in the defeat of these ambitions. Wilson's idea that peoples as well as governments should be directly represented in the councils of the new organization failed to survive the negotiation of the Covenant. A number of other proposals to make the League into an institution of a world society rather than a society of states were also rejected. Moreover, the exclusion of Germany and Bolshevik Russia, together with the rejection of membership by the United States, meant that the goal of universality was undermined from the very start. Unlike the Concert, the League could not even be said to be an association of the great powers. Developments in Italy, Germany, Japan, Russia, and elsewhere destroyed the assumption that consensus within the organization would be increased by the emergence of enlightened publics within the member countries and that the pressure of public opinion would force governments to take

[17] For various conceptions of the character of the League, see Barker, *Confederation of Nations*; Miller, *Drafting of the Covenant*; Zimmern, *League of Nations and the Rule of Law*; and Walters, *History of the League of Nations*.

account of the common interest in trade, disarmament, and the peaceful settlement of disputes. And without such a consensus the procedures for collective security became worthless.

Yet it was in just these ways that the League had attempted to go beyond the Concert. What was left after a succession of developments that challenged the premises of its founders was a more formal and regular association of governments than that of the Concert, to which were appended a number of agencies for the provision of statistical, economic, and social services. The League also enjoyed the services of a secretariat and possessed in the Covenant a full and explicit statement of its tasks and procedures. But it was for the most part unable to act as a single body. Like the Concert, the League functioned largely as a forum for the negotiation of particular disputes and the clarification of the terms of international association in general. But the League was forced to labor against obstacles to agreement with which the Concert did not have to contend. Because several great powers were not members, the League was even less able than the Concert to act on the basis of the united will of the most important members of the society of states. And because the principle of great power primacy was now less acceptable to the minor powers, the Covenant was written in such a way as virtually to require the unanimous consent of all states, great and small, before collective action could be taken. This meant that such action was unlikely.

Reflection upon this experience suggests that the League of Nations suffered from internal contradictions arising from an unhappy combination of cosmopolitan and state-centric premises. Founded in part on an assumption of universal solidarity among the peoples of the world, whose enlightened view of their shared interests and ultimate desire for peace would express itself through the force of world opinion, the League had to operate in an environment in which that solidarity did not exist. Although unquestionably an association of states, with no executive power apart from the united will of its member governments its successful operation presupposed the existence of a world society whose citizens, taking an enlightened view of the common good, would prevail upon their respective governments to cooperate for the promotion of this good. It was the solidarity of this world society that would make collective enforcement of the terms of the Covenant possible. But the actual structure and operation of the League reflected the reality of the states system, not this cosmopolitan ideal.

On the other hand, the conception of international government embodied in the League Covenant remained largely undistorted by purposive considerations. It is true that the League was conceived as an organization for the promotion of presumed common interests in peace and in the integrity of existing political arrangements (in particular, those of the Versailles settlement that certified the reduction of German status and the dismemberment of the Austrian empire), as well as for the promotion of certain social ends through the cooperative regulation of labor practices, public health, and the arms trade. The Covenant begins on what might appear to be a purposive note by stating that those party to it agree to its terms "in order to promote international co-operation and to achieve international peace and security." But, for the most part, these are "purposes" to be achieved through conformity to international law. The means by which these ends are to be furthered makes it clear that states in accepting the Covenant are binding themselves to pursue these ends, and to conduct themselves generally, according to the common practices and principles of the society of states as embodied in international law. This was understood to mean (as it had in the past) that they would behave justly and honorably toward one another by respecting their treaty obligations and the obligations of general international law. It meant that, as a consequence of the new regime of the Convenant, they would accept a new obligation to conduct their relations openly and without resorting to war. Most of the specific provisions of the Covenant represent a working out of the institutional

form of the relationship thus specified. The international society organized by the League of Nations was thus in large
part to be a society of states ultimately united not by the
existence of common interests but by a common acknowledgment of the authority of certain rules governing the pursuit
of all interests, common or conflicting.

The kind of unity presupposed by the arrangements of the
League has often been misunderstood. E. H. Carr gave
expression to a widely held view when he argued that the
League had failed because it presupposed a commonality of
interests which some states, notably Germany and Italy, did
not share with the dominant powers, England and France,
and which the latter were less and less able to impose on the
others after 1919.[18] The implication is that, had the international arrangements more adequately represented the interests of the "dissatisfied powers," the breakdown of the League
and a second world war might have been averted. But the
breakdown of the international society that the League had
sought to govern was not merely a breakdown of a solidarity
based on a community of interest among the peoples and states
of the world. The League might have survived this, taking
the form (as Wilson feared it might) of a "debating society"
in which governments would meet to negotiate their differences within a common framework of rules and procedures,
even if they were unable to reach a level of agreement sufficient to make collective action possible. What completely
shattered the system was the revolutionary attempt of the
Communist and Nazi movements to reconstruct European society along entirely new lines. Each asserted that the society
of states was to be replaced by a new social order in which
the artificial division of mankind into states would give way
to objective arrangements dictated by scientific considerations of class or race. In these circumstances the error was
not merely that of expecting a degree of common interest
among states so broad and uniform as to permit the members

[18] *Twenty Years' Crisis*, ch. 9.

of the League to act in a concerted fashion but of thinking that the conflicting purposes of Germany and the western powers could be reconciled on the basis of negotiation within a common framework of procedures.

In attempting to correct what they perceived to be defects in the League, the framers of the United Nations Charter produced yet another combination of ideas concerning the character of international society and the task of international government. In some ways the Charter would seem to represent a step toward realization of the idea of a cosmopolitan world society. For example, by presenting the organization as a union of peoples and by adopting the promotion of human rights and social progress among the fundamental ends of the organization, the Charter appears to aspire to a cosmopolitan ideal. But other aspects of the Charter contradict this analysis. Despite the claim of the Preamble that the United Nations is based upon the agreement of peoples, the organization is in fact, as Article 2 (1) makes clear, "based on the principle of the sovereign equality" of the states that created it. Nor does the Charter reflect to any significant degree the premise of the League Covenant that the solidarity of the citizens of different countries, expressed through public opinion, would make possible a consensus among states and serve as the force behind the decisions of the organization. The solidarity presupposed by the Charter is no more than that of the convergent will of a handful of major states. The Charter abandons the premise of universal agreement underlying the League, and bases itself instead on the expectation that the common interests of five states defined as great powers will make it possible for the society of states to act for some purpose as a single body.[19]

In this respect, the United Nations is hardly an advance beyond the Concert of Europe. It is true that the society of states it organizes and seeks to govern is now nearly univer-

[19] On the United Nations Charter see Brierly, *Covenant and the Charter*; Kelsen, *Law of the United Nations*; and Goodrich, Hambro, and Simons, *Charter of the United Nations*.

sal, not limited to Europe. Its machinery is permanent rather than ad hoc. In theory it has at its disposal the military might of its members. The scope and magnitude of its economic and social activities is enormous. But in the preservation of international peace and security, which was to be its main concern, the United Nations, like the Concert, is an attempt to govern the society of states through the consultation and agreement of the great powers. From the start, however, the fundamental division between the United States and the Soviet Union has meant that the great powers have in fact done little governing through the organization, with the result that it has become even more marginal to the politics of the powers than the Concert was in its day. In addition, the ever-fragile conception of international government as being concerned above all with the perpetuation of the relationship of states in terms of a common law has far less reality in the world of the United Nations than it did in that of the Concert. The United Nations is not a government administering an authoritative system of law but a divided assemblage of states determined to make the organization an instrument of their separate purposes, and to use it, in the rare instances in which a substantial number of them are in agreement, to impose the consequences of this interest-based unity on the rest.

This situation does not entirely represent a gap between the ideals of the United Nations and the reality of international conduct, for the ideal of practical association—of association in terms of a common law—has in effect been abandoned in the Charter itself. It is true that the Charter appears to establish the organization on the basis of the rule of law. But this appearance is deceptive for several reasons. First, the observance of international law is presented as a goal, not an obligation. Among the ends of the organization specified by the Preamble is that of establishing the conditions for the maintenance of justice and international law. In addition, the Preamble expresses an intention to "save succeeding generations from the scourge of war," to "reaffirm faith in fundamental human rights," and to "promote social progress and better standards of life." The Preamble then goes on to say something about the manner in which these ends are to be pursued. The Charter thus superficially resembles the League Covenant, which also specified both the ends of the organization and the conditions to be observed in their pursuit. But where the Covenant binds states to observe the obligations of international law in pursuing the ends of peace, security, and cooperation, the Charter does not. The members of the United Nations do not promise to make international law the rule of their conduct toward one another. Rather, they commit themselves only to the goal of seeking "to *establish the conditions* under which justice and respect for the obligations . . . of international law can be maintained."[20] The rule of law is no longer even supposed to be the basis of association; it has come to be thought of as an external goal toward which states should work. The members of the United Nations are united not on the basis of their acceptance of law as the rule of their conduct but in an agreement to pursue together certain common purposes, among which is that of establishing the empirical conditions for being associated in terms of law at some future time.

Second, although the organization itself (in contrast to its members acting separately) is assigned the purpose of bringing about the settlement of disputes "in conformity with the principles of justice and international law,"[21] the obligation thereby imposed on it is unclear. As Kelsen has argued, this phrase is ambiguous. If "justice" means "respect for the obligations of international law," then the phrase is redundant. If, on the other hand, "justice" refers to principles different from those of international law, the statement means that in applying the Charter the requirements of "law" are to be balanced by those of "justice." Because the latter concept is nowhere defined in the Charter, and is certainly not self-evident, this provision in effect undermines rather than affirms

[20] *Charter*, Preamble (emphasis added).
[21] *Charter*, Article 1.

the position of international law as the basis for settling disputes.[22]

Finally, in pledging to "fulfil in good faith the obligations assumed by them in accordance with the present Charter," the members may appear to have bound themselves to the observance of at least that body of international law represented by the Charter itself. But in truth they are agreeing only to obey rules that are instrumental to the pursuit of shared substantive ends. They agree to abide by the rules of the organization because the rules are the means to the realization of these ends. But because the Charter binds neither the organization nor its members to the observance of international law as such, there is evidently no formal obstacle to conduct that is indifferent to or even, if the common purpose dictates, deliberately contrary to the traditional principles and practices of international law. The obligations immediately imposed on the members are those that are instrumental to the substantive purposes of the organization. Relationship on the basis of international law, as traditionally understood, is only a distant goal. It is therefore a mistake to regard the creation of the United Nations as an attempt to realize in an institution the requirements of international association on the basis of a common law. It is really an attempt to establish a new regime in which states, associated on the basis of an agreement to pursue together certain specified substantive ends, will follow the directives of the body that is set up to organize the pursuit of these ends.

Among the purposes to which the organization is committed is the improvement of economic and social conditions within its member states. The idea that the United Nations should concern itself with economic and social matters derives in

[22] Kelsen, *Law of the United Nations*, p. 18. The danger that Kelsen discerned in 1945 is evident in the subsequent history of the United Nations. As I argue in Chapter 10, below, the tendency during this period has been toward understanding international justice as a goal of collective action rather than as a constraint upon it, and toward regarding international law as an instrument through which justice, so understood, can be promoted.

part from the establishment, beginning early in the nineteenth century, of international agencies such as the International River Commission, established in 1815 by the Final Act of the Congress of Vienna, the General Postal Union established at Bern in 1874, and the International Labor Organization created by the Treaty of Versailles in 1919. Formed for the purpose of facilitating the cooperation of states in dealing with common concerns of an apparently technical rather than political character, these agencies were typically organized as a conference of delegates meeting periodically to determine the policy of the organization, with a small secretariat to administer the agreement and to provide expertise and continuity between meetings. In the League, these features of the special purpose international agency were combined with the Concert idea of collective governance of the states system by its members. It is therefore not surprising that something of the purposive character of the specialized agency should creep into the Covenant. The founders of the League hoped that the machinery of these agencies, which had been developed for handling the pursuit of common interests in particular substantive areas, might be adapted to facilitating the cooperation of states in furthering what was assumed to be their common interest in peace and security and in promoting social and economic cooperation on a broader scale than had yet been attempted by any existing specialized bureau or commission.

The League was thus to serve as a center for cooperation not only on political but also on technical matters.[23] Underlying this assignment to the organization of social and economic as well as political functions was the premise that there exists an intimate connection between peace and welfare. This idea, implicit in the Covenant, is made explicit in the Constitution of the International Labor Organization. Unlike the Covenant, the latter is not an agreement to abide by certain conditions in acting, but rather to cooperate "for the promo-

[23] *Covenant*, Article 24.

tion of the objects set forth in the Preamble" of the Constitution:[24] to improve the conditions of labor by setting standards of hours, wages, and safety, by preventing unemployment, and by promoting vocational education. These aims are linked to the League's commitment to the preservation of peace, for the latter "can be established only if it is based upon social justice."[25] Thus the International Labor Organization has as its ultimate aim the creation of the empirical conditions of peace. Its purpose is to facilitate the work of the League in the preservation of peace by ameliorating conditions of labor "involving such injustice, hardship and privation to large numbers of people as to produce unrest so great that the peace and harmony of the world is imperiled."[26]

In the United Nations this concern with social and economic welfare, both as a condition of peace and as an end in itself, is brought directly within scope of the main organization. The rather vague social and economic provisions of the Charter (vague, that is, in contrast to the quite explicit provisions concerning dispute settlement and collective security) reflect in part an attempt to rectify the conditions that led to the rise of fascism and to the outbreak of the Second World War. An important aim of the organization was to reconstruct the war-ravaged economies of Europe. With the passage of time and changes in the composition of its membership, the purposes that the organization is supposed to further have come to include the economic development of the poorer states. Out of this there have in turn grown pressures to reform the arrangements of international law and organization in order to effect an international redistribution of wealth and power. This trend has been accentuated by the almost complete failure of the United Nations to maintain international peace through the collective action of the major powers. Thus the purposive conception of the organization as a number of states associated on the basis of a common will to promote

[24] *Constitution of the I.L.O.*, Article 1.
[25] Ibid., Preamble.
[26] Ibid.

certain substantive economic and social goals, which is already fully present in the Charter, has become even more important in the practice of the United Nations. Such a conception can be a source of unity, rather than of division, only to the extent that the members of the organization share the same goals and agree that they should be pursued through the organization.

The virtual abandonment of international law as the basis of association within the United Nations and its replacement by agreement to cooperate for common purposes marks one of the low points in the fortunes of the practical conception of international society in twentieth-century international thought. The result has not been a new purposive consensus, but an incoherence that has further weakened the hold of the practical conception on the conduct of states—the majority of which are new states for whom the experience of participation in the United Nations has a significance that it does not have for the older states of European origin. This incoherence can be seen in the fact that, although international relations on the basis of international law has ceased to occupy a central place in either the theory or the practice of the United Nations, the Charter cannot avoid insisting upon fidelity to it own rules and procedures. But by failing to provide for their authoritative determination it opens the door to arbitrary interpretation of the Charter not only by states acting separately but by the various bodies within the organization itself. The judicial organ of the United Nations is empowered to give only advisory—that is, nonbinding—opinions concerning the resolution of disputes about Charter interpretation that are referred to it by the other organs. Each organ is therefore evidently free to interpret the Charter for itself, with the result that any particular interpretation is authoritative only where there exists substantial agreement. The situation with respect to the authoritative application of international law within the organization is thus not much different from that which prevails in the states system beyond the organization.

Because the application of the Charter is left largely to the

political organs—the Security Council and the General Assembly—its effective meaning is established by bargaining and
therefore tends to reflect whatever combination of interests
is dominant at the moment. Given these arrangements for
interpreting the rules and procedures of the organization, the
use of the United Nations by one and then another dominant
coalition for its own purposes was a foregone conclusion. The
consequence of this partial transformation of the United Nations into the instrument of those powers able to control it
has been not merely to encourage contempt for the Charter
and for the organization itself but to discredit the ideas of
international government and international law in general. The
effort of the less developed states to make the United Nations
the instrument of economic development and international
redistribution is in this respect not an innovation but merely
the latest application of a conception of international government already fully present in the practice of the organization
and in the Charter itself.

The incoherence of the United Nations idea is also apparent in the ambiguous character of the organization as an association *within* international society on the one hand and as
the institutional embodiment *of* international society on the
other. The former is reflected not, as one might think, in the
fact that the organization is based on a compact, for states—
like individuals—can voluntarily bind themselves to acknowledge the authority of common rules as they go their separate
ways, as well as to pursue together some shared purpose. It
is rather to be found in the resemblances between the United
Nations and the special purpose agencies whose administrative structure and procedures the Charter seeks to adapt to
the circumstances of high politics. But, unlike the special
purpose agency, the United Nations has attempted to govern
not merely the relations of its members but international society in its entirety by conferring on itself the authority to
make certain of its decisions binding on states that are not
members of the organization. This intention is evident in the
extraordinary powers granted to the Security Council in Ar-

ticles 39 and 42 of the Charter, enabling that body to determine whether *any* situation constitutes aggression or a threat
to peace and to respond with whatever measures it decides
are appropriate, including those involving economic sanctions
and the use of military force to maintain or restore peace. It
is also evident in the explicit provision of Article 2 (6) that
these powers may be invoked against states which are not
members of the United Nations organization. Thus the United
Nations has created itself as an association among a number
of states for the promotion of certain shared purposes, while
at the same time claiming the authority to impose these purposes on those who do not share them. It is true that the
Charter seeks to limit the circumstances under which such
coercion may be exercised. But because the Charter provisions governing actions by the Secuity Council are interpreted by the Council itself in the light of its own purposes,
the Charter does not constitute an effective bar to the use of
coercion to support the aims of those states that are able to
make their voices heard in the Council's deliberations. It is
therefore not surprising that the authority of the organization
has been repeatedly challenged by states that do not happen
to share the purposes of the moment and that feel themselves
justified in their refusal to cooperate with the organization in
furthering them.

PART TWO

The International Legal System

CHAPTER 6

International Law as Law

I HAVE ATTEMPTED in the first part of this study to show how international law had come, by the end of the eighteenth century, to be conceived by certain thinkers as a distillation of diplomatic, military, and other international usages into a body of authoritative common rules. These rules were understood to consist of generalizations about and abridgments of customary practice, to be discovered through the scientific examination of evidence pertaining to the actual diplomatic practice of states rather than by deduction from the fundamental principles of natural law. Furthermore, the rules whose existence was thus inductively ascertained were regarded as establishing standards of correct international conduct and therefore as prescribing limits to be observed and considerations to be responded to in the formulation of foreign policy. And it was these rules, rather than proximity, interaction, shared beliefs, or common interests, that were understood to define international society. Thus, I have been concerned with the generation and character of a particular conception of international law, one arising from the realization that what makes the states system a permanent *society* of states, as distinguished from either a ruleless anarchy or a temporary alliance of like-minded sovereigns, is toleration by its associates of one another's independent existence within an authoritative framework of common rules and the identification of this authoritative framework with customary international law.

The realization that international law, so understood, could provide a basis for coexistence among a multiplicity of states pursuing divergent purposes was a philosophical insight of primary importance for the understanding of international relations. But far from putting a stop to philosophical inquiry this insight led directly to the question of the character and presuppositions of international law. So long as law is identified with the will of God, the dictates of reason, or the usages of the community, international law fits comfortably enough within the framework of legal thought. But as soon as law is identified with the state and comes to be regarded as having its source in the authority of a sovereign, the idea of international law as law governing rather than issuing from the exercise of sovereignty begins to look more and more like an anomaly. Such a law, if it is possible at all, surely needs some special explanation. Thus the question arises how legal order can exist in the society of states, which manifestly is a society lacking any superior authority.

Preliminary Distinctions

Since the end of the eighteenth century discussion of the character and possibility of international law has taken place within a framework of ideas about law derived from the experience of the modern state. Already implicit in the practice of the increasingly powerful monarchical governments of early modern Europe, the identification of law with the exercise of sovereignty was reinforced by the French Revolution and the example of the *Code Napoléon*. The idea, once revolutionary, that law consists of nothing but the rules laid down by sovereign authority came gradually to be taken for granted. To be sure the identification of law with positive law was resisted by those within the tradition of natural law. In addition, opposition to the idea of positive law arose in the form of a romantic or nationalist jurisprudence that regarded law as an expression of the culture and traditions of a people and opposed codification as an arbitrary interference with the authentic laws of the nation. Despite such opposition the civil order of the modern state is now widely identified with legal order as such. In this civil order standards of conduct derived from the authority of custom, church, or conscience have been

116

pushed aside by new standards legislated within increasingly autonomous systems for making and applying rules. So successful have these systems been in establishing their claim to exclude other standards in matters they choose to regulate that they have even captured for themselves in many contexts, an almost exclusive title to the word "law."

Whatever the merits of this usage, there can be no doubt that from the perspective of history both within and outside Europe it represents a narrowing of the idea of law. One result of this narrowing is that doubts about whether international law, long thought to be based on custom and on natural law, is really law have increased in direct proportion to the success of the narrower conception. The law of nations could hardly be said to originate in the commands of a power superior to the sovereign states, or to be enforced by such a power, for clearly no such power exists. "Law implies a lawgiver" wrote an English judge in 1876, "and a tribunal capable of enforcing it and coercing its transgressors. But there is no common lawgiver to sovereign states; and no tribunal has the power to bind them by decrees or coerce them if they transgress."[1] International law might therefore be *called* "law" but, in the influential words of John Austin, it could not be said to be "law properly so called."[2]

Some theorists of "positive law" find room under this rubric for international law because for them it refers to the rules actually observed within a given society, as opposed to those ideal principles of morality or natural law that might or might not be observed in practice. But, as soon as "law" is taken to mean ónly those rules made and enforced by the sovereign power, the rules of customary practice as well as those of natural law are excluded from the category of law. Yet it does not follow from this narrower conception of law that there are no rules governing the conduct of states. This much Austin himself acknowledged when he labeled the rules

---

[1] Lord Coleridge, dissenting, *R. v. Keyn*, 2 Ex.D. 63.

[2] *Province of Jurisprudence Determined*, pp. 11-12, 142, 201.

of international law "positive morality."[3] Unlike Rousseau and Kant, who regarded as illusory the idea that international relations were to any significant degree rule-governed, Austin merely questioned whether the rules of international society were properly regarded as laws. However, the terminology he proposed has been productive of little but confusion. It is certainly the case that this body of international rules differs in significant ways from the legal system of a modern state, which we have come to regard as constituting the paradigm case of "law." But it is hardly less misleading to refer to this body of rules in its entirety as a "morality."

One unfortunate consequence of Austin's formulation is that it has caused an inordinate amount of attention to be devoted to the verbal question of the proper use of the word "law." The important question for international relations theory is whether a body of rules governing the relations of states can exist in the absence of authoritative central institutions, not whether these rules are "really law." The theorist should be interested in characterizing such rules and understanding the conditions for their existence and efficacy, not merely in how the word "law" is or ought to be used. "The Law of Nations" and "International Law" are names increasingly applied during the modern period to the rules springing from the customs and agreements of states in their relations with one another.[4] That the society of states might be governed by "law" in *this* sense was not denied by Austin, although it has been denied by others for whom the institutions of the modern

---

[3] Ibid., pp. 126-127.

[4] The expression "international law" was evidently introduced by Bentham: "The word *international*, it must be acknowledged, is a new one; though, it is hoped, sufficiently analogous and intelligible. It is calculated to express, in a more significant way, the branch of law which goes commonly under the name of the *law of nations*: an appellation so uncharacteristic, that, were it not for the force of custom, it would seem rather to refer to internal jurisprudence. The chancellor D'Aguesseau has already made, I find, a similar remark: he says, what is commonly called *droit* des *gens*, ought rather to be termed *droit* entre *les gens*." (*Introduction to the Principles of Morals and Legislation*, p. 296.)

state are definitive of law. At the very least one must be clear whether, in discussing the requisites of legal order, one is speaking about the uses of a word or the possibility of a particular mode of association.

Nor is this the only source of confusion concerning international law as law. Discussion of the requisites of international law, as well as of law generally, has been mired in confusion by the persistent failure to distinguish the defining or essential criteria of law from the contingent features of particular kinds of legal order on the one hand and from the empirical conditions for the existence and efficacy of legal order on the other. Lauterpacht, for example, consistently fails to distinguish the criteria of legal order from its conditions. Discussing legislation as a requisite of international law, he begins by concerning himself with whether the existence of a legislative organ is *"essential to the legal character* of a system of rules."* He then goes on to consider the argument that as a method of creating law custom is as important as legislation, concluding that "it is not predominantly through custom that the development, or even the normal functioning, of international law is *likely or possible."*[5] What we have here is an unconscious shift from the question of whether a system of rules lacking a legislature can be said to be a system of law, which is a question concerning the *definition* of law, to an assertion that in the absence of legislation such a system cannot be effective, which is an assertion about the *conditions* of law. Similarly, in discussing enforcement, Lauterpacht does not distinguish between the claim that to suppose public opinion to be a means of enforcing international law "amounts to an admission that . . . *it is not law"* and the quite different claim that such a supposition "is an admission of its *weakness as a system of law."*[6] The frequency with which one meets such unresolved ambiguities in discussions of legal theory suggests that some conceptual clarification is needed, if fur-

[5] *International Law*, 1:14-15, emphasis added.
[6] Ibid., p. 18, emphasis added.

ther progress toward resolving the puzzles about the character and existence of international law is to be made.

The effort to clarify the related concepts of requirement, necessity, essence, possibility, and contingency leads one rapidly into some of the most difficult and controversial topics of philosophy. Two quite ordinary and familiar distinctions are, however, sufficient to suggest a provisional answer to the question of the character and requisites of international legal order. The first is between the features of an object and the conditions for its existence. The other concerns whether a particular feature or condition is necessary or contingent. To say that the existence of legislative or judicial institutions is a requisite of legal order is in most contexts to say one of three things. (1) It may be to assert the existence of such institutions within a system of rules as grounds for identifying that system as a legal system. In this case the presence of such institutions is a *necessary feature* of legal order—that is, an essential or defining attribute constituting the criterion according to which legal order is identified. (2) It may be to claim that the existence of institutions for making and applying rules is a *necessary condition* for the existence of a system of rules, which means that if these institutions were to cease to function the system would inevitably break down. (3) Finally, it may be to claim no more than that the presence of such institutions is a *contingent condition* of the existence or efficacy of a legal system, meaning here that in the absence of such institutions the system is likely to be uncertain, inefficient, or unstable.

Doubts concerning the character or possibility of international law have emerged from each of these views of the requisites of legal order. For those who regard the existence of civil institutions as a necessary feature or criterion of legal order, international law is by definition not law. This was Austin's position. For those who regard the existence of civil institutions as a necessary condition for legal order, international law is an impossibility. This was evidently the view held by Hobbes, Rousseau, and Kant, though each of these theorists can be construed as holding other views on the matter as well. And for those who regard the existence of civil institutions as an important contingent condition of legal order, international law may be law and it may exist, but it exists only as weak law. This is the view defended by Oppenheim,[7] who is careful to note that "a weak law is nevertheless still law." On this view, the existence of civil institutions is neither a criterion nor a necessary condition of legal order. One could go further and argue that the existence of civil institutions is not even an important contingent condition of legal order, at least in some circumstances, and that in these circumstances legal order can do as well without as with it. Some versions of this point of view are considered below. Finally, attempts have been made to argue that civil institutions are indeed either a criterion or condition of legal order, and that it is the existence of equivalent or analogous institutions in the society of states that accounts, either conceptually or contingently, for such legal order as may be found there. The assumption here seems to be that international law is law in just the same way as civil or domestic law, and therefore that the institutions characteristic of the latter must exist, perhaps in a hidden or altered form, in international society. Some arguments of this sort will also be considered in what follows.

LEGISLATION AND ENFORCEMENT AS REQUISITES OF LEGAL ORDER

Let us turn, then, to particular arguments concerning the requisites of legal order, considering first those purporting to show that legislation is such a requisite and therefore that international law is not "law" or that it is not a possible or significant mode of association because international society lacks legislation or legislative institutions. One version of the argument that legislation is a requisite of legal order is that it

[7] *International Law*, 1:14.

is an essential or defining feature of legal order. In fact, there are at least two distinct claims being made here. The first is that any rule properly called a law is one that is the result of legislative activity. In other words, the criterion by which laws properly so called are to be identified is that they must have been created by a law-making institution. But this would appear to be an unduly restricted definition, for it excludes laws created by custom, by the courts, or by an act of political founding or constitution-making, and thus denies to customary, common, and constitutional law the name "law." There are many modern societies in which custom retains an important place and in which it is legally binding even though it has not been enacted by the legislature.[8] Even more conclusive is the logical consideration that the law according to which the legislative power in a given society is identified and its powers defined cannot itself be the product of legislation. Legislation presupposes law of another sort, such as customary law or a written constitution. But if legislative statutes are only one kind of law then the fact of having been created through legislation cannot be the criterion of a law.

The other claim is that existence of legislative institutions is an essential feature of a legal *system*. But this is equally implausible, for it would exclude from the category of legal systems not only international law but many other systems based largely on custom: those, for example, of the various kindreds, clans, *gentes*, segmentary lineage groups, and tribes studied by legal historians and anthropologists and of the great religious traditions, especially those of Judaism and Islam. These bodies of law are lacking legislative institutions, but they are not necessarily lacking in the quality of "system." Integration, uniformity, and adaptation to changing circum-

---

[8] The traditional rejoinder is that customary law, at least, can be regarded as tacit legislation on the grounds that what the sovereign power permits it commands. Hobbes, *Elements of Law*, II, ch. 10, sect. 10; *Philosophical Rudiments*, ch. 14, sect. 15; *Leviathan*, ch. 26; Austin, *Province of Jurisprudence Determined*, pp. 31-32. The weakness of this argument has been shown by Hart, *Concept of Law*, pp. 45-47.

stances is accomplished by means other than legislative co-ordination. And this suggests that the legislation-as-a-requi-site argument in its second version—namely, that the existence of legislative institutions is a necessary condition for legal or-der—is also questionable. The existence of legislative insti-tutions may be a feature of many legal systems, but the di-versity of mankind's legal experience suggests that it is neither a definitive feature nor an indispensable condition of legal order. The absence of legislative institutions in international society therefore provides no grounds for doubting either the legal character or actual existence of international association on the basis of common rules.

As a contingent condition of legal order, some procedure for legislation might still be desirable. This, however, would seem to depend on circumstances. In the circumstances of the society of states it is a moot point whether movement toward the creation of legislative institutions would enhance or undermine the efficacy of international law and the quality of international legal order. Those whose attitudes toward in-ternational law are shaped by the purposive conception of international society are inclined to see the absence of legis-lative powers as a defect and a hindrance. Where law is re-garded as an instrument for the pursuit of shared purposes, some procedure through which the common will could be translated efficiently into law would appear to be desirable. When, on the other hand, law is understood as a set of limits or constraints on the pursuit of purposes, the desirability of legislative powers is less evident. It might be conducive to the efficacy of such constraints to have available some proce-dure for creating and altering them. The danger is that con-trol of that procedure would enhance the ability of some to impose their own purposes on others. From the standpoint of the practical conception, then, international legislation in the world as presently constituted is perhaps more to be feared than wished for.

Finally, it is worth noticing that the identification of legis-lation as a requisite (in any sense) of legal order has often led

123

to the search for some equivalent or analogous procedure in the society of states. Thus it has been argued that if a state that has been injured by another successfully resists the aggression and goes on to impose terms of peace on the defeated adversary, it may be understood as "legislating" for the adversary. But this is playing with words. Only slightly less implausible is the attempt to impute legislative significance to agreements between two or more states acting in concert: i.e., to the making of treaties. By becoming parties to a treaty states make rules for themselves, and may therefore be said to be legislating for themselves. But to speak in this way is of course also to stretch the term "legislation" far beyond its normal meaning. Legislation within the state is law-making by a separate institution, distinguishable from the totality of those subject to the law and possessing the authority to make laws binding on those subjects. When a treaty is made, the states agreeing to a rule are those to whom the rule applies: there is no differentiation between sovereign and subject, and therefore no distinct body that can properly be referred to as a "legislature." Through legislation some members of a society are able to create rules binding on others, but the parties to a treaty bind only themselves. "International legislation" applied to treaties is therefore a misnomer. States making treaties are not legislating for the international community and thereby acting as an organ of it; they are making agreements, as subjects, within the law.

This is true even of those multilateral agreements that seek to codify or reformulate particular substantive areas of international law and that have been signed by most or even all of the members of the society of states at a given moment. Such "law-making treaties," as they are sometimes called, are not—as the expression seems to suggest—of a logically different character from agreements entered into by a small number of states or those concerned with very limited and particular matters. They resemble ordinary treaties more than they do statutes resulting from legislation as it is ordinarily understood. Nor can it be said that the acts of international organizations created through multilateral agreement, such as the United Nations, meet the criteria of legislation. For although in this case there does exist an institution distinct from its members, the extent to which the decisions of this institution are binding on states is limited and controversial. It would certainly be going too far to claim that the law-making activities of international organizations are such as to justify regarding them as international legislatures, or even to confer upon them any significant degree of legislative character. Legislation, if it exists at all in the international legal system, is marginal to its actual operation.[9]

In discussions of whether international law is really law and of the more fundamental question of whether independent states can be related to one another on the basis of common rules, greater importance has been attached to the apparent lack of any effective means of enforcing the common rules. It is said to make little sense to speak of "law" or of conduct according to rules where the rules are not or cannot be enforced, yet this is just the situation that is thought to prevail in the relations of states. And the attempt to find an international analogue of enforcement by a superior power by suggesting that, in the society of states, the common rules are enforced by self-help is dismissed as a sleight of hand intended to create the illusion of law where there is in fact none. The issues here are difficult ones, and we must therefore proceed with care.

First, we must dispose of what is now generally agreed to be the most egregious error made by Austin concerning the relation between enforcement and law. Austin argued that commands (which is what he thought rules were) had to be enforced in order to be legally binding. Unless the commands of the sovereign were backed by an effective sanction, they could not be said to have authority, to be valid, or to create any duty or obligation on the part of those to whom they were

[9] The notion of "international legislation" is effectively criticized by Gihl, *International Legislation*, pp. 26-53, and Lauterpacht, *International Law*, 1:59, 196, 236-237.

directed.[10] This argument finds its way into discussions of international law through the proposition that because international society lacks a coercive power to enforce its rules these rules are not binding. But to advance this proposition is in fact to make two entirely distinct assertions. The first is that because the rules of international law are not adequately enforced they cannot really be said to impose obligations or duties on those whose conduct they purport to regulate. But as Kelsen, Hart, and others have shown, to speak in this way is to confuse matters of fact with matters of right. That one agent is able by force to compel another to act in a certain manner can hardly mean the first has a right to demand such conduct, nor can it mean that the second has a duty or obligation to comply. The latter, as Hart puts it, may be "obliged" to obey, but he is under no "obligation" to do so.[11] To speak of rights and obligations presupposes the existence of rules, but the relationship between coercion and rules is a contingent one. Coercion alone cannot create rights or obligations of any sort, legal or nonlegal. On the contrary, enforcement *presupposes* the validity of the law that is enforced. The point is made succinctly by Fitzmaurice: "the law is not obligatory because it is enforced: it is enforced because it is obligatory; and enforcement would otherwise be illegal."[12]

The second assertion is that because of deficiencies in the manner in which international law is enforced its rules are ineffective—that is, generally disregarded. To say that the rules are not binding means in this context that they are ineffective rather than that they are invalid. But the two senses are often confused, and the deduction mistakenly drawn that, because a rule is ineffective in regulating a particular area of conduct, those to whom it applies have no duty to obey it. To be sure, a system of rules must be minimally effective, if claims about the validity of particular rules that are part of it are to have any point. But effectiveness remains merely an

[10] *Province of Jurisprudence Determined*, pp. 14-16.
[11] *Concept of Law*, pp. 80-81.
[12] "General Principles," p. 45.

empirical condition, and not the criterion, of legal validity.[13] And enforcement by a superior power is, in turn, only contingently related to effectiveness. Enforcement may thus under some circumstances be required as a matter of contingent fact for the existence and effectiveness of a system of rules, but it is a mistake to think that enforcement is a definitive characteristic of rule-based association.

Discussion of the relationship between enforcement and legal order has also been hampered by the frequent failure to resolve certain ambiguities in the term "enforcement." Although this is not the place for an extended analysis of this word and the various ideas signified by it, it may be helpful to notice a few important distinctions. First, to enforce a rule is not necessarily to secure or attempt to secure its observance by employing physical force. It makes perfectly good sense to speak of a rule as being enforced by other forms of coercive pressure such as fines, public censure, or deprivation of privileges. A similar point may be made about the noun "sanction," which is commonly used in discussions of the enforcement of international law. A coercive measure or sanction intended to compel observance of international law may or may not involve physical force: compare military and economic sanctions. Second, one must distinguish the variety of instruments through which rules are enforced. At one extreme there is the practice of self-help, in which the injured party is expected to deter or punish wrongful conduct. Sometimes both the determination that a wrong has been done and the application of sanctions is left to the injured party. Alternatively the injured party may be confined to punishing, or securing redress for, a wrong which has been independently ascertained by an authoritative third party. Or both the determination that a wrong has been done and the application of sanctions may be carried out by a third party. This third party may simpy be the community as a whole, or it may take the form of a differentiated office or institution. We must dis-

---

[13] Kelsen, *Pure Theory of Law*, pp. 211-214.

tinguish, therefore, between sanctions diffusely applied by the community at large (such as "the sanction of public opinion") and those that have been officially authorized. Furthermore, we need to distinguish communities in which there exist a number of such rule-enforcing authorities from those in which there is only one such authority or in which a number of such authorities are combined in a single hierarchy. Which of these various kinds of enforcement is meant when enforcement is asserted to be a requisite of legal order?

Most often, perhaps, what is thought to be required is a single, differentiated enforcing agency recognized throughout the community and capable, if necessary, of bringing overwhelming physical force to bear in order to compel obedience to its rules. Relatively centralized arrangements for regulating the application of sanctions are indeed a feature of many legal systems. But there also have existed and do still exist systems of law in which any such agency is lacking. Jewish and Islamic law know no central enforcing power. Nothing like such a power can be discovered in the arrangement of innumerable primitive societies. The rules that governed the inhabitants of the various empires within which much of mankind lived until the invention and export of the modern European state were those of religiously sanctioned custom enforced by priests or by local tribunals of various sorts rather than by the despot and his agents, whose "ruling" was largely confined to levying taxes and raising armies.[14] Even in the empire of Rome, whose legal institutions most resemble those of the modern state, implementation of the judgment of a court in civil litigation was left to the party winning the case.[15] Nor does observance of the rules that define and regulate many nonlegal practices, such as morality, decorum, and language, depend in any significant way upon enforcement by a superior power. In short, there are many sorts of rule-based order whose existence cannot be accounted for by centralized

[14] Maine, *Early History of Institutions*, pp. 379-385.
[15] Watson, *Nature of Law*, p. 30.

enforcement. Nor is it stretching the point to refer to at least some of these as systems of "law."[16]

Can it be said, alternatively, that legal order requires, if not centralized enforcement, at least sanctions applied by the community at large? The existence of some form of coercive pressure, whether or not applied by an enforcing agency or officials, has often been regarded as a *criterion* of legal order. Kelsen, for example, defines law as a "coercive order" in which disapproved behavior is deterred through the application of "socially organized sanctions."[17] But sanctions can take a wide variety of forms and need not be centralized in a single enforcing authority. In international law, the sanctions are those of reprisals and war. Coercion may be used to enforce the law, even though the application of such coercion is for the most part a matter of self-help. For Kelsen, however, the critical point is that international law does make a distinction between lawful and unlawful uses of force (so that an act of coercion is either a "delict" or a "sanction"); the application of sanctions may be said to be socially organized to that extent at least. Law is distinguished from morality by the fact that the former is and the latter is not a coercive order in the sense defined. Hart too, although he is less interested in reaching a definition of the word "law," identifies enforcement as a critical element in the way the distinction between law and morality is ordinarily made. We are, he suggests, in the realm of the legal when the social pressure brought to bear to secure compliance with the common rules takes the

---

[16] Readers who feel that the definition of "law" *is* being stretched here should ask themselves whether they are not confusing law with its empirical conditions. The question is whether an enforcing power is a necessary condition of law. Suppose I say that primitive law and international law exist without an enforcing power. There is an inclination to reply that these systems are not systems of law. The question must then be asked whether the skeptic is using the term "law" to refer to systems of rules enforced by a central power. The existence of an enforcing power, in other words, appears to have been brought in as a defining feature of law and not as a condition for its existence.

[17] *Pure Theory of Law*, p. 62.

form of physical sanctions, even though these sanctions are applied by the community at large rather than by an agency or agencies specifically authorized to enforce the rules.[18] Thus it is enforcement, though not the existence of an enforcing agency, that is for Kelsen definitive and for Hart characteristic of legal order. Kelsen regards international society as a legal order because it does provide for the (diffuse) application of coercive sanctions, Hart because it sufficiently resembles the coercive order of the modern state, despite the fact that in international society coercive sanctions have a much less important place than within the state.

For these theorists enforcement is a requisite of legal order only because they find it reasonable to follow ordinary usage, which tends to define as law those systems in which it is found. For some purposes it makes sense to define law in this way. It does not follow, however, that enforcement is a defining characteristic or criterion of rule-based association, or that association on the basis of common rules (whether or not *called* "rules of law") is impossible as a matter of contingent fact in the absence of enforcement. Bentham is especially clear and therefore helpful on this point. He distinguishes "a law" from what he refers to as "the force of a law: that is, . . . the motives it relies on for enabling it to produce the effects it aims at."[19] As the motives upon which the law relies are mainly coercive, the ideas of coercion and law have come to be thought of as inseparably connected. But this conclusion is in fact mistaken; the fear of punishment or other pain is simply one among a number of motives inclining people to obedience.

At the time he wrote *Of Laws in General* Bentham regarded punishment by the public authorities as "beyond comparison the most efficacious" means of securing compliance with most of the laws of a society.[20] Elsewhere he made room for "the sanction of public opinion" as a motive inclining states toward conformity with international law (as I have argued

[18] *Concept of Law*, p. 84.
[19] *Of Laws in General*, p. 133.
[20] Ibid., pp. 134-135.

above in Chapter 4). Other legal theorists, such as Maine[21] and Hart,[22] have systematically examined both the variety of laws and the variety of motives through which in different situations their efficacy is secured and are therefore skeptical of claims that enforcement, centralized or diffuse, is an indispensable condition of legal order. Hart, for example, suggests that one of the essential features of a legal system is that it provide "some generally effective motive for obedience (perhaps a sense of obligation and not necessarily fear) when obedience runs counter to the individual's inclination or interest."[23] If so, the provision for sanctions is perhaps no more than one way that legal systems might satisfy this requirement.

This is not to deny that enforcement is an important condition of the effectiveness of many sorts of rules in a wide range of circumstances. But no simple formula is adequate to summarize the forms, occasions, and degree of enforcement by which the efficacy of law is affected. One must be particularly wary of postulating an unrealistic dichotomy between two extreme and abstract states of affairs, one in which the rules are enforced and another in which they are not. It would be false to say, for example, that either there exists an international society constituted and regulated by rules whose observance is guaranteed by a superior power or else there is an international anarchy in the radical sense of rulelessness. Whether the members of a community are related on the basis of common rules is a question that allows a qualified answer. Rule-based association is a matter of degree. The rules may or may not be numerous; they may govern many areas of life or only a few; they may be generally understood, respected, used, and obeyed (in which case the occasions for enforcement may be rare), or they may be widely disregarded. Some members of the community may conduct their relations with one another on the basis of a scrupulous regard

---

[21] *International Law*, pp. 50-51.

[22] *Concept of Law*, pp. 27-35, 38-41, 84.

[23] Introduction to Austin, *Province of Jurisprudence Determined*, p. xiii.

for considerations embodied in the common rules, while others demonstrate their indifference to them. But there can be no logical objection to a system in which the rules are enforced only in certain circumstances. Nor is there anything logically objectionable in a method of enforcement that relies on self-help. The uneven or noncentralized enforcement of a body of rules might lead us to question its fairness or utility but would not justify us in doubting the existence of such a body unless the vagaries of enforcement resulted in the rules being generally ignored. But in that case it would be the general disregard of the rules and not the ineffectiveness of their enforcement that would provide the decisive ground for concluding that a body of common rules did not exist.

To sum up, those who have regarded legislation and enforcement as requisites of legal order and who have therefore doubted the legal character or existence of international law have fallen into the error of confusing certain features of the modern state with the idea of law as such. Often they have failed to distinguish the question of the proper use of the word "law" from the question of the character of association on the basis of common rules. Legislation and enforcement cannot be regarded as essential features or criteria of law. Law cannot be only that which has been legislated, for legislation presupposes the authority of the legislative power, and this can only be established by laws that are not themselves the product of its activity. Law is also not that which is enforced, for enforcement of the law presupposes the authority of that which is enforced. The existence of specialized institutions within a society for enacting and enforcing rules may as a matter of contingent fact be a feature of many legal systems, and it may facilitate rule-based association. But the existence of such institutions cannot be said to be a necessary condition for association on the basis of "law" in some suitably broad sense of the term. The society of states is not the only society whose laws are neither the product of legislation nor enforced by a single superior authority. Regardless of how typical they may be of legal systems, or how contingently important they may be within such systems, legislation and enforcement are not fundamental to legal order in the way that rules and obligation are. It is possible to imagine law without legislation and law without sanctions, but impossible to imagine law without rules and obligation.

The Problem of Uncertainty and Authoritative Determination

If neither a superior legislator nor a superior power to enforce the rules is necessary to legal order, what of the third suggested requisite, a common judge? We have already seen (above, Chapter 4) how a number of thinkers, notably Bentham and James Mill, having reflected on the uncertainty of international law and rejected as both impractical and undesirable the creation of a supranational state, reached the conclusion that some sort of international tribunal would be required if association on the basis of law were to become a significant factor in the relations of states. Although both were convinced that the existence of judicial institutions or procedures was an empirical condition of the effectiveness of international law, they appear to have differed on the question of whether adjudication was definitive of legal order. Mill seems to have regarded international law, in the absence of a tribunal to apply it, as more akin to ceremony or decorum than to law proper, a collection of generally known and approved forms serving the interests of states but falling short of fixing their rights.[24] Bentham on the other hand argues that the judge's work is to carry out the intention of the law; like enforcement, which is in fact attached to and governed by the judicial power, adjudication pertains to the efficacy rather than the character of the laws.[25] Because of the close connection between adjudication and the certainty of law, the exact sense in which adjudication may be said to be a requisite of legal

[24] *Essays on Government*, p. 5.
[25] *Of Laws in General*, pp. 137-139.

order is less easy to discern than in the case of legislation and enforcement.

Historically, the interpretation and application of rules in the settlement of disputes by some person or persons not a party to the dispute—a common relative, an oracle, a priest or official charged with interpreting the outcome of an ordeal or combat, a council of elders, a jury of peers, or a court of law in the modern sense—is a more typical feature of legal systems than is the existence of differentiated legislative and enforcing institutions. But the question of whether association on the basis of law requires a common judge cannot be settled by the merely empirical observation that law and "judges" (in some suitably broad sense of the term) tend to be found together. What needs to be shown is that the application of rules by judges is either a criterion or necessary condition of legal order in a way that legislation and enforcement are not.

The argument that there is a necessary connection between adjudication and law begins with the claim that rules must be identified and applied in particular situations if they are to regulate human conduct. But because of the different values and beliefs, and therefore divergent purposes and interests, of those to whom the rules are supposed to apply, there invariably arise conflicting interpretations of the meaning, scope, or applicability of the rules. What is required, therefore, is some procedure for resolving the resulting ambiguities of the rules as they are revealed in particular disputes. The settlement of disputes on the basis of common rules requires the selection from among various competing interpretations of those that are to count as correct and must therefore be acknowledged as authoritative. The availability of a procedure for authoritative determination of the meaning and application of rules would thus seem to be contingently related to the effectiveness and importance of a legal system. But more than effectiveness is involved. For if, in situations where disputants insist on their own claims and on their own private reading of the rules, the resulting ambiguities and interpretive contoversies cannot be authoritatively resolved, it becomes impossible to say with certainty what the rules are, and the very idea of association on the basis of common rules is brought into question.

The absence of a procedure for authoritative determination thus gives rise to a problem that we may call, following H.L.A. Hart,[26] "the problem of uncertainty." According to Hart, a set of rules may be said to be uncertain where (1) "doubts arise as to what the rules are or as to the precise scope of some given rule," but also where (2) there exists "no procedure for settling this doubt." According to the line of reasoning we have been considering, the absence of such a procedure in a legal system constitutes a defect touching not only its effectiveness but also its very existence and character as law. For it would appear that uncertain rules, if the degree of uncertainty is large enough, cannot be said to be rules at all. And where there are no rules, there cannot be said to be obligations, duties, rights, or any of the other characteristic features of rule-based association. Furthermore, if authoritative determination does indeed have such significance, then we might also wonder whether legal order might require not only adjudicatory institutions, or "judges," to perform the office of authoritative determination but in addition some procedure for reconciling the divergent interpretations of different judges in separate but similar cases: that is to say, a *common* judge in the sense of an integrated judicial heirarchy.

An authoritative determination, it must be emphasized, is not the same thing as an interpretation that can be enforced, for although enforcement may be required for the effective exercise of authority, the relation between enforcement and effectiveness is a contingent one. Conceptually, authoritative determination is prior to enforcement, for compliance with a rule cannot be required until the rule itself has been clarified. A legal system must first of all provide some way of recognizing its own rules, of choosing among divergent interpreta-

---

[26] *Concept of Law*, p. 90.

tions of what its rules require in particular situations, and of deciding upon the adequacy of compliance with them.

When this analysis is applied to international law, the deficiencies of its procedures for authoritative determination appear to constitute a crippling defect. In the legal system of a modern state, the courts are organs of the community authorized to apply its laws. Furthermore, there exist procedures for reconciling the divergent judgments of different courts. That the office of authoritative determination is performed in a comparable manner in the international legal system is doubtful for several reasons. There exist few standing international tribunals of general jurisdiction, nor is resort to ad hoc tribunals of arbitration common except in a few specialized areas. International law is in fact most often applied by domestic rather than international tribunals, and in the absence of any mechanism for higher review the result is often the emergence of significant differences in the interpretation of international law from one country to another. No hierarchical ordering of tribunals exists through which differences of interpretation might be resolved. Moreover, there exist many restrictions on the authority of international tribunals to apply the laws of the international community. The authority of international tribunals is based in the first instance on international agreements that bring them into being and delimit the scope of their jurisdiction, and then upon additional agreements among the parties to particular disputes concerning how the issue in dispute are to be presented to the tribunal for decision. This authority is undermined to the extent that the parties, who have through mutual agreement conferred authority to settle a dispute on a tribunal, retain the right to determine whether the tribunal has exceeded its authority in deciding the dispute, and therefore that its award is null and void. The result is a lack of judicial independence that is especially evident in the case of arbitration tribunals but that also appears in connection with the International Court of Justice and other international judicial bodies. The diversity of tribunals, national and international, in which international law is applied and the deficiencies of many of these tribunals from the standpoint of a concern for judicial independence and integrity raises the question of whether authoritative determination operates in the international system in such a way as to undermine the uniformity and certainty of its rules, thus constituting an obstacle to, rather than a procedure for, the development of a common law of nations.

Skepticism of this sort rightly regards authoritative determination as a more critical feature of a legal system than legislation or enforcement. But the force of this observation has not always been fully appreciated. It is often said that international law is weak or ineffective because of the deficiencies of international tribunals in performing the office of authoritative determination. But the view of authoritative determination we are considering here is more radical in its implications, for it suggests that because it lacks any but the most rudimentary procedure for authoritative determination the international legal system is so uncertain as to bring into question its character and existence as a system of common rules. Authoritative determination by centralized law-applying institutions has thus been regarded to be necessarily and not merely contingently related to the rule of law in international relations.[27]

These arguments, which make authoritative determination by a common judge a necessary feature or condition of legal order, are more persuasive than those that assign comparable significance to either legislation or enforcement. But they are

[27] "Unless the law as promulgated by the legislature or as crystallized in custom is authoritatively ascertained by courts, the very existence of the law becomes questionable." (Lauterpacht, *International Law*, 1:23-24; see also pp. 197-199, and *Function of Law in the International Community*, p. 426.) "The absence of an international court of justice with compulsory jurisdiction over disputes between states does not merely strain the legal character of international law to the breaking point. In truth, it would seem to jeopardize altogether the conception of international law as a body of rules governing the conduct of states." (Gross, Peace of Westphalia, 1648-1948," p. 29; see also "On the Justiciability of International Disputes." pp. 216-217, and *Future of the International Court of Justice*, pp. 764-765.)

contradicted by substantial evidence that in many respects the relations of states are in fact conducted on the basis of common rules in spite of the absence of authoritative determination by a common judge. And this suggests that perhaps the connections between rules, authoritative determination, and the existence of a common judge are not as close as the skeptical view assumes them to be.

First, authoritative determination is not strictly speaking a necessary feature or condition of rule-based association. People often say that something is necessary when in fact they intend a much weaker claim. Thus we often seek to justify or excuse an act by saying that we had to do it or that we had no choice, when we merely mean that it was the least objectionable of the available alternatives. Again, to defend an act of war as a military necessity is not literally to claim that no alternative act was possible but rather that the act in question was expedient for the realization of accepted military ends. We often fail clearly to distinguish stronger and weaker senses of other words related to the idea of necessity, such as "require," "requisite," "impossible," "invariable," "must," "cannot," and so forth. It is not true that differences of interest or belief *necessarily* lead to different interpretations of common rules, or that such interpretive differences *cannot* be reconciled without some procedure for authoritative determination. To say that the lack of such a procedure results in uncertainty is not to say that uncertainty is inevitable, or to say anything about the degree of uncertainty that is likely to arise. The suggestion that an uncertain rule cannot be regarded as a rule at all is surely an exaggeration. Every rule is to some degree and in its application to some circumstances both vague and ambiguous, and therefore to some degree uncertain. The uncertainties of a rule as they may be revealed in future situations are often unknown and unknowable.

Some systems set up procedures for the authoritative application and interpretation of their rules; others do not. Umpires and authorities may or may not be provided to settle disputes about games, decorum, morality, or professional conduct. Anyone who doubts whether a system of rules can maintain itself without any authority to settle disputes of interpretation other than the authority of those to whom the rules apply should reflect on the example of language, for a natural language is a system of rules of just this kind. All natural languages exhibit variations in the linguistic conduct of their speakers. But underlying the diversity of linguistic usages are principles that operate to produce phonetic, syntactical, and semantic uniformity and reliability without the benefit of authoritative administration. The authority of rules of pronunciation, grammar, and spelling is that of general agreement within a community of language users.[28] It is absurd to say that because there is no procedure to decide disputes concerning correct usage authoritatively language is impossible or so undermined by the resulting uncertainty of common rules as to be ineffective or nonexistent. Where the rules in question are those affecting our needs, pleasures, liberties, and security, about which disputes are probable, their effectiveness and value to society may be considerably enhanced by procedures for their authoritative application. But to say this is to claim no more than that authoritative determination is contingently related to the prospects for rule-based association. This is in effect Hart's view when he presents the absence of authoritative determination in a primitive legal order as a defect that is the first to be remedied in many societies because it is more serious than the lack of special agencies for making and enforcing laws.[29]

Because the claim that authoritative determination is a *necessary condition* of association on the basis of common rules is implausible, the argument more often takes the form of an assertion that the existence of some procedure for authoritative determination is an *essential feature* of law. In fact there

---

[28] Dictionaries and other linguistic authorities report linguistic rules, not make them. The authority of such guides depends upon their conformity to acknowledged standards of correct usage. They are, in any case, hardly an invariable feature of natural languages.

[29] *Concept of Law*, p. 91.

are two claims here that need to be distinguished. The first is that authoritative determination provides the criterion by which the laws of a given society can be identified. A procedure for authoritative determination, in other words, provides a society with a way of telling whether a particular rule is or is not a law of that society. The second claim is that the existence of a procedure for authoritative determination permits the observer to distinguish law as a mode of association from other modes of association such as morality or nonobligatory custom. Both of these claims were advanced by the American legal realists, for whom the laws of a society were what its law-identifying agencies, especially the courts, interpreted them to be. "The law," wrote Gray,[30] "is composed of the rules which the courts . . . lay down for the determination of legal rights and duties." It is "the whole system of rules applied by the courts." Statutes should be regarded as a source of law and not as part of the law itself, for "it is with the meaning declared by the courts, and with no other meaning, that they are imposed upon the community as Law." A legal system, by implication, is an order of rules that provides for and is in turn applied by courts or similar institutions. Legal theorists who are not part of the legal realist movement have also made authoritative determination essential to their conception of law. Raz, for example, argues that "a law is part of the system only if it is recognized by legal institutions." (He is thinking mainly of the law-applying rather than the law-creating institutions of a society, and of these mainly the courts.) And he argues that law-applying institutions are "a constant feature of law in every type of society and their existence should be regarded as a defining characteristic of law."[31] Authoritative determination, in other words, is a necessary requisite of law *by definition*. The decision of those author-

---

[30] *Nature and Sources of Law*, pp. 82, 86, 162.

[31] *Authority of Law*, pp. 87-88. Raz also writes that "recognition by law-applying organs" is "a *necessary condition* of the existence of laws" (p. 87, emphasis added), but the context suggests that he has in mind logical rather than causal necessity when he uses the word "condition."

ized to determine the scope and meaning of the law in particular situations is the criterion by which the laws of a particular society may be identified, and it is the existence of such authorities that is the criterion of whether a particular order of rules may be said to be a *legal* order.

Let us consider these claims. In many ways they are plausible ones, and we should reflect on why this is so. It is more than that the conception of law that they imply corresponds to the way in which the word "law" is ordinarily used. Rather, to identify the existence of arrangements for applying the law as an essential or defining feature of legal order makes sense because such arrangements appear to account for the *systematic* character of legal order. We may define "systematic character" as the property displayed by a set of rules constituting a single integrated body within which the validity of some of the rules is determined by criteria specified in other rules. In a legal system there are agreed criteria for recognizing which rules are the rules of that system, and the consistency and uniformity that legal systems typically display are facilitated by the existence of such criteria. A legal system is, in Hart's words, "a system of rules within rules."[32]

Now to be systematic is certainly highly characteristic of law: the laws of most societies, certainly of those organized as modern states, do display this property. Hence the temptation to say (as does Raz, for example, of the law of the modern state) that "one of the defining features of law is that it is an institutional normative system," and that "the existence of certain types of norm-applying institutions" is "a necessary feature of all legal systems."[33] This, as we have seen, is a matter of definition. Such a definition is probably a good one for many purposes. But it is a mistake to equate the systemic quality of a body of rules with the existence of law-applying institutions, for what transforms a mere set of rules into a system is the existence within it of some criterion of recog-

[32] Introduction to Austin, *Province of Jurisprudence Determined*, p. xii.
[33] *Authority of Law*, p. 105.

nition according to which the rules of the system can be identified, and not the existence of law-applying institutions. The existence of such criteria of recognition is an essential feature of legal *systems*, because this is part of what we mean in this context by the word "system." But the existence of law-applying institutions is merely a method—*one* method—by which the validity of rules and interpretations may be tested. Authoritative determination by law-applying institutions, in other words, is a means of securing consistency, certainty, and uniformity within a body of rules; it is therefore a contingent condition of systematic character, not the thing itself.

Where there do exist law-applying institutions such as courts to determine the law, there is also a way of identifying what is to count as a law of the society. But it does not follow that the laws cannot be identified in the absence of law-applying institutions. A society may lack courts and judges yet still possess criteria for distinguishing valid from invalid laws. And it may rely on noninstitutionalized methods for applying those criteria in identifying the laws. The criteria of recognition may be embodied in traditions, moral tales, or sacred writings to which the members of a society refer in order to identify the laws of the society. Such relatively noninstitutionalized arrangements may result in a degree of inconsistency, uncertainty, and inefficiency that the existence of more differentiated law-applying institutions would do much to remedy. But this observation only confirms the conclusion that the existence of law-applying institutions is better regarded as contingently related to the systematic character of a body of rules than as a necessary feature of a legal system.

We have so far focused on the connection between authoritative determination and rule-based association. Our conclusion is that authoritative determination by law-applying institutions is neither a necessary condition nor a necessary feature of legal order. The implications for the related claim that rule-based association requires a *common* judge would appear to be clear: if legal order can exist without any judges at all, it can exist without an integrated hierarchy of judges. But this raises the puzzling question of how determination of the meaning of the rules, and hence the application of criteria identifying which rules and interpretations are valid for the system, can be said to be authoritative in the absence of judges or authorities. The problem exists at two levels: we wonder how interpretive disputes can be authoritatively settled without an independent third party or judge, and we wonder how, even where there are judges, the interpretations of different judges in similar cases can be reconciled without some procedure for deciding which of them is correct.

Authoritative determination is the fixing of the meaning or scope of a rule as it applies to a particular situation. It presupposes a dispute about the proper interpretation of the rule, two or more disputants, and a judge whose decision is acknowledged to be authoritative, that is, binding on the parties to the dispute. The application of a rule to a particular situation should be distinguished from the identification and interpretation of rules, for although it is true that rules must be identified and interpreted in order to be applied in the settlement of disputes, to identify or interpret a rule is not necessarily to apply it. Laws are authoritatively identified in a way that does not involve authoritative application when a legislature adopts statutes codifying customary law. Laws are authoritatively interpreted without being applied when a court issues a declaratory judgment or advisory opinion. An authoritative determination or application, then, is always made in the context of a particular dispute.

Authoritative determination is ordinarily thought to presuppose a third party, although it is not necessarily inconsistent with the concept of authoritative determination for one of the disputants to perform the office. This would be the situation, for example, in a family in which disputes between the mother, let us say, and other members of the family concerning the application of the domestic rules are decided by the former. One might find such an arrangement objectionable, but it does not follow that it is not an example of authoritative determination so long as the mother's decisions are acknowledged as binding. In such a case the mother's ruling is not merely an expression of her private views, on a par with the private views of other family members, but rather takes on a public or authoritative character. We associate the idea of authoritative determination with the decisions of an independent third party because usually the view of one of the disputants (at least in disputes between equals) is not authoritative. But though authoritative determination usually implies a third party or judge, it does not presuppose a common judge, if by the latter we mean either (1) a single law-applying agency to decide all disputes that arise within a society, or (2) a number of such agencies, each with a specified jurisdiction, so related to one another as to constitute a single, integrated judicial system. Thus the judicial arrangements of a legal system such as that of the United States may be said to constitute a common judge because the system is united by rules delimiting the jurisdiction of particular courts, governing when the decisions of one court are to be taken as precedents for the decisions of another, providing an orderly procedure for appeals and retrials, and reconciling divergent judgments reached in similar cases. But a system in which the courts were not integrated in this way would still be one in which authoritative determination was possible: the separate courts would interpret and apply the common rules in particular cases, and their decisions would be authoritative in the sense that they bound the parties to that dispute and possibly laid down precedents within their immediate jurisdiction. In such a system the work of the courts would be less likely to further the development of a uniform body of case law than in a system where the courts were more tightly integrated. But in such a system the courts would nonetheless perform the primary office of a court, which is to settle particular disputes on the basis of law. In doing that, the meaning of the law as applied to the circumstances of particular disputes would be authoritatively determined. These judgments are authoritative because they are made by agencies authorized, within the system of common rules, to apply those rules in the settlement of disputes. It is not an essential feature of authoritative determination that the rulings of particular agencies must be binding everywhere in the system.

The failure to distinguish the office of authoritative determination from the instruments through which it is accomplished has been a continuing source of confusion in legal theory. Authoritative determination requires that there exist procedures for settling disputes, through the application of rules, in a manner that is recognized as binding on those concerned. These procedures do not, however, have to set up a differentiated and continuing organization, such as a court. They may provide for settlement by one of the parties, by an elder, priest, or magistrate, by an ad hoc tribunal constituted through agreement between the parties, or by a fully differentiated and permanent court. Authoritative determination presupposes the existence of a recognized procedure for dispute settlement, but it is compatible with a wide range of institutional forms. To say that authoritative determination presupposes the existence of law-applying *institutions* is therefore to make too strong a claim, unless the term "institution" is being used as a synonym for "procedure." And if this reasoning is correct then it follows that the even stronger claim that authoritative determination presupposes a common judge—i.e., *centralized* institutions—must also be rejected. All that is required for authoritative determination to take place is that the rules should be applied according to generally acknowledged procedures: there must exist institutionalized procedures but not necessarily permanent centralized institutions.[34]

---

[34] For contrasting views on the existence of law-applying institutions as a criterion of legal order compare Raz, *Authority of Law*, pp. 105-111, and *Practical Reason and Norms*, pp. 132-137, with Watson, *Nature of Law*, pp. 28-47. That Raz emphasizes the importance of centralized institutions and Watson does not is perhaps in part accounted for by the fact that the former is seeking to explain the character of law in the modern state while the latter, a Roman Law scholar, bases his discussion on a much wider range of legal experience.

The implications of these conclusions for the analysis of international law are clear. International association on the basis of common rules is possible even in the absence of authoritative determination by a common judge because the latter is neither a necessary feature nor necessary condition of rule-based association. Authoritative determination does not presuppose a common judge: the common rules can be, and in many systems are, authoritatively applied in settling disputes through arrangements far too loosely integrated to be regarded as centralized law-applying institutions. Moreover, authoritative determination itself, although a remedy for the problem of uncertainty, is not the only and therefore not an essential remedy. As the examples of natural language and customary law suggest, it is not true that without authoritative determination the common rules underlying a practice are necessarily so uncertain as to be completely ineffective or nonexistent. Authoritative determination is a contingent but not a necessary condition of rule-based association.

There is little to be gained, furthermore, by adopting the existence of authoritative determination by a common judge as a criterion of association on the basis of *legal* rules. There may be some advantage in doing so where our interest is in explicating the character of the legal systems of modern states. But even here one may question whether making authoritative determination by a common judge the criterion of law does not obscure this character by focusing attention on one of the *means* by which particular laws are identified and interpreted. It is the existence of criteria for the identification of the laws of a system, and of procedures for the authoritative interpretation and application of these laws, that best accounts for the systematic and authoritative character of law, rather than the existence of highly institutionalized or centralized law-applying agencies. If we wish to articulate a conception of law that is going to be useful for understanding societies whose rules are created and applied in ways that differ from those of the modern state—and this includes international society—then we should not tie that conception too closely to the particular institutional features of one species of legal oranization, even if it is today the dominant species.

By relying on a conception of law too closely tied to the particular arrangements of the modern state, those who have written on international law have often misconceived the character and conditions of rule-based association in the society of states. The premise of the present inquiry is that criticism of these misconceptions will lead to a clearer and more accurate understanding of international law by helping to rid international legal theory of unjustified assumptions, derived from the experience of the modern state, concerning the requisites of legal order. But criticism alone is insufficient. It is only by looking at the actual practices and arrangements of the international legal system that one can discover, for example, how the related tasks of authoritative determination, identification, and interpretation are in fact performed. Instead of assuming that, in the absence of the institutions through which law is created and applied in the modern state, international law must be so uncertain as to be virtually nonexistent, we should ask whether and how the society of states has developed alternative methods for increasing the certainty, consistency, and uniformity of its rules. Rather than to conclude a priori that authority in any form is impossible without a superior power to make and apply these rules, we ought to inquire how and to what extent the distinction between private and public judgments, which is essential to the idea of authority, is made and preserved within the international legal system.

Attention to the actual character and conditions of legal order in international society is important for another reason: we cannot say how the rule of law might be more fully realized in the relations of states until we have a clear conception of what it is, in the circumstances of the society of states. It does not follow from the conclusion that legislation, enforcement, or even authoritative determination by a common judge are neither essential features nor necessary conditions of law that international law might not be strengthened if these in-

147

stitutions were to develop in international society. But neither can one simply assume that the remedy for the deficiencies of international legal order lies in policies intended to model it more closely on the modern state. The society of states is not itself a state, and therefore judgments concerning the existence and prospects of legal order within it must take account of the specific character and circumstances of that society.

CHAPTER 7

The Specific Character of
International Law

THE VIEW that international law is in some sense *sui generis* is rejected by those who desire the rule of law to be more fully realized in international relations and whose concept of law includes elements characteristic of the legal order of the modern state but incidental to legal order more broadly defined. Because they regard the institutions of the modern state to be an essential part of legal order as such, they hold that to speak of the specific character of international law is to acknowledge anarchy and lawlessness as the permanent condition of international relations. Thus Lauterpacht, who is representative of this point of view, asks: "Shall international law aim at improvement by trying to bring its rules within the compass of the generally accepted notion of law, or shall it disintegrate it and thus deprive itself of a concrete ideal of perfection?"[1] But concrete ideals are not necessarily appropriate ones. We cannot simply assume that the effort to establish civil institutions in the society of states will necessarily strengthen and improve international law. On the contrary, as I have argued in the first part of this study, there is evidence that efforts to govern the society of states on the model of the modern state tend to corrupt and weaken international law. An appropriate ideal, I would argue, is one that takes account of the specific character of international law and the particular circumstances of its existence and efficacy.

When Lauterpacht posed his question in 1932, he was reacting to the views of those who gave a particular interpre-

[1] *International Law*, 2:8.

tation to the idea of international law, namely that it constituted a body of rules binding on each state only by a consent
that might be withdrawn at any time. He rightly rejected this
conception, which interprets all international law (and not
merely treaties) as a sort of contract and denies what is indeed an essential feature of law, the submission of individual
wills to the limits imposed by a body of common practices
and rules. But it is a mistake to think that by rejecting what
is clearly an inadequate theory of international law as a unique
kind of law one has shown the inadequacy of all such theories.
It remains an open question whether a satisfactory account of
international law as a distinct form of law can be given.

THE PRIMITIVE-LAW ANALOGY

Those who have tried to understand how international relations on the basis of common rules are possible in the absence
of a superior power have often turned to the experience of
primitive or stateless societies. Comparisons between international and primitive law are encountered in studies of international law beginning at the end of the nineteenth century and continuing down to the present.[2] As would be

[2] There is a sense in which the analogy may be said to have its origin in
Hobbes's observation that both the savages of America and sovereign princes
are in a state of nature, subject only to the law of nature. (*Leviathan*, ch.
13.) Compare *Elements of Law*, II, ch. 10, sect. 10, where Hobbes explicitly
identifies the law of nations and the law of nature: "For that which is the law
of nature between man and man, before the constitution of the commonwealth, is the law of nations between sovereign and sovereign, after." But a
more extended exploration of international law as a decentralized body of
customary law made and applied in the manner of primitive societies became
common only with the development of the comparative study of law and the
emergence of social anthropology as an independent discipline. One of the
first writers to notice the similarity, and one who was familiar with the historical and anthropological evidence, was Henry Summer Maine. (*International Law*, p. 13.) Early in the present century the analogy was common in
continental writings on international law. More recent explorations of this
theme include those by Masters, "World Politics as a Primitive System," and
Barkun, *Law Without Sanctions*, as well as the studies by Kelsen and Hart
discussed below.

expected, the analogy between the two forms of legal order is usually made at a very high level of abstraction. It is now common to find the international legal system distinguished from the legal system of the state by reference to the former as decentralized or primitive (the latter being understood as centralized and modern). The distinction is said to lie in the fact that in a modern legal system rules are made and applied by designated officials, whereas in a primitive system the rules are made and applied by the subjects themselves without the mediation of officials. Whether or not there really exist any societies that are primitive in this sense is a question that need not detain us. The relevant point is that, so stated, the primitive-law analogy misleads us about the actual character of international law. The international legal system cannot, despite its lack of a superior law-making and law-applying authority, be regarded as primitive in the sense that it lacks complexity. The limitations of the primitive-law analogy can be seen more clearly by considering the arguments of two theorists, Hans Kelsen and H.L.A. Hart, who have relied on it to explicate the specific character of international law.

According to Kelsen, the legal order of the state is one in which legal rules are created and applied by officials acting as organs of the community. Such acts are performed on behalf of the community and can be attributed to it.[3] But in the society of state there are no centralized organs for creating and applying rules. Instead, the rules of general international law are created and applied by the subjects of the law themselves. General international law is therefore in this respect primitive law.[4] The situation is somewhat different in the case of particular international law, that is, international law that arises by agreement among a number of states or through customary practice that, although of local or regional significance, is not regarded as giving rise to general rules of law automatically binding upon all states. Particular associations of states within the larger international society have some-

[3] *Pure Theory of Law*, pp. 150-151.
[4] *General Theory of Law and State*, pp. 160, 327; *Pure Theory of Law*, p. 323.

times established more centralized and institutionalized arrangements for making and applying law for themselves. In this manner courts, administrative agencies, and even lawmaking bodies representing various degrees of confederation can come into existence. Such arrangements, being based on agreement, establish organs within general international law but not of it. The general rules, based on custom, continue for the most part to be applied by the members of the international community themselves, that is, by states. It is in this respect that the international legal system resembles the legal order of a primitive society whose members must rely upon self-help and diffuse social pressure to guide the application of the customs of the community and to enforce conformity with them.

States, on this view, are not organs of the community, even when they act in concert to make or enforce rules. The term "organ" implies a body authorized to create and apply rules for the community, one whose decisions can be attributed to the community. But the acts of a state do not in themselves create international law, nor are they authorized by the international community as a whole. These limitations apply to the collective action of states in concluding treaties or establishing international agencies and tribunals, as well as to unilateral state acts. Although the joint action of some number of states may in various ways modify general international law as it applies to themselves, it does not alter the law as it applies to other states. These principles are reflected in the common observation that treaties bind only those states party to them, and in the less common but equally cogent observation that even a universal treaty, to which every state is party, does not in itself create general international law. Such a treaty would not, for example, bind a new state that did not exist at the time the treaty was concluded. The nonofficial character of collective state action is also reflected in the principle that the decisions of international organizations and tribunals, where they give rise to legal obligations at all, are binding only on members of the organization or parties to an arbitral or judicial proceeding. In keeping with this principle, the Statute of the International Court of Justice lays it down (in Article 60) that "the decision of the Court has no binding force except between the parties and in respect of that particular case." The international legal system does not, strictly speaking, recognize the principle of *stare decisis*. Collective state acts, like unilateral acts, may indirectly affect the creation of general international law only to the extent that they may give rise, through the accumulation of state practice, to customary international law.

Although Kelsen's exploration of the implications of the international legal system as a primitive legal order appears to leave little room for authoritative determination, neither does it support the view that the decentralized character of this order means that international law is a law "between" rather than "above" separate states.[5] Kelsen is, on the contrary, the leading critic of this conception which, as an expression of the view that international law exists only by the consent of states, verges on the denial of the existence of any international law apart from that created by the particular transactions of states. As a decentralized order, the international legal system lacks a hierarchy of offices. But it does not lack the hierarchical arrangement of norms that Kelsen takes to be one of the differentia of a legal system. This hierarchy of norms does not create but is on the contrary presupposed by the hierarchy of offices that distinguishes the legal order of the modern state. It is, for example, presupposed by the idea of the sovereign as an office authorized to legislate by a law more fundamental than the rules that are the product of its own legislative activity. A fatal defect of the Austinian command theory is that it cannot account for how the sovereign has acquired the authority to enact laws. For Austin the criterion of a valid law is a particular factual occurrence—the issuance of a command by a superior who is obeyed by all in

[5] Oppenheim, *International Law*, 1:4; cf. Lauterpacht, *International Law*, 2:8-14.

153

a particular society and who is not obliged to obey the commands of any (human) superior beyond the society.[6] But for Kelsen that occurrence can only create law because it takes place in circumstances governed by a more fundamental rule according to which the identity of the sovereign is established and the authority to command conferred on it. Kelsen thus restates Hobbes's view, which nineteenth-century legal positivists like Austin were neither the first nor the last to misunderstand, that "law, properly, is the word of him that *by right* hath command over others."[7] By the same reasoning, treaties can give rise to binding legal obligations only because there exist more fundamental rules that define what treaty is and specify that a treaty shall have such an effect. Legislation and treaty-making equally illustrate the proposition that particular acts or transactions presuppose procedures according to which they can acquire legal effect. Kelsen's analysis of the international legal system as a primitive or decentralized legal order preserves these insights because, while it denies the existence of any hierarchy of offices, it still allows for a hierarchy of basic and subsidiary rules in which the validity of the latter is derived from that of the former. In this repect his account is superior to that implicit in the distinction between horizontal and vertical legal systems favored by a number of more recent theorists of international law.[8] This terminology is potentially misleading because it obscures the fact that there may exist a "vertical" hierarchy of rules even in a "horizontal" system—that is, one without central law-creating and law-applying institutions.

According to Kelsen, then, a legal system is a stratified structure of rules that may or may not provide for special law-making and law-applying organs. The existence of such organs is therefore neither a necessary condition nor an es-

---

[6] *Province of Jurisprudence Determined*, lecture 6.

[7] *Leviathan*, ch. 15, emphasis added.

[8] Falk, "International Jurisdiction," pp. 295-320; Kaplan and Katzenbach, *Political Foundations of International Law*, pp. 20, 355; Barkun, *Law without Sanctions*, pp. 14-17, 31-35.

sential feature of legal order. From this it follows that the absence of such organs in the society of states neither means that international association on the basis of common rules is impossible nor deprives the rules of this society of their character as law. But international law nevertheless remains a species of primitive law because it lacks specialized organs for creating and applying rules.

Hart reaches similar conclusions, for although he criticizes many aspects of Kelsen's analysis the two share substantially the same conception of legal order. For Hart the existence of judicial agencies is one aspect of the complex structure of rules governing conduct, together with procedures for recognizing, changing, and applying the rules, that constitutes "the heart of a legal system."[9] The distinctive character of the legal order of the modern state is to be found in the manner in which it systematically combines what he refers to as "primary" and "secondary" rules. Primary rules of obligation are rules that directly regulate the conduct of the members of a society. Secondary rules apply not immediately to conduct but to other rules, and state the criteria according to which the primary rules of a society may be identified, altered, and applied in particular situations. Among the secondary rules, those by which the primary rules of a society are authoritatively identified or ascertained—the so-called "rules of recognition"—occupy a particularly important place, for they constitute the criteria of validity within the legal system of that society.[10] Only if a system includes such rules of recognition can the validity of its rules be determined by some procedure other than general acceptance. The actual rules or recognition in a given system may be extremely intricate; they may not, indeed, even be stated or easily statable, but may remain implicit in a variety of procedures for determining which rules are valid rules of that system.[11] But a legal order whose rules of recognition are vague, ambiguous, contradic-

---

[9] *Concept of Law*, p. 95.
[10] Ibid., pp. 92, 100, 102, 106.
[11] Ibid., pp. 107-108, 110, 113.

tory, or nonexistent must be to some degree an incoherent and uncertain one.

In addition to the existence of rules of recognition, Hart emphasizes the importance, in fully developed legal systems, of judicial institutions authorized (by secondary rules of application) to determine the scope and meaning of primary rules in the contingent circumstances of particular situations. In a primitive or decentralized legal order, such law-identifying and law-applying institutions are missing or rudimentary. How, in such a system, can disputes about the meaning and scope of the rules be resolved? It is at this point that the radicalism of Hart's account, in contrast to Kelsen's, becomes evident. There exist in legal systems of this sort, Hart argues, no rules of recognition—no criteria which, applied by a law-identifying agency, serve to determine the validity, within the system, of a contested rule. Instead, it is acceptance by the members of the community at large that determines whether a rule constitutes a valid part of the legal system. A primitive system is therefore not only decentralized, in the sense that it lacks institutions for the creation, identification, and application of its rules, but it lacks moreover the hierarchical or multilevel structure of higher and lower rules, a property that for Hart is characteristic of modern legal systems and for Kelsen is definitive of law as such.

Even though he sees international law as lacking this hierarchical ordering of rules, Hart does not draw the conclusion that it does not exist or that it is not law. Instead he follows Bentham's judgment that international law is "sufficiently analogous" to other systems of law to be numbered among them.[12] Like the noninstitutionalized arrangements of primitive law, however, international law is a borderline case. Because it lacks rules of recognition, international law is not strictly speaking a *system* of law at all. It is in fact no more than a *set* of separate rules related to each other only because all are more or less regularly observed by states. There are

12 Ibid., p. 231.

no generally accepted tests of legal validity in international law, and it is therefore merely a matter of fact that states regard certain practices as obligatory. Consequently if a dispute should arise concerning the exact requirements of such a practice concerning a particular situation, there is no generally accepted way of reaching an authoritative resolution of the matter. If different states consistently interpret the requirements of the practice differently, the practice in question simply ceases to be one that is generally obligatory. Indeed, it may cease to count as a practice of the community at all. General international law is thus best understood as a set of customary rules that are binding on states simply because they are generally acknowledged to be binding and not because they have passed the test embodied in a rule of recognition.[13] Thus, it is acceptance by the members of the international community at large that determines whether a rule is a valid part of international law.

For Hart, then, a procedure for authoritative determination is neither logically nor materially necessary for legal order, although it is a distinctive and perhaps even definitive feature of the legal order of the modern state. But the sort of rule-based order that exists without such a procedure is doubly primitive because it lacks not only rule-applying institutions and a structure of secondary rules but above all rules of recognition according to which the other rules of the system can be identified apart from the mere fact of their acceptance by members of the society. Such a system is purely a customary one, and the relevant customs are those of the population generally, not those of some differentiated class of interpreters possessing an authority to say what the law is.

Is this an accurate picture of the international legal system? Only in part. The primitive-law analogy certainly illuminates some of the system's most striking and characteristic features, but it neglects others that, if not as visible, are fully as important. In the first place, international law is applied in a

---

[13] Ibid., pp. 228-230.

variety of international and transnational disputes by authoritative third parties. Second, whether a rule is a valid rule of
international law depends not only upon customary state
practice but also upon the customs and judgments of a differentiated body of interpreters: the profession of international
law. And, as a consequence of these two features, it follows
that there exist in international law criteria for identifying the
rules of international law that are distinct from the mere acceptance of those rules by states. Because there exist within
it procedures for authoritative determination and authoritative interpretation, international law does in fact contain rules
of recognition and therefore does display to at least some degree the systematic character of a modern legal order. Let us
turn to the arguments that support these conclusions.

AUTHORITATIVE DETERMINATION WITHOUT A COMMON JUDGE

Those who emphasize the importance of adjudication for legal
order pay particular attention to one means for performing
the office of authoritative determination: the application of
rules of law by courts. We have already noticed some of the
deficiencies of authoritative determination in international law
as it is performed by the International Court of Justice and
other international tribunals. But we should also ask whether
authoritative determinations are not also made in other ways,
by rule-applying institutions other than courts. Authoritative
determination implies a decision in which a particular dispute—one, that is, between named disputants—is settled on
the basis of law. This is the sort of decision that is at the
center of what courts do. But the identification is not perfect.
Courts also do other things, such as determine the facts rather
than the law of a case, issue particular orders, and interpret
the law apart from the settlement of particular disputes (as
happens when courts issue declaratory judgments or advisory
opinions, or pronounce *obiter dicta*). The office of authoritative determination, moreover, is one that is performed by

public officials other than judges. Criminal law, for example, is applied not only by courts and judges, but also by policemen, grand juries, prosecutors, sentencing boards, and probation officers. Similarly the courts are only one part of the law-applying machinery in the many branches of administrative law, such as those regulating taxation, labor relations, immigration, and nuclear power. In order to administer the law, its meaning in particular situations must be ascertained and interpretive disputes thereby settled. This is something that is done routinely by administrative officials as well as by judges.

The fact that administrative determinations are typically subject to review, by higher officials and by the judiciary, does not deprive them of their character as acts of authoritative determination. Judicial decisions are also often subject to review. A concern with the rule of law might suggest that there should exist procedures whereby administrative determinations can be submitted to judicial guidance and review, but such judicial involvement is neither an essential feature nor an empirical condition of authoritative determination. That legal systems differ in the degree to which their rules are administratively rather than judicially applied reinforces the point that adjudication and authoritative determination are contingently, rather than logically, related. It is true that adjudication is the ultimate recourse for the resolution of legal disputes in many legal systems. But the existence of this close contingent link should not blind us to the fact that authoritative determinations are also made by nonjudicial officials.

In the international legal system the rules are applied within international organizations and by international administrative authorities as well as by international judicial and arbitral tribunals. In addition a great many disputes in which questions of international law are raised are decided in national courts and by national administrative officials. Indeed, because adjudication and arbitration occur relatively infrequently at the international level, the authoritative determination of international law is largely carried out by agencies other than international tribunals. In terms of the sheer number of disputes settled, domestic courts are more important than international tribunals, although the decisions of the latter are in general of greater significance for the development of uniform principles of international law. The decisions of domestic courts, and of national administrative officials, thus represent one of the main ways in which the meaning of rules of international law is specified in particular situations, despite the fact that at times these decisions may appear to be incompatible with one another or even contrary to international law. The question of whether and how international law is applied to particular cases should be distinguished from the question of how consistency and uniformity of application thoughout the system as a whole is achieved.

When international law is applied in proceedings before a domestic court, the meaning and scope of its rules in the circumstances of the case at hand are authoritatively determined by the court in the sense that the latter has interpreted the rules in a way that is binding, within the national legal system, on the parties in that case. The same is true when international law is applied domestically by nonjudicial officials. That the manner in which international law is applied in one country does not establish a rule or precedent that judges or administrators in other countries must follow, or that foreign courts may sometimes even refuse to give legal effect to decisions taken elsewhere, does not mean that the law has not been authoritatively determined. It has been determined in a way that is binding on and hence authoritative for the parties to the dispute: it determines the legal situation of the deciding state. The legal significance of judicial and administrative decisions beyond the immediate case and outside the jurisdiction of the deciding court or official, on the other hand, is largely a matter of comity, judicial deference, and custom. The same may be said of the legal significance of the decisions of international agencies and tribunals. The question of the extent to which the laws and decisions of one place are to be given effect elsewhere is, moreover, one that is not unique to international law. Every modern legal system has a branch of its law (often referred to as "conflict of laws") dealing with this issue. For authoritative determination to occur it is not required that there be general acceptance either of particular decisions or of particular interpretations of law upon which they are based.

International law, then, is applied by domestic as well as international tribunals, and it is applied at both the international and domestic levels by administrative as well as by judicial officials. These applications are not equally important, nor are they of identical legal significance. But the variety and complexity of the procedures according to which international law is applied suggests that to regard the international legal system as a primitive legal order can interfere with our perception of important dissimilarities between international law and the law of societies lacking differentiated law-applying institutions. The customary legal order of a primitive society is one in which general acceptance by the individual members of the society determines the identity of its laws. In the absence of official judges and interpreters it is the meaning assigned to the rules by the subjects whose conduct they regulate that determines what the laws require both in general and in particular cases. There is no way that the distinction between correct and incorrect interpretation and application can be drawn except through the recurrence, in the practice of the society, of similar judgments—that is, through the development of custom. But the reality of international law is more complex than this, because although the correctness of a rule of international law in general depends ultimately upon custom, its correctness as applied to particular cases is frequently determined by a procedure more specialized than the judgment of general opinion. The international legal system is a decentralized one, to be sure, but unlike the legal order of a primitive society it is one within which there exists a distinction between public and private persons. If states are subjects of international law and therefore in their disputes with other states in effect private persons, they are also in other kinds of disputes agencies through which international law is applied. These are for the most part transnational disputes between individuals or corporations of different nationality, or between the government of one country and nationals of another. But there are also certain kinds of interstate disputes, such as those concerning jurisdictional immunities of foreign states and their diplomatic, military, and commercial representatives, in which the authorities of one state authoritatively determine the rights and duties of other states under international law. In such cases administrative and judicial officials apply rules of international law and therefore must be regarded as acting in a public and authoritative capacity with respect to the parties and issues in such disputes. Thus the international legal system, far from being simple and undifferentiated, is in fact an extremely complex system displaying characteristics of both the customary order of a primitive society and the differentiated order of a modern legal system within which law is applied according to specified procedures and by designated officials.[14]

That international law is authoritatively applied in transnational and in certain kinds of international disputes by state officials does not, however, mean that the latter may be regarded as organs of the international community. Clearly they are not, if by "organ" we mean an agency whose rulings are automatically binding on other states and attributable to the international community as a whole. Nor can existing inter-

---

[14] This feature of the international legal system has been analyzed by Georges Scelle under the label *dédoublement fonctionnel* or "functional division," referring to the application by courts and officials of foreign as well as domestic law. (*Précis de droit des gens*, 1:43 and 2:10, 21, 51; *Manuel de droit international public*, pp. 22-23; and "Phénomène juridique du dédoublement fonctionnel," pp. 324-342.) But Scelle thought that to rely on domestic institutions for the application of international law was no more than a makeshift, a dangerous substitute for centralized law-applying institutions, for state officials must be expected to apply international law "only as they conceive it" and therefore "only in the light of their particular interests." ("Some Reflections on Juridical Personality in International Law," p. 57.)

national agencies, including international judicial and arbitral tribunals, be said to be organs in this sense, either. On the contrary, the application of international law by states or by particular international agencies may often amount to little more than the basis for an adversary claim, so far as the correct interpretation of international law is concerned. It would appear to be particularly pointless to regard state officials who invoke international law in disputes between their own government and that of another state, concerning matters beyond their jurisdiction to enforce, as acting in the capacity of organs of the international community. A subject of the law cannot in general authoritatively determine, either for itself or for another subject, the rights and obligations of the parties to a dispute in which it is itself involved. A state's interpretation of international law in such cases is a claim, not an authoritative judgment. On the other hand, state officials do authoritatively apply international law in transnational disputes, as well as in a limited range of international disputes in which enforcement of the outcome is by right and in fact clearly within the power of the deciding state, and in such cases the state is no longer in the position of a subject of the law. It is not a party to the dispute, but a third party applying the law that will determine its outcome. In such situations state officials are able to determine authoritatively the rights and duties of the parties to the dispute under international law. But it does not follow that they are thereby acting as organs of the international community, for authoritative determination by a third party or judge is not the same thing as authoritative determination by a *centralized* third party or common judge—which is what the term "organ" implies.

But if the international legal system is without law-applying organs, it does not lack procedures for the authoritative application of international law in certain kinds of disputes. It recognizes a variety of means for applying international law and provides rules delimiting their jurisdiction and defining the scope and significance of their authoritative determinations. The existence of such procedures means that authoritative determination is to some extent institutionalized in the society of states, even if it is not performed by *centralized* institutions. The office of authoritative determination, to put it differently, is to some extent regulated by common rules, even if it is not performed by a common judge. To use the term "institution" as a synonym for "centralized institution" or "organ," as does Raz,[15] obscures the possibility of degrees of institutionalization falling between centralized law-applying institutions and no law-applying institutions or procedures at all. The International Court of Justice is an institution within the international legal system, but it cannot, despite the prestige of its judgments and opinions, be regarded as an organ of that system. That it is not an organ of the system as a whole is a consequence not only of limitations on its jurisdiction but more fundamentally of the fact that it has been established by treaty. The court is therefore the particular instrument of those states that have participated in its creation, rather than an instrument or organ of general (customary) international law. In the same way domestic courts, because they apply international law, may be regarded as institutions within the international legal system as well as organs of their own national systems. But they cannot, even more clearly than in the case of the International Court, be said to be organs of the international legal system. The system, in short, is one that contains institutionalized procedures for rule-based dispute settlement even though it lacks centralized law-applying organs.

Two important conclusions may be drawn from this analysis of the specific character of the international legal system as one characterized by the lack of centralized law-creating and law-applying organs, as well as by the presence of recognized, institutionalized procedures for the authoritative settlement of disputes on the basis of law. The first is that there is no necessary connection between authoritative determination and

[15] *Practical Reason and Norms*, pp. 132-137; *Authority of Law*, pp. 87-88, 105-111.

the existence of centralized law-applying institutions. The international legal system is one in which the office of authoritative determination is performed without a common judge. International law is applied by a variety of officials in a variety of forums, including those of states. And while the domestic application of international law may be no more than an adversary claim in controversies to which the state is itself a party, it authoritatively determines the outcome of controversies over which the state has jurisdiction. Limitations on the authority of a decision by state officials applying international law are paralleled by similar limitations on the authority of the decisions of international agencies and tribunals. In each case to say that international law has been authoritatively applied in settling a dispute is to say little concerning the larger authority and legal significance of the decision.

This leads to a second conclusion, that there is also no necessary connection between authoritative determination and an intepretation of international law that is authoritative in the quite distinct sense that it is recognized as correct or given legal effect beyond the jurisdiction of the court or official making the determination. The authority of particular interpretations of international law thus has two dimensions that must be distinguished: the authority to determine the outcome of a dispute within the jurisdiction of the deciding official, and the recognition throughout the system that the interpretations underlying such determinations are legally correct. Whether the interpretations of international law that are made when particular national or international officials apply its rules in deciding disputes are authoritative, in the larger sense that their persuasiveness and legal force is generally acknowledged by other states, depends upon customary international law. The interpretations of law-applying officials, whether judicial or administrative, national or international, are thus ultimately validated, so far as general international law is concerned, not through review by some higher agency but through the collective judgment of the international community as it is reflected in the cumulative re-

165

sult of various nonbinding reviews by statesmen, judges, and legal commentators. If an interpretation of international law made in the handling of a particular dispute receives general support, its validity as a part of general international law is thereby confirmed. The primitive-law analogy would appear to be more accurate as a description of the way in which a rule or interpretation is recognized as part of interntional law than as an account of how international law is applied, although even here it oversimplifies. To understand why it is inadequate in this respect we must look more closely at the way in which customary international law comes into being.

INTERNATIONAL LAW AS CUSTOMARY LAW

The international legal system is one that has developed so as to accommodate itself to the fact that for much of its history nothing remotely resembling a central law-applying institution has existed. Even now, following establishment of the United Nations (whose various branches, committees, and associated agencies provide a forum for the application of international law), the International Court of Justice, and a few other putatively general agencies and tribunals, centralized law-application exists only in a most rudimentary form. The manner in which international law is created is likewise decentralized. But although the resulting uncertainty and inconsistency of international law are defects that a centralized and compulsory institution for adjudicating disputes might do much to remedy, if one were possible, it does not follow from the lack of such an institution that the degree of uncertainty and inconsistency within the system must be so great as to render association on the basis of common rules impossible or insignificant.

Like a natural language, international law is based ultimately on the practice of its users. Like the rules of language, those of customary international law are not the outcome of particular decisions to create them, but rather the indirect consequence of innumerable and substantively motivated acts,

166

decisions, and policies. The result is a body of rules that rests "upon a consensus of . . . states, not expressed in any code or pact" and that in the absence of express agreement is capable of proof "only by evidence of usage to be obtained from the action of nations in similar cases in the course of their history."[16] The rules of customary international law are a distillation of the constantly changing practices of states, and they reflect the collective will of the international community only in the sense that certain patterns of conduct from time to time attain a degree of acceptance sufficient for them to be acknowledged as a distinct practice entitled to govern future conduct. The rules of customary law are not, like those created by treaty, the direct and explicit expression of a wish to pursue certain substantive ends or observe certain formal restraints. Customary international law arises wherever there exists a general or uniform practice together with the general acceptance of this practice as law.

A great deal of attention has been given to the question of what is to count as general practice and general acceptance, which is in turn connected to the even more fundamental question of how the rules of international customary law may be identified. Certain agreed principles have emerged as a result of this reflection. It is agreed, for example, that the opposition of a few states cannot prevent the emergence of a rule of customary international law, but also that the rule that does come into being through the practice of a large number of states is not binding on those who have resisted it, provided they have explicitly denied its legal validity throughout the history of its development. It is likewise generally agreed that, in order to invoke a rule of customary international law against a state, it is not necessary to demonstrate that it has accepted that rule. On the contrary, such acceptance is presumed and the burden of proof is on the dissenting state to show that it has consistently opposed the rule in question. But these principles are themselves part of customary inter-

---

[16] *West Rand Central Gold Mining Co. v. The King*, 2 K.B. 391.

national law. The criterion or test of what is and what is not a rule of customary international law is, in other words, to be found in custom itself.

This characteristic of international law as customary law has been a source of perplexity. The validity of a law within a particular legal system, it has been thought, can be determined only by reference to some more fundamental law that provides the criterion according to which it can be identified as a law of that system. But then the question naturally arises as to the source of the validity of that more fundamental law. Kelsen's theory of the "basic norm"[17] was an attempt to solve the problem of infinite regress to which this line of reasoning seemed to lead. The existence of a basic norm within any particular legal system, from which the validity of all the other laws is derived, is simply postulated. Applied to international law, the theory of the basic norm accounts for the validity of the rules of customary international law by postulating a norm that establishes general state practice, together with the general acceptance of that practice as law, as a "law-creating fact."[18] As there does not seem to be any more fundamental rule from which the validity of customary international law can be derived, the "basic norm" of international law has appeared to be nothing more than the principle, itself a part of customary international law, that states are legally obligated to obey customary international law. Such a formulation seems, however, to put an end to infinite regress only by introducing circularity.

The simplest way out of these perplexities would be to abandon the idea that every legal system must contain a "basic norm." In some systems the validity of the laws may depend simply on whether or not they are accepted by the bulk of the population. According to this line of reasoning, the rules of customary international law are valid because they are accepted as valid by the members of the society whose conduct

[17] See, e.g., *Pure Theory of Law*, pp. 193-205.
[18] *Pure Theory of Law*, p. 324; *Principles of International Law*, pp. 556-562.

they govern—that is, by states. There is, in other words, no higher source from which the validity of customary international law may be deduced. To determine whether a rule of customary international law exists as a valid rule of the international legal system, one must search evidence pertaining to the conduct of states for a pattern of uniform practice and general acceptance of that practice as law. The validity of such a rule is not deduced from other rules, but rather established inductively on the basis of empirical investigation.[19] There is, to borrow Hart's terminology, no "rule of recognition" by which the validity of the rules of customary international law can be determined in advance—no test that allows one to say, before a rule comes into existence, that "it *will* be valid *if* it conforms to the requirements of the rule of recognition."[20] To insist upon the existence of a "basic norm" or "rule of recognition" in a customary system is pointless. To do so would lead, in the case of international law, to the empty and useless principle that states should recognize as valid those rules that states recognize as valid. All this can be avoided if we accept the view that the rules of customary international law simply exist, as a matter of empirical fact, in the conduct of states, just as the rules of a natural language are those that may be discovered in the conduct of the members of a linguistic community.[21]

The absence within the international legal system of any independent criterion for identifying the rules of the sytem, apart from the actual acceptance of those rules by states, would seem to constitute yet another aspect of the primitive character of that system. But although the primitive-law analogy is in this respect substantially correct, it must be qualified if

[19] Gihl, "Legal Character and Sources of International Law," p. 69.

[20] *Concept of Law*, p. 229.

[21] The view that the rules of customary international law are simply those that are acknowledged and are effective in the relations of states is most articulately defended by Gihl, *International Legislation*, chs. 1 and 2, and "Legal Character of International Law," pp. 53-71; Ago, "Positive Law and International Law," pp. 691-733; and Hart, *Concept of Law*, pp. 226-231.

it is not to distort the actual character of the international legal system. The analogy with primitive law oversimplifies the actual complexity of international law in two important ways. First, it ignores the systematic complexity that arises from the hierarchical relation between international customary law and treaties. And it exaggerates the primitive character of the system by ignoring the role played in establishing the validity of customary law by the activities of a specialized legal profession.

With respect to the first of these points it should be noticed that, in addition to customary rules, international law includes rules based on explicit agreement among particular members of the society of states. In contrast to the general international law that arises from custom, treaties create a special or particular international law for those party to them.[22] The particular character of treaties has led a number of theorists to the conclusion that they do not constitute law in the same sense as the rules of customary international law, just as contracts among private parties within a state are not law in the same sense as legislative statutes.[23] To refuse to refer

[22] Special law may also be created by custom where a practice is observed among some *particular* group of states that is not *generally* recognized as law; the present discussion ignores this complexity and therefore all references to custom should be understood as references to general custom.

[23] Gihl, *International Legislation*, pp. 20, 46-47; Fitzmaurice, "Some Problems Regarding the Formal Sources of International Law," pp. 157-160. "It is incorrect to speak of treaties as 'sources' of international law. They are no more than contracts between the parties, and their significance as legal acts derives from the existence of rules of customary law by which their validity and their binding quality is determined, and according to which they are interpreted." (O'Connell, *International Law*, 1:21.) The distinction between contract and law is emphasized by Hobbes, who distinguishes between "simple covenant" or contract and law proper, arguing that the former "obligeth by promise of an action, or omission especially named and limited" while a law "bindeth by a promise of obedience in general. . . . So that the difference between a convenant and a law, standeth thus: in simple covenant, the action to be done, or not done, is first limited and made known, and then followeth the promise to do or not do; but in a law, the obligation to do or not to do, precedeth, and the declaration what is to be done, or not done, followeth after." (*Elements of Law*, p. 221.)

to treaty rules as "international law" would certainly represent a departure from accepted usage, but the point that the rules of treaties and those of custom are of a different character is an important one. Customary international law is basic. It provides the fundamental principles regulating the conduct of states in the absence of special agreement. And, because it specifies the procedures according to which special agreements are created, interpreted, invalidated, and terminated, customary international law embodies the criteria by reference to which the identity of valid treaty rules can be determined.

The international legal system is ultimately a system of customary law because the existence of international custom is logically prior to the particular rules created by treaty. This is true even though treaties have become more and more important both in regulating whole areas of international relations not governed by customary law and in codifying and developing customary law in those areas traditionally governed by it. Treaty-based law cannot replace custom as the ultimate foundation of international legal order no matter how widespread treaty-making and codification become. There will always be states that are not party to particular treaties, or that have accepted them only with reservations. There will always be disputes of interpretation that written rules of treaty interpretation cannot resolve, for such rules of interpretation will not be accepted by everyone and will themselves require interpretation. Furthermore, the existence of obstacles to amending existing treaties means that the practice of even those states that are party to them will tend over time increasingly to depart from the rules embodied in the texts. Because of changing circumstances and the gradually evolving customary practice of states, the adoption of codes paralleling customary international law makes the task of finding the law more rather than less complicated. The notion that customary international law might in time be completely replaced by treaties is an illusion. On the contrary, the scope and importance of customary international law grows in proportion to the growth of treaty-based law.

That customary law is logically prior to the treaty is most clearly seen in the core principle of the treaty institution itself. *Pacta sunt servanda* is a rule of customary international law and not itself the product of explicit agreement, for if it were one would have to ask why the agreement to respect agreements should itself be respected. The duty to observe agreements arises from the customary-law principle that to make a treaty has the consequence that those who are party to it are bound by its provisions. Customary law is thus the foundation upon which the entire edifice of treaty-based international law rests. Custom can exist in the absence of treaties, but treaties cannot exist without custom.

Because treaties and custom are related in this hierarchical way, the international legal system can be regarded as a completely primitive system neither with respect to the manner in which its rules are created nor with respect to the way these rules are applied. Although the validity of a rule of customary international law rests upon its acceptance in the society of states, the validity of a treaty rule depends upon criteria other than mere acceptance. To say that a particular treaty rule is binding upon a state is to identify it as a valid rule of international law not on the grounds that those states to whose conduct it applies do observe it (in fact, they may not), but because it is the outcome of a procedure (the practice of making and interpreting treaties) capable of generating valid rules of international law. The validity of custom rests on acceptance, but the validity of treaties rests on those rules that together make up the customary international law of treaties. These rules contain the criteria of identity or rules of recognition by which the validity of international laws embodied in treaties may be determined. Therefore the international legal system must be said to display, to some extent, the multilevel, hierarchical character of more complex legal systems united by a rule or rules of recognition. Because there exists no rule of recognition for customary international law, the system is not completely united by a single criterion of identity. But then given the diversity of sources of law it is not clear that *any* legal system can be shown to be so united. The unity of a legal system is a matter of degree rather than kind.

The primitive-law analogy also simplifies reality by identifying custom entirely with state practice. Here again the actual working of the system is more complex. Although customary international law is a distillation of state practice, the interpretation of what constitutes state practice belongs to a community of professional interpreters whose judgments, if unofficial, are nevertheless extremely influential. To a significant extent international law exists in the practice of states because it exists as an idea in the minds of a class of legal professionals, and because what these professionals understand to be international law is accepted by others. As this acceptance varies, so does the reality of international law as a factor in the relations of states. It is true that the professional community of international lawyers encompasses a diversity of views, that it is unevenly distributed across the globe, and that it enjoys—or suffers—fluctuations of acceptance and respect with the passage of time. But these facts tend to reinforce rather than undermine the conclusion that the fortunes of international law as a significant factor in world affairs depend upon the strength and integrity of those who know best what international law is and who are committed to its preservation. International law may therefore be said to be founded not only on the customs of the community of states but on those of the community of international lawyers.[24]

[24] The importance of the legal profession in the origin and propagation of international law was stressed a century ago by Maine, *International Law*, pp. 19, 26, 51. More recently the dependence of international law on the ideas and practices of the international legal profession has been emphasized by McDougal et al., *Studies in World Public Order*, pp. 42-154; Schachter, "The Invisible College of International Lawyers"; and Lachs, *Teacher in International Law*. Johnson, *English Tradition in International Law*, p. 30, argues the importance for international law of a body of lawyers whose regular practice includes work involving international law and suggests that the

The reasonings favored by this community of professional custodians determine the character and development of international law even though according to orthodox doctrine the views of lawyers, scholars, and even judges are not a formal source of international law. According to that doctrine, treaties and custom are formal sources of international law in the sense that they provide grounds for the validity of particular rules: a rule is a valid part of international law because it has been created by custom or explicit agreement. But judicial decisions and scholarly commentary do not themselves create valid rules; we look to them only for evidence concerning what the valid rules of international law might be. What is interesting in the present context is that this distinction between a formal source of law and mere evidence of it—a distinction that has struck many both within and outside the legal profession as a rather fine one—is one that is insisted upon from time to time by judges in deciding cases and by scholars in commenting on the law and in speculating about its character and sources. The idea that the ultimate source of international law is state practice, as manifested in treaties and custom, is an idea that exists at all because it exists in the collective mind of the international legal profession.

Furthermore, despite the authority of this idea, the community of international lawyers accords great significance to judicial decisions and scholarly commentary. Judicial decisions—especially those of international tribunals and of courts in countries with independent judiciaries, and above all those supported by intellectually compelling written opinions—are often cited as authority for particular rules and interpretations. This is not to say that the weight attached to judicial opinions of any sort is uniform throughout the international system. They are, for example, much more frequently cited

---

paucity of such professionals is a factor in the incomplete understanding and appreciation of international law within the legal profession as well as among the public. The argument that international law as a distinct profession is in danger of disappearing is considered by Vagts, "Are There No International Lawyers Anymore?" pp. 134-137.

by judges and scholars in common law countries than else-where. But it is undeniable that the significance of judicial decisions goes considerably beyond the direct legal effect of the ruling of a court within its prescribed jurisdiction. It is, for example, the informal rather than the formal authority of decisions of the International Court of Justice that explains their prestige and influence. These decisions have an impact on international law that extends far beyond the limits tech-nically imposed by the Statute of the Court and by the nar-row formal authority accorded its decisions. The same may be said of the great influence on general international law of certain decisions of domestic courts, such as those of the United States Supreme Court in boundary disputes between states within the American federation. The immense and continuing influence of legal scholarship on international law also has more to do with what the legal profession itself finds accept-able than with any formal status accorded to it as a source of law.

It follows from the absence of centralized law-applying in-stitutions and from the great influence of legal scholars in international law that the boundary between official and pri-vate interpretations of the law is less clearly defined here than in domestic law.[25] Ordinarily the authority of a judicial ruling is based largely on the formal position of the judges who make it and only secondarily on the quality of their rea-soning; the reverse is the case with the interpretations of scholars. In the international legal system, however, the im-pact of a judicial decision beyond the immediate case de-pends largely upon how it is argued and what conclusions are reached and upon the reception accorded these arguments and conclusions by practitioners and scholars of international law. The same may be said of the effect of administrative decisions at both the domestic and international level. The legal significance of the resolutions and declarations of inter-

[25] The existence of a sharp boundary between what is and what is not law is of course a matter of controversy in legal theory generally. For an analysis of the common law as a body of ideas and practices belonging to the legal profession, see Simpson, "Common Law and Legal Theory."

national political bodies like the Security Council and General Assembly of the United Nations, on the other hand, is a curious mixture of formal and informal authority. Even nonbinding resolutions by these bodies are widely regarded as having legal significance beyond that of merely serving as evidence of state practice, although the precise character of this significance is a matter of continuing controversy. According to an ideal conception of a legal system, the criteria of legal validity are maintained by being accepted by public officials, whose consistent and uniform application of these criteria prevents the legal system from disintegrating into an uncoordinated congeries of contradictory rules, orders, and judgments. But in the international legal system consistency and uniformity depend upon the maintenance of a consensus in which the acceptance of these criteria by nonofficial specialists and commentators plays an extremely important role. The history of international law suggests that this role was formerly even more important than it is today, but the fact that claims and judgments are now more often bolstered by appeals to treaties and state practice than to the opinions of Grotius or Vattel does not mean that the judgments of private commentators are unimportant. Given the richness of modern international law, their influence is less direct and comes largely in the interpretation, criticism, and reconciliation of a diversity of legal materials. The system is still one that is developed to a significant degree "by the antiquated method of writer commenting on writer."[26]

The importance of the international legal profession for international law constitutes yet another way in which the international legal system displays a degree of complexity and institutionalization that distinguishes it from the legal system of any primitive society. International law is interpreted not only by the public officials who apply its rules in a variety of judicial and administrative settings at both the domestic and international levels but also by nonofficial interpreters whose

[26] Maine, *International Law*, pp. 52-53.

judgments possess an informal authority without which the identification and development of international law cannot be fully understood. International law exists ultimately as a body of customary ideas and practices, but these ideas and practices are those of international lawyers as well as of statesmen.

AUTHORITATIVE INTERPRETATION AND THE RULE OF LAW

The primitive-law and domestic-law analogies represent extreme models of the international legal system. In fact, the system falls between these extremes. It is, on the one hand, more complex and differentiated in the way that its rules are made, applied, and identified than most versions of the primitive-law analogy recognize, although the primitive-law analogy certainly reflects the important truth that the international legal system is one in which common rules are perpetuated without reliance on centralized institutions for making and applying law. Criticism of the system from the perspective of the domestic-law analogy, on the other hand, is useful in focusing attention on the real problem of rule-based international association: can subscription to certain, consistent, and uniform rules of conduct be secured in the absence of some of the devices through which this is achieved in the legal systems of modern states? But it does not follow from the fact that rule-based international association faces problems that have been solved through the development of the centralized law-creating and law-applying institutions of the state that this solution is possible or desirable at the international level.

I have already considered the threat to diversity and liberty posed by a world state. Without fully embracing the views of Rousseau, Kant, and other theorists of international society that such a state would necessarily be despotic, one can still doubt whether the centralization of power in a single government would materially advance the rule of law in world society. In this respect the prospects of more centralized arrangements for applying international law appear both less ambitious and less dangerous. But here too one must be wary of simply assuming that movement in the direction of a common judge would necessarily strengthen rule-based international association. Greater use of international arbitration and adjudication, and increased reliance on a single international tribunal such as the International Court of Justice, might result in the development of more certain and more uniform rules of international law to be applied by domestic courts and by national and international administrative officials. A broader and more consistent realization of international association on the basis of common rules might come about if the system were to acquire more centralized and authoritative law-applying institutions. But international law would not necessarily be strengthened by such a development. On the contrary, the effects of international adjudication might well be destructive.[27] And to the extent that international tribunals are influenced to settle disputes on the basis of extralegal principles rather than on the basis of law (a direction in which some evidence suggests that the International Court has been moving in a number of cases), international law may be undermined rather than strengthened.

This is not an argument against efforts to increase the reliance of states on arbitration and adjudication in their relations with one another. I wish only to challenge the assumption that in the circumstances of the society of states more centralization of arrangements for applying international law would necessarily strengthen that law, and the assumption that rule-based association is impossible in the absence of such arrangements. The legal values of certainty, consistency, uniformity, and impartiality are no more guaranteed by centralized institutions than they are precluded by decentralized

---

[27] Jenks has argued this with respect to the decisions of the International Court concerning the requirements for proving the existence of customary international law, which have given support to the position that a state is bound by custom only where its own consent can be proved. (*Prospects of International Adjudication*, p. 237.)

procedures. Certainly the gaps and contradictions that exist in international law leave considerable discretion to those who interpret and apply its rules. But this discretion is not unlimited. There are limits, it is known that there are limits, and many of these are a matter of widespread consensus. There are degrees of uncertainty, and considerable uncertainty is not the same as legal anarchy. The same must be said for the legal values of uniformity and impartiality.

A clear perception of the ways in which certainty, uniformity, and impartiality are secured within the international legal system is obscured when one exaggerates differences in the interpretation of international law or fails to understand the specific methods by which such differences are reduced. With respect to the first point, it is important not to forget that, in spite of the prejudice of state officials in applying international law in some areas, a high level of agreement and impartiality may be achieved in others. Where there does exist a firm international consensus, as for example in the area of diplomatic immunities, the application of international law by state officials is more likely to conform to what is generally understood to be the law than where such consensus is lacking. Where a state departs from this consensus, as Iran did by making hostages of American diplomats, the illegal character of the act is nearly indisputable. Departures from widely acknowledged rules are more striking and harder to justify than departures from rules that are unclear or controversial. It is often the case that acts that are claimed to constitute violations or misapplications of international law are in fact taken in areas where the law has in some respect become uncertain because the consensus of states and legal commentators has broken down. It is not clear, for example, that national courts that display a parochial bias in applying international law in expropriation cases are departing from the requirements of the international law regulating the rights of foreign investors, if that area of law is itself in disarray. It is most unlikely that such disagreement could be overcome by the rulings of an international tribunal, for the realities of the

179

situation are such that until a political and legal consensus is reestablished there exists no general international law to be applied. An international tribunal would be required to engage in judicial law-making under the most inauspicious circumstances. Thus, situations in which the application of international law by national courts and administrative officials appears most partisan are often situations in which the law itself is uncertain.

Secondly, the reestablishment and maintenance of consensus is an end that is sought in a great variety of ways. Widely shared and thus authoritative interpretations of contested rules often develop even in the absence of authoritative determination by a third party. Although it is true that the interpretation of rules typically occurs when they are applied to particular situations, interpretation and application are not the same thing. The application of a rule involves questions of fact as well as of interpretation. Interpretation of a rule may involve clarification of its scope or meaning in general, that is, apart from its scope or meaning in the particular circumstances of a given dispute. And while rules are often authoritatively interpreted by being applied to particular situations, this is not the only method of securing authoritative interpretations. Thus, the certainty, uniformity, and authority of international law are advanced in part by efforts to reach agreed or authoritative interpretations apart from the application of the law to particular cases. The question of how authoritative interpretation of international law is achieved apart from its application is thus an important one for the theory of international law. By answering this question we also provide an answer to the narrower question of how the consistency, uniformity, and authority of common rules is maintained in the absence of centralized law-applying institutions.

We have already considered the most important way in which interpretive agreement is reached in international law: through the practice of states and of the community of international law professionals, each of which contributes in its own way to the development of general rules acknowledged as law. But agreement is often sought and sometimes reached through more deliberate methods such as the restatement and codification of customary international law, or through the clarification of treaties by agreement among the parties. It is now common, moreover, for treaties to make provision for the settlement of interpretive disputes by the International Court of Justice, by arbitration, or by some other agreed procedure. The uniformity and authority of international law is also strengthened when domestic courts and officials interpret and apply rules in a consistent manner, as well as by the policy that is sometimes followed in areas of disagreement, such as expropriation, of giving legal effect to the official acts of foreign states based on a contrary interpretation of international law.[28]

In the absence of centralized law-applying institutions the need for certainty and consistency also appears to have found a response in the emergence of a variety of rules limiting the discretion of states unilaterally to interpret, alter, or claim exemption from international law, especially the general rules of customary international law. Among these are rules that limit the sources of international law by recognizing the preeminent authority of treaties and custom and relegating all other sources of international law, such as judicial decisions, the resolutions of international organizations, private commentary, so-called general principles, and equity, to a distinctly subordinate position. Appreciation of the dangers of uncertainty is also apparent in the principle that considerations of morality beyond those already embodied in customary international law cannot be allowed to override rules of law, even in exceptional cases. Something like this principle would appear to underlie the evident reluctance of the international legal community to accept the argument that the kid-

---

[28] Such "judicial deference" in the application of international law in areas of persistent disagreement is advocated by Falk, *Role of Domestic Courts in the International Legal Order*. See also Justice Harlan's opinion in *Banco Nacional de Cuba v. Sabbatino*, decided by the U. S. Supreme Court in 1964 (376 U.S. 398, 84 S.Ct. 923), section 4.

napping of Adolf Eichmann by Israeli agents did not constitute a violation of Argentinian sovereignty. The certainty and uniformity of international law are upheld by the position that such an act, even if morally justified, remains unlawful.[29] Rules limiting the ease with which acts may be justified by appealing to diverse sources of positive law, or to higher law principles capable of overriding positive law, reflect an awareness of the dangers of interpretive discretion in the absence of centralized institutions for maintaining certainty and uniformity.

Such awareness is also reflected in stricter restraints in international law on unilaterally altering the terms of agreements than is usual in the domestic law of commercial contracts, and in the development of relatively conservative doctrines of treaty interpretation. For the same reason, it is common in drafting international agreements to spell out the scope of a concept or rule by means of examples, and even at times to attempt to provide a complete enumeration of the kinds of contingencies anticipated, rather than to rely on statements of general principle or connotative definitions. Extradition treaties, for example, typically list specific offenses as extraditable, instead of or in addition to defining such offenses in general terms. Thus the treaty on extradition presently in force between the United States and Japan enumerates forty-seven extraditable offenses.[30] Another example is provided by the statement on aggression produced within the United Nations after years of negotiation,[31] which lists seven prohibited acts of aggression as well as providing a general definition of the offense.

The international legal system, then, is a system that has developed its own imperfect remedies for uncertainty, its own characteristic methods for promoting uniform and authoritative interpretations of its rules. It is also a system that has been forced to accommodate itself to an even more basic dif-

[29] Merrills, "Morality and the International Legal Order," pp. 533-534.
[30] *Treaties and Other International Agreements Series*, no. 9625.
[31] General Assembly Resolution 3314 (XXIX), December 1974.

ficulty than the absence of centralized law-applying institutions, a difficulty of which this absence is more symptom than cause: that the very idea of the rule of law is imperfectly understood and little valued by many of those who in every country are responsible for the conduct of foreign affairs. By the rule of law I mean a particular interpretation of the idea of rule-governed association according to which authorities are accountable for their decisions and there exist procedures for evaluating these decisions and thus implementing the principle of accountability. More specifically, the criteria according to which the evalution of official conduct is made are known, public, alterable only by some regular procedure, and consistently applied. To the extent that such procedures exist, the conduct of authorities may be said to be governed by rule rather than by discretion, allowing of course for the fact that no system of rules can be applied without some discretion and that the relationship between rule and discretion is therefore one of balance and degree. Those who have been concerned to articulate the ideal of the rule of law have not sought to do away with administrative and judicial discretion but rather to point out the incompatibility between rule-based association and unfettered discretion.[32]

The concept of the rule of law was developed in reference to the modern state; it concerns the internal operations of the state, not the relations among states. Therefore, although the ideal of the rule of law clearly has application to the realization of rule-based association in the society of states, this application is indirect and complex. One way in which the exercise of arbitrary state power may be checked is through the subjection of legislation and of administrative decision to judicial scrutiny. But foreign affairs has been one of the areas of national policy in which governments have been most re-

[32] On the idea of the rule of law, see Hayek, *Road to Serfdom*, ch. 6, and Raz, *Authority of Law*, ch. 11. Oakeshott's *On Human Conduct* is interpreted as an exposition of the essential core of the idea of the rule of law by Auspitz, "Individuality, Civility, and Theory," pp. 278, 284, 287, a view reaffirmed by Oakeshott himself in "Rule of Law."

luctant to submit to being monitored even by their own courts, and the courts most reluctant to perform this monitoring office. The reliance of American courts on a rather amorphous "political questions" doctrine to avoid direct confrontation with the executive branch in the area of foreign affairs illustrates this reluctance. And even when the courts hold government to the rule of law, the rule of *international* law is not guaranteed. The regular principles and procedures upheld by the judiciary in one country may be very different from those observed elsewhere, so that the foreign policy of different states may be rule-governed without necessarily being governed by the *same* rules. That is why a society of republics, or constitutional states, is not necessarily an international society governed, to the degree that many internationalists from Kant to Woodrow Wilson hoped it might be, by international law. Obstacles to international association on the basis of common rules would exist even if all states were governed by the rule of law in their internal affairs.

The reluctance of states to conduct themselves according to the ideal of the rule of law in their relations with each other is thus a problem with several dimensions. At one level there is the reluctance of governments to subject their decisions in any area to the oversight of their *own* courts, and indeed in many states an independent judiciary with the authority to check the exercise of arbitrary state power scarcely exists. And even where there does exist such an independent judiciary, the scope of its powers of criticism and review may be quite circumscribed. They are particularly likely to be minimal in the area of foreign affairs. At another level, there is also an even stronger reluctance on the part of governments to submit their conduct to *external* examination, whether by the courts of another country, by the United Nations or other international organizations, or by an international tribunal. This reluctance is illustrated by the advocacy by many states of dispute settlement provisions in multilateral treaties according to which compulsory arbitration or judicial settlement is to be replaced by what is referred to as "free choice of means," which has evidently been taken by some states to mean "free choice in the fulfillment of their international legal obligations."[33] Hostility toward third party settlement on the basis of international law is perhaps less marked in constitutional states than in states with communist or military regimes. But American resistance to accepting an obligation to submit disputes to the International Court of Justice, and the widespread imitation of this position by other states that might otherwise have followed the United States in accepting such an obligation, suggests the magnitude of the obstacles facing the rule of law internationally, even among states that observe it in their internal affairs.

International law exists in the absence of institutions for securing the rule of law in the strict sense because regular international relations presuppose general rules. Whether they recognize it or not, statesmen act on the premise that international transactions—the exchange of diplomatic representatives, trade, regulated warfare, cooperation through international organizations—are impossible except on the basis of shared practices and procedures according to which agreements are concluded and interpreted, judgments of conduct formulated, and claims advanced, rebutted, and judged. As an agent acting within this framework of general practices, even the most narrowly self-interested state cannot ignore the fact that any claim formulated as a legal right, and thus as imposing legal duties on other states, may if generally accepted come to impose limits on its own conduct that in other circumstances might be inconvenient. "States are thus, more or less against their wills, driven to follow Kant's exhortation to act according to maxims that one could wish to see elevated to the position of general laws."[34] The process may be too haphazard to inspire confidence in the degree of security that could be expected from it, and it is this insecurity that most of all inhibits any decisive movement away from reliance

[33] Gross, "Justiciability of International Disputes," p. 217.
[34] Gihl, *International Legislation*, p. 43.

on self-help, with all that that implies. But it is not so hap-hazard as to foreclose rule-governed association altogether.

The international legal system is a system in which conduct according to common rules is secured, to the extent that it is, by methods very different from those that prevail within the state and that have been regarded, in the legal theory derived from reflection on the state, as characteristic of law as such. But in its preoccupation with the internal order of the state, legal theory has confused certain contingent features and conditions of legal order with the idea of legal order itself, and this has made it more difficult to see how it is that rule-governed association can exist outside the state. A clear view of the possibilities—and limits—of rule-based international association cannot ignore the actual and specific manner in which the society of states maintains its common rules, and thus perpetuates itself as a society.

CHAPTER 8

Rules and Purpose in International Law

ACCORDING TO the view of international society explored and defended in this book, there exists a society of states in which a number of independent states conduct their relations on the basis of authoritative common practices. Hence my name for this view: "the practical conception" of international society. International law, according to the practical conception, consists of rules distilled from the common practices of the society of states, expressing more precisely and explicitly the terms of association embodied in them. Because they constrain the conduct of states pursuing different and sometimes incompatible purposes, the authority of these rules does not depend on their contribution to the realization of particular substantive purposes.

The immediately preceding chapters have been concerned with certain fundamental questions raised by this conception of international society and international law: whether a framework of common rules is possible in the absence of central institutions for making and applying rules and how the unity and persistence of such a framework can be accounted for. But we have yet to consider a number of objections to the practical conception that arise within an essentially purposive view of international society as based ultimately on the existence of shared ends, interests, and values and a desire to pursue them in concert, and of international law as the product of this coincidence of desire and the instrument of its realization.[1] International law, it is argued, is an expres-

[1] The objections with which I am concerned in the present chapter question whether the practical conception can provide an adequate account of the *character* of international law. Another kind of objection, that shared beliefs and purposes are a necessary *condition* for the existence of international legal order, is considered in the concluding chapter.

sion of will, not usage; it is the servant of this will, not its master; and it can have no authority apart from its utility in furthering the ends it is intended to serve.

Such doubts have been most forcefully expressed in recent years by a number of American writers on international law—above all those who have expounded the "policy-oriented jurisprudence" of Myres S. McDougal and his colleagues and students at Yale Law School—by Soviet and East European theorists of international law, and by those who have attempted to articulate an international jurisprudence responsive to the presumed interests of the new states. Although diverse in origin, motivation, and style, all these attempts to specify the true character of international law are united by their rejection of the distinctive features of the practical conception. In particular, these views share a propensity to regard international law as an instrument of shared substantive purposes, and an insistence (which may take a variety of forms) on the relative independence of states from the obligations imposed by general rules. In addition, the arguments that are advanced to support these conclusions are sometimes linked to a repudiation of the preoccupation with rules and constraints that is said to characterize the traditional view of law as a body of rules. The common conclusion to which these various arguments lead is that the practical conception of international society is largely irrelevant to the conduct of international relations and to the actual place of international law in world affairs because it misconstrues the character of international law and indeed of law as such.

RULES AND RULE-SKEPTICISM

The present study continues a long-standing tradition of speaking of international law as a body of rules. Oppenheim was merely repeating what had by the end of the nineteenth century become a stock expression when he suggested that "Law of Nations or International Law (*Droit des gens, Völkerrecht*) is the name for the body of customary and conventional rules which are considered legally binding by civilized States in their intercourse with each other."[2] Most subsequent definitions, although less quaint, do not depart significantly from this formulation. "International law," wrote Hackworth in 1940, "consists of a body of rules governing the relations between states."[3] "International law consists of a set of norms prescribing patterns of behavior. . . ."[4] These and similar definitions of international law do indeed vary in significant ways, but they vary along a limited number of dimensions. International law is said to be a body (set, system, or other ordered arrangement) of rules (norms, principles, procedures, or standards) that regulate (govern, prescribe, or guide) conduct. Despite terminological variations, the concept of a rule is central to all such formulations.

The proposition that to identify law with rules is to adhere to an unnecessarily limiting conception of law is one of the main contributions of the American legal realists during the first half of the present century. The realists sought to shift attention from the law conceived as a body of rules abstracted from the activity of making and applying rules to that activity itself. Law, they suggested, could not be rightly understood so long as it was regarded as a body or system of rules. They called upon legal scholarship to pay greater attention to the legal process: a complex and in many ways disorderly congeries of decisions, actions, practices, and arrangements in which the work of the courts held an especially important place. And, as legal scholarship was supposed to pay more attention to the actual conduct of judges and other participants in the legal process, it followed that it should make greater use of the theories and methods of the social sciences. The famous slogans of the realist movement—such as Holmes's "the life of the law has not been logic: it has been experience,"[5] or Llewellyn's "what officials do about disputes is . . . the law

[2] *International Law*, 1:3.

[3] *Digest of International Law*, 1:1.

[4] Coplin, *Functions of International Law*, p. 7.

[5] *Common Law*, p. 1.

itself"[6]—are epigrammatic expressions, and of course exaggerations, of this point of view; their purpose is to get us to look at law in a new light. These suggestions are no longer revolutionary, or even particularly controversial, although they have had less impact in the field of international law than elsewhere. But they are not necessarily incompatible with traditional ideas of law as a certain kind of rule-governed activity or practice. It is only insofar as realism tends to the conclusion that rules of law do not exist that it raises a challenge to one of the central postulates of the practical conception of international law.

The view that rules of law do not exist, and that what we think of as legal rules are no more than attempts to generalize about the decisons of various public officials and institutions, is commonly referred to as "rule-skepticism." The latter is not, however, a single unified doctrine, but rather a collection of quite diverse propositions not all of which are compatible with one another, and some of which are quite false. For present purposes we might usefully distinguish three versions of rule-skepticism.

The first and most acceptable is one that arises out of the realists' concern with legal education and reflects their conclusion that what textbooks and other written materials identify as the rules of particular areas of law are, on closer inspection, no more than crude and often mistaken efforts to formulate abstractly the much more complicated and ever-changing considerations embodied in legal practice. The point of this form of rule-skepticism is not that there are no rules of law, but that the textbook rules are not *the* rules that in fact account for the decisions of judges and other officials. This suspicion of textbook formulations was soon extended to the written opinion of judges. A well-known expression of this point of view can be found in Justice Cardozo's reconsideration of the rules of manfacturer's liability in *MacPherson v.*

---

[6] *Bramble Bush*, p. 9.

Buick Motor Co.,[7] in the course of which he argues that the actual rule of earlier cases bearing on this issue cannot be deduced from the written opinions of the deciding judges but only from the actual pattern of the decisions themselves. To speak of law as a body of rules may be misleading to the extent that it implies that rules of law are identical with the verbal formulations of them appearing in textbooks and judicial opinions. But there is otherwise nothing in this mild version of rule-skepticism that is incompatible with the traditional view of international law as a body of rules. Indeed, to characterize this body of rules as rooted in the customary practices of states and as a distillation of these practices is simply another way of emphasizing the insight of the realists that rules are corrigible attempts to formulate statements of legal practice.

A second and somewhat stronger version of rule-skepticism appears in the suggestion that talk of rules is misleading because the law consists not only of rules but also of other sorts of standards that are not properly called rules. A number of legal theorists have noticed, for example, the importance in certain contexts of distinguishing between "rules" and "principles." According to this distinction, "rules" are standards "precisely determining what shall take place upon a precisely determined set of facts,"[8] whereas "principles" simply add weight on one side or the other. Rules are criteria of decision framed in such a way that, if the factual conditions they stipulate are met, then the rule governs the decision, and other rules or reasons for deciding the dispute another way are excluded from consideration. If two rules conflict, one or the other of them must be regarded as inapplicable in the immediate circumstances and the decision wholly determined by the other, whereas conflicting principles are capable of being reconciled through compromise.[9] The point, taken by itself and apart from any implications for legal theory that

[7] 217 N.Y. 382, 111 N.E. 1050.

[8] Pound, *Introduction to the Philosophy of Law*, p. 56.

[9] Dworkin, *Taking Rights Seriously*, pp. 22-28.

may be thought to follow from it, is unexceptionable. But nothing in the view of law as a body of rules need imply an insistence on rules in a narrow sense that would exclude principles as part of the law. On the contrary, it is usual to employ the term "rule" in an inclusive sense to refer to both rules and principles. It is certainly one of the distinguishing aspects of the practical conception of international law that it emphasizes the rich variety of rules, principles, procedures, standards, precepts, customs, routines, and other sorts of practices accepted by the international community and constituting its common law. The tradition of regarding international law as a body of rules is one that does indeed, as the legal realists protest, sometimes lead to a rigid and unrealistic conception of the actual character of international law. But this is an incidental rather than an essential defect of the traditional conception.

The objection to talk about rules is perhaps inspired by the mistaken belief that rules are prohibitions, together with the sound conviction that there is more to law than prohibition. But, as Hart and others have emphasized, many rules are permissive, either because they expressly permit an act or else because by not forbidding it they tacitly permit it. Still other rules define and thus constitute new forms of activity and empower both private persons and public officials to engage in legally defined and protected undertakings. The traditional terminology of obedience that is used to describe the relation between law and those whose conduct is (in part) based upon it is unfortunate because it imples that law consists only of rules that either require or prohibit action. It is misleading to say that we obey permissive rules; it would be more accurate to say that we act on, take advantage of, or avail ourselves of them.[10] The suggestion that the term "conformity" be used to cover both obedience to and action on a rule is perhaps a good one, for "nonconformity" implies action on some other basis and not necessarily disobedience.

[10] Hart, "Kelsen's Doctrine of the Unity of Law," p. 185.

To the extent that it identifies rules with prohibitions, then, rule-skepticism labors under a misapprehension and gives rise to objections that cease to be persuasive if we allow that the term "rules" can be used broadly to refer to several different kinds of standards of conduct.

Another misapprehension is the notion that rules completely and unequivocally prescribe particular acts, and that particular acts can always be clearly identified as compatible or incompatible with a rule. This may explain the charge that a conception of law as rule-based association is rigid. But in the application of rules there are always circumstances to be considered, distinctions to be made, ambiguities to be resolved, borderline cases and novel situations to be classified, disputes concerning jurisdiction to be settled, pleas of justification and excuse to be accepted or rejected, and an indefinite number of other doubts, qualifications, exceptions, and considerations to be taken into account. Moreover, when rules are expressed in verbal form, a degree of uncertainty arises from the fact that the language in which they are expressed can be vague (there is a "penumbra of uncertainty"[11] surrounding a settled core of meaning) or ambiguous (because a word may have more than one settled meaning). Because of these features of language, rules are to some extent indeterminate, and because no verbal formulation can anticipate all possible circumstances and contingencies they are necessarily incomplete.[12] On the other hand, although these complexities mean that rules cannot uniquely determine particular acts, it does not follow that rules are completely indeterminate. Although rules do not provide unequivocal answers to all puzzles they do provide tentative answers to many puzzles, and although they cannot unequivocally prescribe or forbid particular acts they do delimit ranges of conforming and nonconforming conduct. The attempt to identify the precise scope

[11] Hart, "Positivism and the Separation of Law and Morals." p. 607.
[12] On the relation between law and language, see Hart, *Concept of Law*, pp. 121-132, and Twining and Miers, *How to Do Things with Rules*, pp. 110-128.

and meaning of a legal rule always creates an impression of disagreement and confusion, for our attention is directed to the areas of uncertainty and away from the common ground that is taken for granted. But the context of interpretive controversy is always interpretive agreement; the possibility of a dispute concerning the meaning of a rule in a marginal case presupposes agreement concerning core cases, for without that there would be no rule to be applied to the doubtful case.

The strongest version of rule-skepticism is that which insists that law cannot be understood as a set of standards at all, but consists of conduct itself. The point here is not that judges and officials apply various sorts of legal standards other than rules, but that all legal standards are so embedded in and inseparable from the actual conduct of lawmakers, judges, and administrators as to be incapable of satisfactory statement apart from a detailed description of their decisions and the circumstances in which they are made. This is an amorphous doctrine, itself open to a number of interpretations. According to one interpretation, law is a "decision process" through which shared "values" are articulated and common "policies" deliberated. A legal system is not a structure of rules but a process of bargaining in the course of which agreed policies evolve through the continual exchange of claims and counterclaims. From this it follows that legal theory should focus on the actual, observable phenomena of this process and not on mysterious abstractions ("rules"). This manner of speaking does in fact capture an aspect of law that the traditional terminology sometimes causes us to neglect. But it goes too far in its suggestion that the law consists of whatever outcomes emerge from the activities of public officials. The view that there is no law apart from what officials decide is indeed self-contradictory, for the very idea of an official presupposes rules according to which public offices are created, their lawful incumbents identified, and the scope of their jurisdiction delimited. Even more questionable is the identification of law with the activities not only of officials but of everyone powerful enough to affect the outcome of important decisions.

The study of law at this point becomes a kind of sociology. All the conceptions that have long characterized both the practice and the study of law—"rules," "duty," "right," "validity," "authority," "office," "jurisdiction," and many others—are either abandoned or reinterpreted in wholly descriptive or predictive terms. The result is a conception of law that leaves out the idea of standards of lawful conduct. The realist urge to debunk the received notions of jurisprudence and to substitute for them a supposedly hardheaded and scientific empiricism thus culminates in a new dogma that is as blind to the distinctive character of law as any of the doctrines it is intended to replace.

The truth is that law consists both of conduct and of standards of conduct, and it is therefore misleading to stress either at the expense of the other. The rule-skeptic is certainly correct in arguing that one cannot state the rules embodied in legal activity without paying attention to the ongoing practice of those involved in that activity. But the converse is also true: one cannot describe legal activity apart from the rules implicit in it. To speak of a legal system as a body of rules does not exclude consideration of it as an activity, but rather points to what is surely a characteristic feature of law: that it is an activity defined and governed by rules and one in which the effort to discover, clarify, and make explicit rules of conduct is regarded as supremely important.

The distrust of commonly employed words and concepts that is characteristic of rule-skepticism is sound, but it needs to be supplemented by criticism of the new theoretical vocabulary to which legal realism has given rise. It is not likely that eschewing the word "rule" is going to solve the problem of how to talk and think about law. The new vocabulary either misses the dimension of legal activity to which the term "rule" refers or else it implies the existence of such a dimension while avoiding explicit analysis of it. Those who reject "rule" as rigid or metaphysical sometimes prefer a word of sociological origin like "norm" for its presumed freedom from these defects. That word seems better adapted to the program of creating a descriptive and predictive science of law. Whereas the term "rule" implies a standard of conduct to which the members of some group are expected to conform, even if they do not in fact conform to it, a norm—in this descriptive sense—is a generalization about regularities observed in the actual conduct of particular persons. But the term "rule" can also be used descriptively, just as there are contexts in which "norm" is used in the sense of a standard.[13] This ambiguity, which indeed pervades the language of human conduct, reflects the fact that most human activity is defined, shaped, and guided by standards of one sort or another.

The conception of rules repudiated by the rule-skeptic is a straw man. Although examples of the view of law as a body of rules in the sense condemned by the skeptic are easily found, it hardly follows that to speak of law as a body of rules is necessarily to speak in this sense. Language provides a helpful analogy. It does not follow from the fact that linguists refer to rules of phonetics or syntax that the speakers of a given language are to be regarded as consciously and conscientiously applying precepts of correct speech. All that is claimed is that their speech reflects the tacit application of standards capable of being expressed as rules, most of which the average speaker would be completely unable to state. It is one of the remarkable features of language that speakers,

---

[13] See Chapter 1, n. 3. Legal theorists are sometimes urged to speak of "practices" rather than "rules" as a way of breaking the grip of the excessively formal intellectual habits that are believed to have hampered jurisprudence in the past. Instead of confronting us with ontologically awkward questions such as "Is the rule that cousins cannot marry part of the Russian legal system?" it leads us to raise altogether more sensible and answerable questions such as "Under Russian legal practice, are cousins permitted to marry?" (Dworkin, "Comments on the Unity of Law Doctrine," p. 206.) While such a manner of speaking may well correct certain unfortunate tendencies in the language of "rules," it should be noted that it does not at all dispense with the idea of standards of conduct and therefore has little in common with the more extreme forms of rule-skepticism that seek to confine discourse about law to descriptive and predictive statements about "behavior," "decision-making processes," and the like.

exercising the competence represented by their tacit knowledge of linguistic rules, can produce novel combinations of phonemes, words, sentences, and other linguistic units that are correct in the sense that they conform to the underlying rules that account for the patterns of speech in a particular linguistic community. Furthermore, the range of expressions that are linguistically correct in a given situation is vast. The rules of a language do not require its speakers to say particular things, for there are always in any situation an indefinite number of possible utterances that are linguistically correct. There is nothing rigid or mechanical in the conception of language as rule-governed in this sense. Nor does thinking of languages as rule-governed mean that one's conception of language is necessarily static, another frequent claim of rule-skepticism. Continuous change is in fact one of the more striking features of language, as it is of many other rule-governed human activities. The rules of a language are continuously affected by the manner in which they are applied in practice. No rule of a language is immune from alteration as a result of the linguistic performances of its speakers.

The term "rule" is a convenient shorthand for the variety of practices, principles, procedures, and other considerations that underlie and account for legal conduct and are essential for legal discourse. To speak of law as a body of rules is a way of expressing an understanding of law as rule-based conduct and of focusing attention on the standards of conduct implicit in the legal practices of a community. It does not commit the legal theorist to the view that law involves the conscious and mechanical application of precise, completely specifiable, absolutely determining, and unchanging criteria of conduct. Rules of law, as of language, are used and applied tacitly as well as explicitly, creatively as well as mechanically, skillfully and ineptly, correctly and incorrectly. Like linguistic rules they cannot avoid being altered by the manner in which they are applied in the particular performances of officials, advocates, scholars, and citizens. And, just as linguistic rules can be looked at both from the perspective of the speaker as standards of

197

correct usage and from the perspective of the linguistic theorist as generalizations about linguistic conduct, so legal rules can be regarded both normatively and descriptively. These are evidently all points to which rule-skepticism wishes in one way or another to call attention; but, to the extent that it rejects all talk of rules and insists on reducing the discussion of law to statements about behavior, legal theory founded on rule-skepticism must fall back upon an impoverished vocabulary in which generalizations about legal conduct are emphasized at the expense of attention to the relation between conduct and standards of conduct.

Law as an Instrument of Shared Purposes

Rule-skepticism is closely related to the view that law is a means or instrument for facilitating the pursuit of shared purposes. I shall refer to this view as "instrumentalism." It comprises both the analytic or descriptive argument that law is, by definition or in fact, an instrument for the pursuit of shared purposes and the normative argument that law should be used and regarded as such an instrument. For the rule-skeptic the essence of law is to be found not in rules of conduct but rather in conduct itself: in the "legal process." Instrumentalism describes this process as one through which agreement is reached concerning the purposes to be served by collective action and through which policies are devised for furthering these shared purposes. The legal process includes all activities that contribute to the identification of shared values, the articulation of shared purposes, the pursuit of common interests, and the implementation of agreed policies. Whereas the rule-skeptic questions the identification of law with rules, the instrumentalist attacks the idea that law consists primarily of formal limits within which people must act. According to the instrumentalist the law is not a set of constraints on the pursuit of substantive ends but rather an instrument of that pursuit. Instrumentalism thus questions the most central and distinctive claim of the practical conception of international society and international law.

198

There are many versions of instrumentalism in international law, just as there are of rule-skepticism. Most, however, share certain common characteristics. Most regard shared aims and interests, rather than the observance of constraints imposed by common practices and procedures, to be the basis of international association. In Eastern Europe, for example, relations among socialist states are officially regarded as governed by principles whose authority is derived from their contribution to the end of preserving socialism. The sovereignty of socialist states is therefore limited by this superior purpose, which justifies their existence. A socialist government is free to determine how the ends of socialism can be best promoted for its own people. In other words, it is constrained by the duty not to hinder these ends, either internally or in other socialist countries. The international law governing relations among socialist states must reflect and serve the common interests of the socialist community.[14] Similar arguments, though postulating other ends, are made outside the socialist community.

Another characteristic of instrumentalist theories of international law is their tendency to draw very indistinct lines between law and policy. Because law is a means of furthering shared aims and interests, it is largely coextensive with politics. Law and politics become aspects of a single process through which values are authoritatively allocated and collective decisions reached.[15] Finally, such authority as law possesses derives from its adequacy as an instrument for the pur-

---

[14] These arguments, sometimes called the "Brezhnev Doctrine," have been invoked by the Soviet Union to justify the suppression of deviations from socialist orthodoxy in Hungary, Czechoslovakia, and Poland. This could not be done without overriding the constraints of general international law on armed intervention.

[15] Thus traditional—that is, noninstrumental—conceptions of law are criticized for assuming, wrongly, that law is "autonomous" and "separable from community processes." (Falk, *Status of Law*, p. 14.) In the more extreme versions of instrumentalism adjudication becomes a kind of bargaining in which no distinction is made between the common interest and the common good and respect for forms and procedures is regarded as merely one interest to be weighed against others.

suit of shared purposes. These three central propositions of instrumentalism in international law—that the law is a means of furthering shared purposes, that it is a process scarcely distinguishable from politics, and that the authority of the bargains that emerge from this process depends ultimately on their relation to the pursuit of shared purposes—reflect an essentially purposive conception of international society.

Although instrumentalist arguments can be found throughout the literature of international law, they have been put forward with particular fullness, vigor, and influence in the work of Myres S. McDougal.[16] Like the realists of an earlier generation by whom he has clearly been much influenced, McDougal's aim is to create a descriptive and predictive science of the legal process that can serve as a basis for choosing and implementing policies intended to promote shared purposes. The task of jurisprudence has usually been held to be the clarification of legal rights and duties, although since Bentham there has been a tendency to make room within jurisprudence itself for reflections on policy ("the principles of legislation") that have traditionally been regarded as falling within the province of politics rather than law. McDougal's conception of jurisprudence requires not only that the traditional separation of law and politics be abolished but also that jurisprudence include sociological inquiries designed to describe and explain the process through which the important decisions for a society are made. Such a descriptive science is required if policies are to be rationally devised and pursued. This conception of jurisprudence echos the conviction of earlier realists such as Pound and Llewellyn that the discipline of law should become a kind of social engineering aimed

---

[16] Despite the vast volume of writing produced by McDougal and his collaborators during the past two decades, the relatively early synthesis of his instrumentalist theory of law in *Studies in World Public Order* (1960) remains of fundamental importance. A number of studies in international legal theory are assembled in McDougal and Reisman, *International Law Essays*. There is a good bibliography of materials by and about McDougal in Reisman and Weston, *Toward World Order and Human Dignity*, pp. 579-593.

at promoting the realization of socially desirable ends on the basis of a sound descriptive science of law.

The view that jurisprudence has a descriptive as well as a normative dimension is no departure from a more traditional understanding of its character and aims. What is novel is the uniting of a particular conception of science with an instrumentalist reinterpretation of the normative character of law. Legal science works within its proper sphere when it confines itself to describing, explaining, and predicting legal behavior such as the decisions of judges, whereas law should devote itself to using the propositions of legal science for the achievement of substantive policy goals. Conversely, if the pursuit of goals is at the heart of the legal enterprise, the lawyer cannot be content with the traditional task of identifying and applying rules, for rules are mere abstractions that provide no sufficient basis for explaining and predicting actual conduct. Legal science must broaden its focus to include the study of "social and power processes" if it is to succeed in predicting conduct and evaluating the consequences of alternative policies.[17] "The problem-solving tasks with which the legal scholar, adviser, and decision-maker are faced can be most successfully managed in the 'process' frame."[18]

It is thus a central premise of McDougal's conception of jurisprudence that theory and practice are closely linked and that the form of this linkage is an instrumental one. In approaching the traditional problems of legal practice—those of legislation, advocacy, dispute settlement, administration, and counsel—the lawmaker, judge, lawyer, and legal scholar are all to proceed in much the same manner. The first step in legal analysis is to clarify the goal or goals that it is the object of policy to achieve. Although these goals might presumably have any substantive content, McDougal often writes as if there existed some internal connection between the policy-oriented approach to jurisprudence and commitment to a par-

---

[17] *Studies in World Public Order*, pp. 164-165.
[18] "World Constitutive Process of Authoritative Decision," p. 78.

ticular set of goals that he identifies as promotion of a "world order of human dignity." Once the goals of policy are determined, the next step is to examine relevant events and trends from the perspective of their implications for the realization of the chosen goals and seek to understand why the present state of affairs is as it is and not as one would like it to be. It is at this stage that the ideas and methods of the social sciences are most important for the legal analyst. On the basis of the relevant data and theories, the analyst attempts to predict what the future will be like if various alternative courses of action are pursued. Finally, a policy to further the chosen goals is formulated, and this policy becomes the basis of action in the form of decisions, judgments, interpretations, or advice. Applied to international law this conception of jurisprudence leads to the conclusion that the proper function of the international lawyer is to estimate future developments and identify alternatives that will promote the goal of human dignity.[19]

With the clarification and pursuit of values elevated to the position of a central concern of jurisprudence, the instrumentalist is confronted with the problem of deciding which values are to be clarified and served by legal science and the legal process. McDougal's proposed solution to this problem is a kind of utilitarianism. Natural law is rejected as a source of values: value clarification is not to be confused with the "ancient exercises" through which natural law thinking achieves the "transempirical derivation" of values. The values to be served by law are to be discovered by empirical study of the values that people actually hold. Moral values are "preferred events, social goals,"[20] and value clarification is "goal thinking." The preferences discovered by empirical inquiry, which McDougal summarizes under the comprehensive rubric of "human dignity," are not arbitrary but rather the result of a systematic clarification of "community values."[21] The ration-

[19] *Studies in World Public Order*, p. 39.
[20] Ibid., p. 53.
[21] "International Law, Power and Policy," p. 183.

ale for making the promotion of human dignity the ultimate goal of international law is thus that the set of values it represents are in some sense empirically founded: an international jurisprudence devoted to the creation of a world order of human dignity is one that "harmonizes with the growing aspirations of the overwhelming numbers of peoples of the globe" and "is in accord with the proclaimed values of human dignity enunciated by the moral leaders of mankind."[22]

Despite these claims to the universality of the values to be served by international law, it is obvious that not everyone shares these values. This is in effect acknowledged by McDougal's exclusion of the values of those to whom he refers as "totalitarians" from the category of human dignity. This exclusion reveals that one of the motives underlying McDougal's commitment to policy-oriented jurisprudence is a desire to combat the threat to liberal democracy posed by fascism and communism. "The policy task of a free society is to put its own distinctive value-variables into practice and to control the factors that condition their attainment."[23] The enemies of liberal democracy conceive government as an instrument for the promotion of a certain conception of the good—one that is in fact mistaken and evil. Therefore those who are committed to "human dignity" and "democratic values" must use the resources of government and law to promote the conception of the good embodied in their own values. In particular they must attempt to create a world order in which the ideological diversity of the present system is replaced by ideological uniformity, for "a society of human dignity presupposes a high degree of unity as to goal values."[24] This identification of law with the promotion of a particular set of substantive purposes would appear to leave little room for the traditional conception of international law as a framework of rules within which the divergent policies of diverse states might be reconciled, irreconcilable differences

[22] *Studies in World Public Order*, p. 39.
[23] Ibid., p. 61.
[24] Ibid., p. 35.

tolerated, and coexistence made possible. There is no response in McDougal's writings to the argument that freedom, as an aspect and consequence of the rule of law as traditionally conceived, might be threatened by the very instrumentalism he defends. The circularity and arbitrariness of the proposed "value clarification" is also overlooked. The clarification of values is supposed to be a purely empirical activity uninfluenced by preconceived moral principles, but at the same time certain values are excluded from the empirical canvas because they are morally offensive. The contradiction is evident. Policy-oriented jurisprudence must be guided by values that are neither transcendentally derived nor, McDougal's own evidence and arguments suggest, universally shared. In the end, therefore, the value of human dignity is simply postulated.

McDougal attempts to provide an account of how the unity of values presupposed by a world order of human dignity might be reconciled with the actual diversity of human values reflected in the states system by arguing that consensus on values is shaped by the international legal process. "Community policy" for the promotion of shared values is the product of a "world constitutive process of authoritative decision."[25] This is essentially a bargaining process in which differences are reconciled, areas of common interest explored and delimited, and mutually satisfactory policies agreed upon. Conformity with the bargains struck in this ongoing process is ensured by the interests of states, which are served by their agreements and by their power to retaliate against violations of these agreements.[26] Clearly something like the bargaining process McDougal describes is central to international politics, and results from time to time in agreement, and sometimes in nearly universal agreement. But this agreement does not necessarily represent a consensus on values: on the contrary, it often reflects no more than an agreement on procedures, con-

[25] Ibid., pp. 169-171.
[26] Ibid., p. 168.

ditions, limits, and restraints on the pursuit of divergent values. Nor does the ability of states to reach agreement about various matters of mutual concern mean that they have reached consensus in support of the value of human dignity as conceived by McDougal's policy-oriented jurisprudence. The outcome of the "world constitutive process of authoritative decision" is not necessarily a policy for the promotion of shared values, much less the particular value of human dignity. The expression "community policy" is in fact merely a label, and a rather misleading one, for whatever combination of interests happens to be served by the bargains and cooperative arrangements of states at any particular historical moment.

In collapsing the traditional distinction between law and politics, McDougal's analysis erases a number of other distinctions often thought to be characteristic of legal order. The term "decision," for example, is used to refer both to the judgments and choices of participants in the international legal process and to the outcome of this process. The term "decision maker" applies to several distinct offices and roles: those of the administrator, the legislative assembly, the cabinet, the court, the diplomatic conference, the legal scholar and occasionally even the legal adviser or advocate. "Authoritative" decisions are not those that have been authorized by the appropriate rules, but rather those that are effective. Using this terminology McDougal portrays international law in ways that resemble the familiar and accepted picture of the international legal system as a decentralized one in which legal rules are interpreted and applied largely by states and in which the authority of these rules is ultimately dependent upon their general acceptance as reflected in general state practice. McDougal's analysis thus seeks to clarify just those aspects of international law that have puzzled other observers and, although it eschews the traditional vocabulary of international law by refusing to speak of "rules," it arrives at conclusions that superficially resemble those of more conventional accounts. But the gap between policy-oriented jurisprudence and the analysis of international law as a body of rules rooted in the customary practices of states and constituting a framework of formal restraints governing their relations with one another is nevertheless profound.

McDougal's reinterpretation of the idea of *dédoublement fonctionnel* illustrates this gap.[27] It is not that this reinterpretation is mistaken as an account of international politics, for in this respect it is indeed illuminating. But as an account of the character of international law it is unsatisfactory because it dispenses with the distinctions between rules and interests, making and applying law, and authority and efficacy upon which law, as a mode of association distinct from one governed wholly by considerations of interest and power, rests. McDougal's version goes like this: Certain national officials make authoritative decisions affecting both their state and the international community. Their role in the international system is thus a double one. As representatives of a state they make adversary claims, but they also serve "as authoritative decision-makers of the general community" because they are engaged in "prescribing and applying inclusive policies for all states."[28] To the objection that state officials cannot make decisions that are authoritative for other states because they reflect parochial rather than community interests, McDougal responds plausibly that their double role discourages these officials from advancing claims that, if generally accepted, might prove inconvenient in the future, and therefore that the international decision process operates in such a way to reject idiosyncratic claims and decisions.[29] But despite certain resemblances between this account and Scelle's concept of *dédoublement fonctionnel*, the two in fact have little in common. According to Scelle, national officials apply both domestic and international law. But officials, according to McDougal, do not apply law. They make and implement policies. Their double role requires them to balance the interests of their own state with the interests of the world community as a

[27] On the concept of *dédoublement fonctionnel* see Chapter 7, n. 14, above.
[28] *Studies in World Public Order*, p. 171.
[29] Ibid., p. 174.

whole. It is therefore misleading to suggest, as does Falk,[30] that McDougal builds on Scelle, for the latter argues only that national officials apply the law of both their own state and the international community, not that their decisions "serve the interests" of both. On the contrary Scelle argues that the primacy of national interests forecloses the possibility of impartiality in the application of international law by state officials. McDougal thus departs from Scelle both because he substitutes an account of politics for the latter's account of law and because he replaces Scelle's pessimism concerning the prospects for impartial decision making in the double role with an optimistic account of these prospects.

The gap between McDougal's instrumentalism and the practical conception is also evident in his treatment of the topic of administrative and judicial discretion. Because it is committed to promoting particular substantive purposes, policy-oriented jurisprudence gives much more scope than do more orthodox views of law to the discretion of those who interpret and apply international law. Where there is disagreement about whether to comply with what is asserted to be a legal obligation, or concerning how a contested rule should be interpreted by a government, judge, or legal scholar, it should be settled by choosing an alternative that is reasonable given the situation and goals of the relevant decision makers. In deciding such matters the administrator, judge, advocate, or scholar must take account of a variety of factors that bear on the implications of the decision, for there are no precise rules to be applied. Rule-skepticism is thus an integral part of policy-oriented jurisprudence. International law consists not of rules but of "complementary principles" (such as "freedom of the seas" vs. "maritime jurisdiction" or "military necessity" vs. "humanitarianism") that must be balanced in any particular decision.[31] To imagine that policy decisions are governed by rules is to be blind to the substantial discretion that deci-

---

[30] *Legal Order in a Violent World*, p. 81.
[31] "Ethics of Applying Systems of Authority," p. 223.

sion makers in fact enjoy and are supposed to exercise on behalf of community goals.

This analysis leads McDougal to reject the traditional approach to treaty interpretation.[32] The international lawyer ordinarily relies on canons of interpretation that give primary weight to the text of a treaty as evidence of the intentions of the parties to it. McDougal's view, in contrast, is that the interpretion arrived at by this method is not to be given effect if it is incompatible with the goal of "public order." The danger in this view is obvious. Given the number and diversity of those who have occasion to interpret treaties, together with the extremely vague content of the notions of public order and human dignity that McDougal puts forward as the ultimate grounds for decision, the consequence of such a doctrine of treaty interpretation is to permit the interpreter so much discretion as to undermine the institution of treaty making. McDougal's proposal is far more radical than the argument that rules of law must often be balanced against other sorts of considerations in making decisions. According to this proposal considerations of policy determine not only the observance of legal rules but their very content. The legal decision becomes a matter of balancing a number of policy considerations against one another, with considerations embodied in legal rules having scarcely any independent significance. McDougal's view of treaty interpretation thus reveals another facet and implication of the identification of law and politics.

The attempt to ward off the most extreme consequences of the doctrine of discretion underlying this view of treaty interpretation by relying upon reasonableness as a standard is almost certain to be futile in a system as diverse and unstructured as that of international law. Such a standard can help to secure consistency and uniformity in a legal system only where there is substantial agreement among those responsible for carrying on the customs and traditions of the law. As

[32] See McDougal et al., *Interpretation of Agreements and World Public Order*, and the critical review of it by Fitzmaurice, "Vae Victis, or Woe to the Negotiators!"

a criterion guiding the interpretation and application of law, reasonableness can avoid leading to extreme flexibility and discontinuity only if there is substantial agreement concerning what is reasonable. Furthermore, such a criterion can serve to advance some particular value, such as human dignity, only to the extent that there exists agreement with respect both to the meaning of that value and to the decisions that are reasonable when evaluated from the perspective of a concern for it. Given the diversity of beliefs, values, purposes, and interests that must be reconciled by international law and that affect the manner in which it is interpreted and applied, the states system would seem to be among societies least likely to be successfully governed according to so open-ended a conception of legal reasoning.

Instrumentalism attacks not only the formalism of traditional international jurisprudence but also the very idea of international association on the basis of common rules, of which formalism is merely a (sometimes distorted) expression. There is indeed a sense in which instrumentalism, if carried to its limits, is corrosive even of association on the basis of shared purposes. Rules cannot serve as an instrument for the achievement of shared purposes unless those united for the joint pursuit of these purposes are willing to defer to rules. Part of the rationale for having rules is that they record and preserve the results of past decisions. In making decisions we allow our judgment to be guided by rules because we understand that it is impossible to consider afresh every factor that would have to be taken into account were we to refuse to accord rules any special weight and because we realize that without some shared procedures and reliable agreement nothing whatsoever can be accomplished. And where agreement on ends is lacking there is the additional consideration that deference to common rules provides the only basis of association and coexistence.

By making shared purposes the ultimate basis of international association, instrumentalism both underestimates the importance of rules for the pursuit of shared purposes and ignores the importance of common rules as the only conceivable basis for the relations of those pursuing different and often incompatible purposes. Moreover, it fails to take account of the fact that cooperation to further shared purposes presupposes agreement at the level of procedure that can be drawn upon in making and implementing agreements. It fails to grasp that the pursuit of shared purposes itself presupposes acknowledgment of the authority of common practices and rules according to which cooperative agreements can be created, altered, interpreted, and preserved.

Consent as the Basis of Legal Obligation

The instrumentalist view of how international law should be interpreted and applied implies a theory of legal obligation according to which states have a duty to observe, as law, only those considerations that are consistent with the pursuit of their own purposes. The instrumentalist approach to obligation is thus a version of the view (which I shall label "voluntarism") that the only source of obligation is consent. Policy-oriented jurisprudence ends in voluntarism in effect, if not by intention, because the criteria according to which those who apply international law must interpret it are so vague. In place of the often uncertain standards embodied in common rules, policy-oriented jurisprudence proposes to rely on even more uncertain notions like public order and human dignity, together with a permissive conception of interpretive discretion. The result is a theory of legal obligation according to which the obligations binding on a state are those that its officials determine are compatible with the goals of public order and human dignity as they interpret them.

These views strongly resemble earlier theories of consent or autolimitation, according to which states have obligations under international law only because they have voluntarily incurred them and continue to regard themselves as bound by them. The basis of international obligation is, according to such theories, a consent to be bound that may be withdrawn at any time. This view rests in turn upon a particular understanding of state sovereignty according to which the will of the state is the ultimate source of legal obligation. Sovereign states are "independent beings, subject to no control, and owning no superior," from which it follows that "a state is only bound by rules to which it feels itself obliged in conscience after reasonable examination to submit. . . ."[33] This point of view, common in all countries in the nineteenth century, was developed most fully by German writers around the turn of the century into the claim that the only limits on the conduct of a state were those that it imposed on itself, and furthermore that the state might at any point alter those limits unilaterally. Hence the terms "auto-" or "self-limitation."

The view that the basis of international legal obligation is the consent of states to be bound by particular rules of international law reappears in the view of Soviet and East European writers that treaties are superior to custom as a source of international law. More is meant by this than that treaty making is now the most important method of creating new rules of international law, an opinion that is shared by many Western international lawyers. Custom is defective because it is only an imperfect expression of consent. The basis of obligation in international law is the will of states, and this will is more directly and clearly manifested in treaties than in custom. In place of the traditional view that rules of customary international law are presumed to bind a state unless it has specifically opposed the rule in question in word and deed from the very start, Soviet doctrine substitutes the view that the rules of customary international law reflect tacit agreements among states and are thus binding only on those states that are parties to these agreements.[34] Like treaty rules, the rules of customary international law bind only states that have in some way indicated their acceptance of them. The

[33] Hall, *Treatise on International Law*, p. 4. Hall does not, however, subscribe to the extreme version of autolimitation, according to which the consent to be bound may be unilaterally withdrawn at any time.

[34] Tunkin, *Theory of International Law*, pp. 124-125.

effective difference between the traditional and the Soviet view is that according to the former a state must prove that a customary rule is not binding on it, whereas in the Soviet view the burden of proof is on those trying to show that a state had accepted a customary rule where it denied that acceptance.

The view that a state is bound only by rules to which it has given its consent also leads to the argument that existing rules of international law are not binding on "new states"—that is, states that have not participated in the creation of a rule because they were not in existence as states when the rule came into being. It is evident that existing treaties do not bind such states for the straightforward reason that treaties bind only those states that have explicitly accepted them. A new state is in exactly the same relation to a treaty predating its existence as an existing state that is not party to the treaty. And if it is argued that certain treaties (such as those creating international organizations possessing international status and immunities, which all states are obligated to respect) do in fact have legal consequences affecting nonsignatories, still it can hardly be argued that a newly created state was in a more privileged position with respect to escaping such consequences than an existing state that was not a party to the treaty in question. It is therefore true, but only trivially so, that new states are not bound by treaties to which they have not given their consent.

The main burden of the voluntarist argument, of course, is that customary international law is not binding on new states, either, without their consent. "The State's will is the basis of the binding force of a customary norm."[35] Because this view allows for the expression of tacit consent, it really covers a spectrum of opinions ranging from the argument that a new state is free to reject any rule of customary international law in effect at the moment of its creation to the much more moderate position that entrance into membership in the so-

[35] Bokor-Szegó, *New States and International Law*, p. 63.

ciety of states signifies consent to existing rules of customary international law. But even this most moderate version of voluntarism implies both a fiction (that by assuming responsibility for their foreign relations states indicate an intention to be bound by international law) and an inconsistency (that new states may exercise more discretion than existing states in deciding whether or not to conform to customary international law). The idea of tacit consent is a fiction because a new state is in fact automatically bound by customary international law as a consequence of having achieved the status of statehood. Merely to exist as a state and to have regular dealings with other states is to recognize the authority of at least some of the existing practices and rules embodied in customary international law. The inconsistency follows from the fact that the rules of customary international law create rights as well as obligations affecting new states. The voluntarist view of legal obligation, however, cannot explain why, if a new state is free to ignore a rule of customary international law in its relations with an existing state, the latter should not be equally free to ignore the rule in its relations with the new state. Only if the rule in question is regarded as a general rule of international law rather than as a kind of tacit agreement between the two states, can this inconsistency be avoided.[36] The view that new states are not automatically bound by customary international law entails the view that there is no such thing as a general international law, that all international law is the special law of states that have consented to it.

All these theories share the premise that the obligations of international law are binding on states only to the extent to which they share similar values, interests, and purposes. International law is regarded simply as the product of the common will of states as it exists at any moment, giving rise to obligations only to the extent that such a common will can be identified. But if the basis of obligation is the common will,

[36] Sørensen, "Principes de droit international public," p. 46.

then any rule of international law ceases to be binding on a particular state as soon as it decides that it no longer wishes to be bound by it, for in that case there is no longer any common will uniting that state with the others. What the doctrine of autolimitation achieves by allowing states unilaterally to determine how they will be bound by the common rules, policy-oriented jurisprudence achieves by allowing state officials to interpret international law according to their own conception of the common will. The freedom or discretion of the state, on either version of voluntarism, is manifested not only at the point of law-creation (a state is free to determine the obligations to which it will submit itself) but also at the point of law-application (a state is free to interpret and apply the law in such a way as to determine for itself the scope and meaning of its legal obligations in particular situations). Consent, in other words, is required not only in the creation but also in the application of international law.

Such an understanding of legal obligation rests upon two confusions. The first is a confusion between two senses in which an agreement (for example, the agreement to submit to a rule) can be said to be voluntary: on the one hand that the agreement is entered into freely, and on the other that it may be terminated at will. To deny the latter proposition is not to say that states have no part in the making of international law. On the contrary, they make it both by explicit agreement and by what they do—provided enough of them do it consistently and so make a practice of it. But that international law may be said to be voluntary in the first sense hardly supports the proposition that it is therefore voluntary in the second, and indeed to hold the latter is not merely to deny the binding force of both treaties and custom but to display a complete failure to understand the idea of obligation. To say that a state is at all times free to ignore the general rules of customary international law or the specific rules embodied in the treaties to which it is party says nothing about the specific character of international law: it is an admission that, whatever may be claimed to the contrary, states are in fact related to one another on the basis of interest rather than law. The freedom of states to terminate treaties is clearly limited in a variety of ways and must be limited if treaties are to have any significance. The point of a treaty, like that of a contract or promise, is precisely to limit the freedom of the parties to it by placing them under an obligation that is not easily terminated by a unilateral decision. To regard all agreements as terminable at the will of one of the parties defeats the point of making them in the first place.

The second confusion in the voluntarist view of legal obligation is between the way in which an obligation comes into being and the basis of its authority. With respect to legal obligation specifically, the confusion is one between the method of creation of a law and the source of its validity. A particular legal rule may be created by an act of legislation or agreement, but it is valid—if it is valid—within a particular legal system only because of the existence of other rules that specify that the rule thus created shall give rise to legal obligations. The failure to appreciate this point vitiates even the least extreme versions of voluntarism in international law, such as Triepel's, according to which international law represents the "common consent" of the two or more states.[37] According to this view the source of international obligation is not the will of any individual state but the joint will of at least two states. Thus, a treaty can be terminated by the agreement of those party to it, but it cannot be terminated by a single party acting unilaterally. Such a view, however, is incapable of explaining how the common consent of states can give rise to international obligations, for it fails to explain how will is converted into duty. The practical conception of international law, on the other hand, does provide the needed explanation: the common will of states, as manifested in international agreements, can have legal effect because there already exist rules of customary international law according to which becoming party to a treaty shall have this effect. The practical concep-

---

[37] "Rapports entre le droit interne et le droit international," pp. 82-83.

tion helps us to see that a voluntaristic theory of international legal obligation necessarily results in paradox: if an agreement can be terminated unilaterally, then it creates no obligations; if it cannot, then the obligation it creates must be based on something other than consent alone, namely on rules of a more fundamental character that spell out the meaning and consequences of agreement.

The theory of common consent is also unable to provide a coherent account of the obligation to conform to customary international law. The theory explains the binding force of customary international law in terms of the fiction of tacit consent. Even if we accept this fiction as plausible, it would still be necessary to discover rules according to which the tacit consent implied by state practice could give rise to legal obligations. Now either these rules are binding independently of the consent of states, which is excluded by hypothesis, or they are binding because they are the product of consent. But if the latter, then we must postulate still more fundamental rules . . . and so on, ad infinitum. These difficulties can be avoided only by dropping the assumption that the obligation to conform to customary international law must have its source in consent.

International association on the basis of common rules presupposes acknowledgment of the authority of the common rules. The defining feature or criterion by which we may recognize the existence of true legal order in the relations of states is their deference to considerations embodied in authoritative common rules. To be related as subjects of a common body of law states must acknowledge the independent authority of this law or, which is the same thing, acknowledge its rules as obligatory. And this in turn has a number of implications. It means for one thing that judgments concerning whether or not the rules serve purposes that are considered to be desirable, however relevant they may be to the creation or revision of rules of law, are irrelevant to the question of whether or not they are authoritative and obligatory. Where the considerations embodied in the common rules clash with other considerations, the latter must give way; to hold otherwise is to abandon the rule of law in favor of some other kind of relationship. What distinguishes international law from other modes of international association is that the considerations embodied in it are understood to override other considerations. This much is implied by the very idea of association *on the basis of* common rules rather than on some other basis such as shared purposes.

The absence of law-creating and applying institutions in the international legal system has made the concepts of international legal authority and obligation particularly elusive. But these circumstances are not the main reason for the difficulty; they merely compound a difficulty that pervades jurisprudence and political theory in general. The notion persists that there is some mystery about the correlative ideas of authority and obligation that can only be dispelled by explaining the authority of rules, and the obligation to conform to them, in other terms. Only if we can locate the sources of authority and the bases of obligation in something outside the law, it has been thought, can any satisfactory account of these concepts be given.

The demand for some exogenous account of legal authority and obligation can take one of two forms. The first amounts to a demand for an explanation in broadly empirical or causal terms of how some are able to command and others obliged to obey, or of why those subject to a particular system of law obey its rules. Such inquiries may explain why legal rules have a particular content, help us to understand the motives for obedience, or suggest factors that promote conformity with law. But they cannot *replace* discussion of law in its own internal language of rules, rights, obligation, and authority. To think that such inquiries can account for legal authority and obligation is to confuse what are sometimes referred to as the "material sources" of law and legal obligation with the formal sources of legal validity. The two sorts of inquiry are different. It may be, for example, illuminating to discover that the origin of the principle of freedom of the seas is to be found in the fact that the maritime powers were for several centuries able to enforce a regime of the high seas advantageous to themselves, but such an explanation of this part of the law of the sea cannot by itself answer questions concerning the validity of the principle and the rights and duties of states according to it.

The gap between the internal perspective of the participant and the external perspective of the observer has sometimes been thought to have been bridged by a second kind of exogenous approach, one that is concerned with questions of authority and obligation from the internal point of view but that finds the answer to these questions in a moral realm outside the law. On this view, the formal sources of legal authority and the basis of legal obligation are discovered in such places as the law of nature as known through revelation or through reason, in consent as a manifestation of the sovereignty of the will, in man's natural sociability, in human needs, in the common good, and elsewhere. That there exist so many answers to the question of the basis of legal obligation illuminates the very predicament that the concepts of legal authority and obligation were developed to overcome: that, where there exists controversy over the true grounds of human conduct, what is needed is general acceptance of a common standard that everyone will acknowledge as supreme in the sense that it excludes other standards in case of conflict. The common standard recognized as law is accepted not because there is agreement on its truth or on the values served by conformity to it but on the contrary precisely because such agreement is lacking. The authority of law is a substitute for such agreement, and rules of a legal system are therefore arbitrary with respect to the beliefs and values of particular members of the society governed by it. But it does not follow that the decision to submit to these rules is irrational. On the contrary, it is the conclusion to an argument that, where people disagree on matters of substance, agreement on matters of procedure and form assumes a position of unique importance.

A society governed by law is one governed by a system of rules whose criteria of validity are internal to the system itself. No exogenous account of legal authority and obligation is either necessary or possible. Legal obligations exist because there exist legal rules giving rise to them, and not as a result of any reasons or considerations outside the law. This self-contained aspect of legal authority is well illustrated by the distinction between having a legal obligation and having an obligation to obey the law. That there is a legal obligation to obey the law is a tautology: it merely restates the fact that where there is law there is legal obligation. But it does not follow from the existence of law and legal obligation that there exists some other sort of obligation, usually understood as moral, to obey the law. The moral question, "Why should I obey the law?" is not one that can be answered in legal terms. "What are my legal obligations?" and "Am I morally obligated to meet them?" are different questions that can be answered in different ways without logical contradiction.

The discussion of international obligation has suffered from a failure to keep these questions distinct.[38] If international law gives rise to legal obligations it is because this fact is inherent in the idea of law and not because the rules of international law are morally valid, expressions of the will of states, or instrumental to the realization of desirable ends. International law, like all law, is association on the basis of common rules that constitute the decisive standards for judging the legal validity of claims. Legal systems do sometimes admit considerations of morality, equity, utility, or policy as grounds for legal judgment. In that case, however, such con-

---

[38] Brierly's well-known account of international obligation founders on his mistaken assumption that no satisfactory account of legal obligation can be given except by invoking moral principles. ("Basis of Obligation in International Law," p. 65.) A different kind of mistake is illustrated by Schachter's identification of "authority" and "obligation" with "legitimacy" and "compliance." ("Towards a Theory of International Obligation," pp. 19-20.) The latter is yet another example of the reductionism characteristic of both Austinian positivism and twentieth-century legal realism.

siderations function not as exogenous standards but as part of the legal system itself. The obligation to conform to international law lies, in short, in recognition of the authority of international law as a whole, and not on judgments of the desirability of particular rules. Acknowledgment of the authority of international law is not to be confused with approval of its particular content.

PART THREE

International Law and Moral Conduct

CHAPTER 9

International Law
and International Morality

THE PRECEDING discussion has been largely concerned with
the practices and rules of the society of states regarded as
law. This is how they are usually understood by international
lawyers and by diplomats, judges, and other officials. But these
same practices figure in the judgments of many others who
know little of international law and for whom the rights and
wrongs of states and statesmen are a matter not of law but of
morality: a matter of viewing international conduct from the
perspective of a tradition, sometimes religious, over which
lawyers and politicians by no means have a monopoly and
which is indeed often opposed to the particular usages of law
and government.[1] Yet the legal and moral realms are intimately connected in a number of ways. Each has influenced
the development of the other. Moral and legal discourse rely
upon a similar vocabulary (such as "obligation," "justice," and
"rights") and often on similar principles, reflect similar ways
of viewing conduct as comprising the acts of responsible agents,
and are often affected by similar controversies. And because
these similarities extend to international society there is a
close connection between the ideas and principles of international law and those of international morality.

---

[1] There are also those for whom international relations is a realm neither
of law nor of morals but of power and necessity. These are the skeptics—the
"deniers" or "realists," as they are sometimes called—who think the idea of
international society is an illusion. Yet those who profess to be moral skeptics
often think and argue about international affairs in moral terms. The claims
of moral skepticism are effectively rebutted by Walzer, *Just and Unjust Wars*,
ch. 1, and Beitz, *Political Theory and International Relations*, Part 1.

223

The following pages are intended to explore and clarify this connection. In the present chapter I continue the discussion, begun in the first chapter, of law and morality as different kinds of authoritative practice; consider the different ways in which the expression "international morality" can be interpreted; and argue that international law and international morality must be understood as related but distinct traditions of thought and practice. The remaining chapters spell out some of the implications of the practice/purpose distinction for both legal and moral discourse concerning international relations. Because of its importance in discourse concerning international conduct and association, I give particular attention to the idea of justice. Two chapters are devoted to the investigation of conflicting conceptions of international justice in the context of disputes about the distribution of social and economic goods (Chapter 10) and about the initiation and conduct of war (Chapter 11). In both chapters a practical conception of international justice is defended against various purposive alternatives and objections. The concluding chapter seeks to restate the theory of international law and international morality underlying these investigations and to defend this theory against the argument that all international association, including practical association, depends ultimately on the existence of shared purposes.

MORALITY AND MORAL CONDUCT

The words "morality" and "moral" are used differently in different contexts, so to fail to specify the context is to invite misunderstanding. The adjective "moral" once pertained to human activity in general, to the world of human rather than natural things (as in "the moral sciences"). Something of this inclusive connotation remains in the identification of "moral" with a kind of autonomy or freedom, as when we refer to persons as "moral agents" in virture of their capacity to choose and not in relation to the evaluation of their choices. The related word "ethics" refers in some contexts to the responsiblities of those who are members of a profession, and in others to the whole realm of values and ideals guiding human conduct. The concept of morality to be considered here is broader than that indicated by the term "ethics" in the sense of a professional code but narrower than that which the discipline of ethics takes as its subject matter, and very much narrower than the concept of human agency. Its scope may be roughly indicated by saying that it has to do with principles or rules of conduct based on, though not necessarily identical with, the "manners" and "morals" (in Latin, *mores*, French *moeurs*) of a people, that is, with the generally acknowledged standards of conduct by which the acts and character of the members of a particular community are judged. A morality in this sense is an authoritative practice, and moral conduct is conduct that conforms to its standards. Each element of this definition requires clarification.

A morality is not, in the first place, identical with the *mores*—and certainly not with the actual habits or ways (*manières*)—of a people. Human beings are intelligent, and one of the things they are intelligent about is their own conduct and their own standards of conduct. Thus people often think about the *mores* of their community, especially where they have an opportunity to compare them with the ways of outsiders. Such reflection and criticism leads, in turn, to the elaboration of revised or alternative standards of conduct— ideal standards—by which not only the conduct of individuals but also the *mores* of the community may be evaluated. Morality, then, has to do not only with *mores* but also with moral reflection and moral ideals. Moralities that arise from critical reflection on customary morality often take the form of an explicitly articulated and rationally arranged system of principles, or code, which necessarily departs more or less noticeably from the customary morality from which it is derived. It is usual to mark this distinction by speaking of "social" or "positive" moralities on the one hand, and of "critical" or "ideal" moralities on the other.[2] Moral conduct, by extension,

[2] Here "critical" means thoughtful or self-conscious, not censorious. Crit-

is either that which conforms to the relevant *mores* or that which is in accord with the standards embodied in an ideal moral code.

Most moralities are a mixture of customary and ideal elements and are characterized by tensions of various sorts that arise from differences between the *mores* of particular communities and moral ideals generated by critical reflection. Moralities can therefore be distinguished according to the manner in which these tensions are resolved. Some show a tendency toward moral purity and perfection, a tendency that might be displayed in the teachings of a moral reformer, in the writings of a builder of moral systems, or in the ascetic practices of a community of sectarian or utopian nonconformists able for a time to find a niche within the larger society or to escape from it. Other moralities are more worldly, seeking to accommodate conflict and change through adaptation and to resolve the tension between ideals and conduct through compromise. Moralities of this sort often arise out of the effort to articulate minimum standards of conduct for the vast majority of every community that is unable or unwilling to blend life wholly to an ideal. Their principles are those of compromise, toleration, coexistence, and mutual accommodation, their methods those of casuistry, the interpretation of general principles in the light of particular cases. Such moralities are particularly likely to develop in societies within which there exist a diversity of peoples, and hence a diversity of social and critical moralities to be reconciled. They are, as

---

ical moralities are typically linked, more or less closely, to the social moralities from which they draw their inspiration. The influence of social upon critical morality is evident even where the inspiration is almost wholly negative; Nietzschean ethics is hardly intelligible except as a reaction against the Christian moral tradition. And no social morality is wholly inhospitable to and unaffected by criticism. Moral conduct is always to some extent the product of self-conscious reflection. The *mores* of a community reflect both the habits of its people and the fruits of generations of experience and reflection upon that experience. The distinction between a body of *mores* and a rationally reconstructed system of moral principles is therefore in part one of degree.

Strawson puts it, "systems—though the word is too strong—of recognized reciprocal claim that we have on one another as members of human communities. . . ."[3] Unlike the reconciliation sought by moral idealism, the reconciliation implied by a common morality is sought at the level of practice. Where a common morality takes root new customs emerge that may, in time, themselves become the object of moral criticism.

The history of morals can thus be read as a story of movement back and forth between moral idealism and moral realism, between perfection and accommodation, between life according to self-consciously articulated ideals and life within a tradition of conduct. At a certain point we may find a people governed by an accepted body of *mores*: its morality is a morality of custom, tied to the life of the community and shaped largely by its traditions. Such a morality, Oakeshott has suggested, is one in which moral life is "a habit of affection and conduct" rather than the outcome of the self-conscious consideration of alternatives, application of principles, or estimation of consequences.[4] Here the responses of a person to the exigencies of life are determined by habits acquired through the experience of living with people who habitually behave in a certain manner: that is, through the experience of having been educated in a tradition of conduct and having thereby acquired the values and tastes characteristic of the tradition. As soon as reflection and criticism enter the picture, the future of such a morality is rendered uncertain. It may continue largely as a tradition into which are incorporated the results of moral reflection and criticism, so that the tradition evolves

[3] "Social Morality and Individual Ideal," p. 117. Moralities of this kind, Strawson suggests, may be thought of as "a kind of public convenience: of the first importance as a condition of everything that matters, but only as a condition of everything that matters, not as something that matters in itself" (p. 103). A common morality is an authoritative practice that both defines and makes possible the common good of a community and thereby enables the members of the community to pursue their own self-chosen ends. See Chapter 1, n. 12, and accompanying text for further discussion.

[4] "Tower of Babel," p. 61.

without ever being radically altered, at least, not all at once. Alternatively, reflection and criticism may bring a moral tradition to the point of crisis by leading to the development of a critical morality or moralities significantly at odds with the tradition. A morality in which the critical element is large tends to give rise to the self-conscious pursuit of ends or the self-conscious formulation of rules. In either case the criterion of moral conduct takes the form of an ideal abstracted from (and in extreme cases articulated in opposition to) some aspect of the tradition. Critical morality thus tends to become a morality of ideals: ideal ends, ideal virtues, or ideal rules. And, because ideals are abstractions, they are necessarily to some degree narrow and exclusive. A community in which ideal moralities begin to flourish may therefore become one in which the common life is disrupted by a chaos of conflicting ideals.[5] The stage is thus set for the emergence of a new morality of mutual accommodation, perhaps in the form of a reaffirmation of the principles of the traditional common morality that have come to be challenged. Nothing guarantees that such a morality will in fact appear. Should it do so, however, and go on to become generally accepted, a new tradition, a new body of *mores*, may be said to have developed. The stability of a morality of custom has been reestablished to last until it, too, is undermined by the corrosion of critical scrutiny and the articulation of new ideals.

I do not offer this account of moral change as a description of any historical occurrence, although it may fit the historical data at certain points. Moral change need not occur in discrete stages; life according to a tradition, reflection on that tradition, the articulation of ideals, and the attempt to live by them may all go on simultaneously; some aspects of the moral life of a community may be altered as a result of reflection and criticism while others are untouched. The tides of moral change may move simultaneously as well as sequentially, and may either reinforce or cancel each other. Nor would I wish

[5] Ibid., p. 59.

to claim, as many others have, that the kind of breakdown of traditional forms that I am here attempting to characterize is unique to the modern world. The breakdown of tradition is, to be sure, characteristic of Western civilization since, let us say, the sixteenth century, but it is not limited to it. It can occur among any people whose traditional morality has been disrupted by the emergence of ideal moralities, the development of moral pluralism, and the subsequent generation of doubts concerning the basis of association within an increasingly divided community. And the recurrent solution, the invention and sometimes the widespread acceptance of a morality of mutual accommodation, is one which, although fundamental to modern secular moral and political thought, is by no means limited to it.

Although moralities of mutual accommodation have appeared at various times and places, the theory of this kind of morality appears to have achieved its fullest and most articulate expression in modern European moral and political philosophy, above all in the writings of two thinkers often thought of as defending very different moral views, Hobbes and Kant. We have already considered Hobbes's suggestion that, in the absence of agreement at the level of ideals, the most reasonable course is to reach agreement at the level of procedure: that is, to give up the expectation of uniformity with respect to ideals but to acknowledge the authority of certain restraints upon individuals in the pursuit of their several ideals. In opposition to the sort of moral idealism that insists on imposing its own ideals on everyone, and thus in effect denying any distinction between the private and public realms, Hobbes suggests a morality founded on a sharp distinction between public and private: a morality of common rules according to which individual ideals must be pursued within publicly circumscribed limits that all are obligated to respect. These limits are derived from certain fundamental "laws of nature"[6]

[6] *Philosophical Rudiments*, I. 2, 3; *Leviathan*, I. 14, 15.

that state the conditions of individual coexistence and security and can be apprehended through the exercise of reason.

The other side of Hobbes's analysis concerns the institutional requirements for the realization of association among
individuals on the basis of common rules: a sovereign power
authoritatively to declare, interpret, and apply the positive
laws through which the laws of nature are to be adapted to
the exigencies of particular societies. It is this theory of the
state, together with his extreme individualism, that sets Hobbes
apart from the tradition of natural law. But if his moral theory
is divorced from these elements Hobbes can be seen to be
concerned with one of the tasks that occupied Jewish, Stoic,
and Christian thinkers engaged in moral reflection and criticism: exploration of the idea and content of a common morality. This common morality gradually separated itself from
the *mores* of particular Jewish, Hellenistic, Roman, and
Christian communities, and took the form of a body of principles binding on individuals as rational beings rather than as
adherents to a particular faith or members of a particular political community. It is a morality whose content is not, or
not only, divinely revealed, but is discoverable through the
use of reason. And it is understood for the most part to be a
morality of rules or "law": "the law of nature," "the moral
law," or simply "morality."[7]

[7] I am aware that in classing Hobbes with those in the tradition of natural
law more narrowly conceived I am departing from the view (argued, for
example, by Strauss, *Natural Right and History*, pp. 166-202) that Hobbes
effected a revolutionary departure from that tradition. But Hobbes did not
challenge the traditional understanding of the law of nature as a set of principles that could be known by reason and thus defended rationally. There is
no necessary connection between Hobbes's view that peaceful association is
unlikely to be established on the basis of agreement concerning moral and
religious truth and the view of Weber, Sartre, and others that the truth of
particular moral judgments or religious beliefs cannot be defended rationally.
It is a mistake to think that modern individualist or liberal political thought
necessarily entails what is sometimes called "emotivism," the view that moral
judgments are subjective, a matter of feelings or preference, not rationally
defensible. All that liberalism need postulate is the political fact that agreement on such matters is unlikely, not the epistemological premise that moral
truth is impossible.

The presuppositions of morality as a body of common rules for rational beings are explored in Kant's ethical writings. Kantian ethics is fundamentally philosophical in its effort to separate the idea of morality from the contingencies of moral conduct in particular communities and situations. Kant's fundamental moral principle, the categorical imperative, is in its various formulations a way of expressing the idea that moral conduct consists in acting in accordance with that moral law accessible to reason. The categorical imperative does not tell people what they must do to survive, be happy, or realize other good ends; it helps them to identify the limits they must respect in their efforts to achieve these ends. To pursue an end is to seek to alter the world so as to bring it closer to an imagined ideal world. Ideals give rise to maxims governing the lives of those committed to them. As imperatives they are, in Kant's terminology, "hypothetical" rather than "categorical." A maxim or hypothetical imperative is a rule of skill or a counsel of prudence concerning what must be done to promote a particular end. But these maxims do not constitute duties and they are not moral. Duty and morality appear only when observance of maxims is itself governed by the categorical—or moral—imperative to conduct oneself in the pursuit of one's ends in a manner that conforms to the moral law.[8] The categorical imperative is not itself a rule of conduct but a criterion or test of the moral validity of particular rules. It expresses the common insight of many theorists of both natural law and civil association that moral conduct is defined not by the ends sought in acting but rather by the respect the agent shows for certain fundamental limits that together constitute the common good of a community of individuals who may be motivated by different beliefs, values, ideals, and interests.[9]

[8] *Foundations of the Metaphysics of Morals*, pp. 30-33.

[9] This conception of the common good is fundamental to Kant's account of law as well as of morality. "*Right* is the restriction of each individual's freedom so that it harmonizes with the freedom of everyone else (in so far as this is possible within the terms of a general law). And *public right* is the distinctive quality of the *external laws* which make this constant harmony

Restating Kant's distinction between hypothetical and categorical imperatives, we need to distinguish practices that are *instrumental* (that is, specify procedures to be followed in order to achieve a particular result) from those that are *authoritative* (that is, specify procedures, forms, and limits to be observed regardless of the substantive end pursued).[10] A common morality, or morality of accommodation, is an authoritative practice composed of considerations to be taken into account in judging and acting. Such a morality does not itself specify the particular ends to be sought in action; on the contrary, it presupposes and seeks to regulate the conduct of persons engaged in pursuing their own self-chosen ends. It consists of standards of conduct for "individuals" or "persons," that is, for intelligent beings who may have a variety of beliefs, values, desires, and aversions, and who are engaged in a variety of projects and activities. Thus it typically reflects in various ways, though often only imperfectly, the idea of impartiality among persons and their ends. And it is concerned with procedures rather than purposes, means rather than ends, and compromise rather than perfection. Purposes, ends, and ideals are all within the sphere of individual freedom; it is the duties and rights of those pursuing particular purposes, ends, and ideals that fall within the sphere of common morality.[11]

---

possible. Since every restriction of freedom through the arbitrary will of another party is termed *coercion*, it follows that a civil constitution is a relationship among *free* men who are subject to coercive laws, while they retain their freedom within the general union with their fellows. Such is the requirement of pure reason, which legislates *a priori*, regardless of all empirical ends (which can all be summed up under the general heading of happiness). Men have different views on the empirical end of happiness and what it consists of, so that as far as happiness is concerned, their will cannot be brought under any common principle nor thus under any external law harmonizing with the freedom of everyone." (*Political Writings*, pp. 73-74.) This passage contains the kernel of the conception of law as a morality of accommodation that is developed in other writings, especially *Metaphysics of Morals*.

[10] For a statement of the distinction between "authoritative" and "instrumental" practices, see Chapter 1, above.

[11] The preceding account of the character of moralities of accommodation

INTERNATIONAL MORALITY

The expression "international morality" introduces a new level of complexity into the discussion of morality and moral conduct, for to the questions concerning the character and forms of morality so far considered we must add those that arise when our attention is focused on relations between the citizens or officials of different states. Notice that according to the conception of a common morality just considered, something like a common morality of international conduct is to be found embedded in international law. For international law is a body of authoritative practices and rules constituting a common standard of conduct for states in their relations with one another. One must exclude as nonmoral those parts of international law that are instrumental to the realization of particular substantive purposes: that is, much of the special law embodied in treaties and in the charters and regulations of international organizations. The moral element in international law is to be found in those general principles of international association that constitute customary international law, and above all in the most fundamental of those principles, such as the ones specifying the rights of independence, legal equality, and self-defense, and the duties to observe treaties, to respect the immunity of ambassadors, to refrain from aggression, to conduct hostilities in war in accordance with the laws of war, to respect human rights, and to cooperate in the peaceful settlement of disputes. Customary international

draws on Oakeshott's discussion of morality in *On Human Conduct*, pp. 55-70. Most of Oakeshott's book can be read as an attempt to explicate the presuppositions of such a morality in its civil or legal aspect. But legality is only one of the forms that a common morality can assume. Some are informal and uninstitutionalized, resting on custom and communal sentiment or opinion, while others are interpreted and applied by priests, elders, sheiks or other custodians. Moralities of accommodation often appear as part of religion, notwithstanding the tendency of religions to connect moral principles with theological premises and religious ideals. Two notable recent works that seek to explore the presuppositions and to expound at least part of the content of the common morality as understood within the tradition of natural law broadly defined are Donagan, *Theory of Morality*, and Finnis, *Natural Law and Natural Rights*.

law, according to one point of view, *is* the common morality of international society because it contains the authoritative practices and rules according to which that society is defined and the conduct of its members directed and judged.

There are, however, certain difficulties with this view. The most obvious of these arises from the fact that there exist other conceptions of morality from the perspective of which customary international law appears to be nonmoral. For example, moralities are often understood as pertaining in one way or another to the conduct of individuals rather than groups or organizations. One can reasonably ask, therefore, whether the ideas of morality and moral conduct have any application to the relations of states. It should be noticed that the issue here is a conceptual one, not to be confused with the moral issue of whether the provisions of customary international law are morally justified or just.

One question to be considered is whether one can speak of states as agents capable of engaging in conduct. The question is in fact a special case of the more general question of whether any group, association, or collective entity can be interpreted intelligibly in terms of the concepts of human action. Certainly there are instances in which to do so is to put an unbearable strain on these concepts. To speak of the motives or beliefs of a corporation or government, in contrast to those of its members or officials, would seem to involve significant danger of confusion. On the other hand, it is not usually misleading to speak of the deliberations, choices, decisions, acts, or policies of a collective body. It is usual and proper in many contexts to speak of states, governments, and government agencies as if they were moral persons, agents whose acts can be judged by moral standards, just as in legal discourse it is usual and proper to regard them as legal persons enjoying various rights, powers, and immunities and subject to various duties and liabilities. Perhaps the notion of collective conduct is always an abstraction or fiction, but if so it would seem to be an indispensable one for both moral and legal discourse.

Even if we accept the convention of conceiving states as agents, however, the objection might still be made that it is misleading to refer to state conduct as either moral or immoral, on the grounds that the terms "morality" and "moral conduct" apply only to individuals. From this it follows that the principles of customary international law cannot be moral because they are not principles for individuals. But the assumptions concerning both morality and international law underlying this conclusion are unwarranted. Although it is true that for the most part international law applies to the conduct of states, it does in some circumstances apply directly to individuals. It includes, on the one hand, principles of responsibility that bring the conduct of individuals directly under international law: in the past, piracy, and more recently, crimes of war, provide the main examples of individual activity directly regulated by international law. And, on the other hand, international law has for some time been moving in the direction of setting minimum standards for the treatment of individuals by states, and thus toward the direct recognition and protection of individual—or, as they are now often called, "human"—rights. Thus, the claim that international law does not directly regulate relations between states and individuals and thus does not concern itself with individual conduct is correct only if it is qualified to take account of certain clear exceptions.[12]

Nor is it correct to say that morality applies only to individuals. A moral tradition, even though it may be concerned primarily with personal conduct, may also have something to say about the acts and policies of collectivities such as the state. Much of the just war tradition is concerned with precisely such judgments. The law of nations was originally simply natural law applied to sovereigns. We can say that it would be wrong for one country to invade another, or that a government ought to keep its promises, where the oughts in question are neither prudential nor legal but moral oughts. Be-

---

[12] See the last section of Chapter 10, below.

cause we imagine and speak of corporate persons, we pass judgment on them, and the resources upon which we draw in making such judgments are often those of morality. It is false to say that moral discourse and moral principles apply only to individuals and that it never makes sense to speak of the moral obligations of states. Morality consists of principles for individuals and, by extension, for individuals acting in concert. While it is correct to say that moral concepts and principles apply largely and fundamentally to individual conduct, it does not follow that the conduct of states cannot be judged in moral terms.

The real difficulty with the view that customary international law constitutes or embodies an international morality arises not from doubts concerning whether this body of law applies to individual conduct, or whether moral principles apply to states, but from the conviction that principles cannot be regarded as moral unless they demand respect for the freedom and rights of the individual. Therefore it might be argued that, even on the definition of common morality as a form of practical association, the principles of association represented by customary international law cannot be regarded as moral principles because they do not adequately recognize and protect what we have come to think of as individual rights. The principles of international association embodied in international law are not moral, according to this view, because on the one hand they permit governments too much liberty to violate the rights of their own citizens and on the other restrict governments too much from intervening to redress the violation of individual rights abroad. Thus, to the extent that the idea of morality is tied to the ideas of individual liberty and rights, one may plausibly wonder whether customary international law falls under it.

Two different responses can be made to these doubts. The first is that there is no reason to insist, in all contexts, on certain particular principles of individual liberty and rights as definitive of morality. If one does, few social moralities would count as instances of morality. One must be careful, in other words, to avoid confusing the question of whether the concept of morality applies to customary international law from the quite different question of the moral adequacy of that law according to some particular set of moral standards. The first is a conceptual question, the second a question of moral judgment. It is not necessary to demonstrate that customary international law is above criticism in order to conclude that it falls under the concept of morality in an important sense of that term.

The other response one can make to doubts about whether customary international law is properly regarded as a morality in the narrow sense of an authoritative practice reflecting a concern for individual liberty and rights is that customary international law does in fact reflect such a concern. Thus it is sometimes suggested that international law gives weight to individual liberty by recognizing the existence of independent political communities—states—and by placing limits on intervention by one state in the internal affairs of another. In this way, it is argued, international law seeks to protect the liberty of a people to govern itself according to its own laws and traditions. The principles of state sovereignty and nonintervention, according to this view, are based on the assumption that a state is a community united through common laws and institutions reflecting an inherited culture and shared history. Foreign intervention is therefore presumed to constitute an interference with the liberty of the citizens of a state to live according to their own traditions and to govern themselves. The liberty of states served by the principle of nonintervention, on this account, is merely the liberty of individuals to live in a political community whose arrangements have been determined without external interference.

But this "communal liberty," as it has been called, is related only tenuously to the liberty of the individual. It is merely one liberty among others, and is compatible with the denial of other liberties. As Hobbes long ago pointed out, the liberty of a political community is not the same as the liberty of its citizens: it is "the liberty of sovereigns, not of private men."[13] "The Athenians and Romans were free—that is, free commonwealths; not that any particular men had the liberty to resist their own representative, but that their representative had the liberty to resist or invade other people." But it is precisely the liberty of a people to "resist their own representative" that critics of international law have in mind in challenging its moral adequacy. If the principle of nonintervention protects tyrannical states as well as those in which individual liberties are recognized and protected, how can international law be said to reflect a concern for individual liberty? The right of individuals "to a state of their own"[14] is unquestionably important, but it is only one among a number of morally important liberties.

There is, however, another argument for a connection between collective and individual liberty, namely that the two are contingently related. The principles of state sovereignty and nonintervention reflect the consideration that, in a world organized as a society of states, individuals have rights largely as members of a political community—that is, as citizens of a state. Although citizenship hardly guarantees that they will be treated in a manner that respects their personal autonomy or dignity, it is clearly related to such treatment. The rights of citizenship are at least an obstacle to enslavement and massacre. Furthermore, there is a contingent connection between the international pluralism respresented by a multiplicity of states and individual liberty. As Gibbon and others have argued, the alternative to a world of independent political communities is a single universal state in which there would be "no place left for political refuge and no examples left of political alternatives."[15] International law therefore expresses a concern for individual liberty not only insofar as the states whose integrity is preserved by adherence to the prin-

13 *Leviathan*, ch. 21.
14 Walzer, "Moral Standing of States," p. 228.
15 Ibid.

ciple of nonintervention are those in which individual liberty can flourish but because it reinforces global pluralism.

I have spoken so far as if the principles of state sovereignty and nonintervention were without exception, but this is far from the case. Because the presumption of a connection between state sovereignty and individual liberty is not always warranted, international law also reflects a concern for the latter by placing limits on state sovereignty and by permitting foreign intervention in circumstances in which this liberty is gravely threatened. In particular, great crimes such as occur when a government sets out to massacre a number of its own subjects have long been recognized as justifying foreign concern and action.[16] International law has also traditionally included the idea of an "international minimum standard" regarding the treatment of aliens by the government of the country within which they reside. More recently it has come to embody minimum standards governing the relations between a government and its own citizens, under the label of "human rights." These limits on state sovereignty constitute a second way in which a concern for individual liberty is reflected, however inadequately, in customary international law.

Customary international law, then, does express a concern for individual liberty. But because international law deals primarily with regulating the relations of states with one another, this concern is necessarily circumscribed and indirect. In a world organized into states, some version of the principle of nonintervention is required by the idea of rule-governed relations among them. Yet the principle is not absolute. The existence of a body of international law regulating these relations does not exclude the existence of rules governing the relations between governments and individual persons falling within their respective jurisdictions. Such rules must, how-

[16] On the scope of the principle of nonintervention see, inter alia, Mill, "A Few Words on Non-intervention"; Stowell, *Intervention in International Law*; Vincent, *Nonintervention and International Order*; Walzer, *Just and Unjust Wars*, ch. 6; Hehir, "Ethics of Intervention"; and Wicclair, "Human Rights and Intervention."

ever, be reconciled with those that are fundamental to the idea of international society as a rule-governed association of states, one in which a multiplicity of diverse and independent political communities can accommodate themselves to each other's continued existence. It is true, as one critic of the principle of nonintervention has argued, that "if human rights exist at all, they set a limit to pluralism."[17] But it is not clear that weakening the traditional restraints on intervention, especially armed intervention, will do more to promote individual liberty than continued respect for the principle of nonintervention (together with its recognized exceptions). Nor, given the hazards of intervention, is it clear that the compromise between state sovereignty and foreign concern embodied in international law is as morally indefensible as it is sometimes claimed to be.

Because customary international law reflects a concern for individual liberty, in a manner shaped by the circumstances of the society of states, it may be said to have moral significance even on a fairly stringent definition of morality. However, it hardly follows that "customary international law" and "international morality" are synonymous. The most we can say is that the law partially embodies a morality of state conduct, and to that extent expresses what may plausibly be represented as a moral point of view in regard to the relations of states. But it does not have an exclusive claim to represent such a point of view. A morality is a particular kind of authoritative practice governing the conduct of some community: that is, containing standards according to which the conduct of members of that community may be judged. It presupposes not only a community of moral agents whose conduct is judged but also a community of *judges*. Now the most striking feature of customary international law is that, although its standards are standards of conduct for states and statesmen, the judgments upon which the creation and application of these standards rest are those of a specialized

---

[17] Luban, "Romance of the Nation-State," p. 396.

community of international lawyers. Customary international law is international morality as interpreted by lawyers. This suggests the possibility that there exist other international moralities constituted by the judgments of other communities of judges. Clearly there exist other moralities or moral traditions that have sought to articulate standards of international conduct. One of them is the natural law tradition as understood within the Catholic church. Another, more inclusive, international morality is to be found in the application of the inherited concepts and principles of the entire Hebrew-Christian moral tradition. Still another is the tradition of Islam, which despite its militant origin has worked out an elaborate morality of mutual accommodation among separate peoples both within and outside the Moslem faith.[18] If these traditions have from time to time in their long histories countenanced genocide, slavery, conquest, and holy war, they have also provided the basis for self-criticism. It would appear, then, that there exist many international moralities, each based on the principles and judgments of a different community or tradition.

These various moralities or moral traditions have in common one feature that they do not share with international law. The latter is a distinct system of principles of international conduct with its own sources and an identity distinct from any other system of law. What we today call "international law" is not only a *kind* of law but a particular *instance* of that kind: the international legal system. The other moral traditions, however, are not distinct systems of international morality. Unlike customary international law, which is essentially a morality of state conduct, the great moral traditions are essentially moralities of personal conduct. As international moralities they must to a significant extent be regarded as personal moralities applied to the problems and taking account of the circumstances of international affairs. Their

[18] Kedourie, " 'Minorities,' " pp. 286-316, and *Nationalism in Asia and Africa*, pp. 33-34.

standards of international conduct therefore reflect both the general principles of the tradition and the specific practices, such as those of statecraft or warfare, to which these general principles must be adapted. For example, the morality of war as it is understood within the Christian tradition reflects the application of moral principles derived from other areas of experience to military conduct. Indeed, to put it this way is to oversimplify, for these principles have themselves been altered as a result of having been tested in the circumstances of war. The theory of the just war as explored by Christian moralists from the earliest times is tied on the one hand to the larger structure of concepts and principles that define the Christian tradition itself and on the other to the particular practices and circumstances of military conduct, including those of positive law. From the perspective of Christianity, neither the morality of war nor international morality constitutes a distinct and autonomous body of principles. If this is understood, it would seem permissible as a matter of convenience to speak of those parts of particular moral traditions that deal with international affairs as "international moralities."

I have spoken so far of international moralities in the plural. Are there any grounds for accepting the view that underlying the various moral traditions of different human communities there can be discerned a common, even universal, morality of international conduct? Historically, the argument for a single common morality underlying the diversity of moral traditions has tended to take one of two forms. The first is to seek to transcend the customs of different moral communities by abstracting general principles from particular practices. One searches for evidence of moral agreement and locates the common morality in principles common to various traditions. The second is to look for some rational justification for moral principles, apart from the mere fact of general acceptance. The principles of the common morality are deduced from certain theoretical assumptions concerning the nature of human beings and their world rather than arrived at inductively from a survey of customs and beliefs. The moral traditions of dif-

ferent communities—and these include both social and critical moralities—can then be seen as more or less adequate
approximations to God's will, the law of nature, the impartial
judgments of imaginary rational beings, or whatever criterion
of right is adopted as correct. As many moralists have recognized, however, generally accepted principles are not necessarily rational, nor are rational principles necessarily generally accepted. Hence the recurrent appeal of an approach that
combines both forms of argument, thereby giving weight to
the reason of experience and tradition as well as to that of
analysis and argument.

No single moral tradition can claim fully to represent the
common morality of international conduct, for each is tied to
the specific practices and assumptions of those whose activities sustain it. Customary international law is bound up with
the decisions of statesmen and the procedures of lawyers, while
the moralities of the religious traditions reflect the ethical
ideals and theological premises of particular faiths. If there
does exist an international morality transcending the contingent features of particular moral communities and traditions,
it is likely to be found in the ongoing conversation or dialogue
among them. Its general principles will be those that are widely
accepted and continually reaffirmed in this conversation, and
its "reason" those considerations and modes of argument that
have survived repeated critical examination.

The most articulate recent attempt to give systematic
expression to the principles of a common morality of international conduct, one that meets the criteria just suggested,
may be found in Michael Walzer's discussion of the morality
of war in *Just and Unjust Wars*. Morality for Walzer is essentially casuistical—that is, its principles are shaped by reflection on cases.[19] The chief defect of positive international law,
from this perspective, is not the lack of centralized rule-making and sanctions so often mentioned by its critics but rather

[19] Walzer's conception of moral reasoning and argument as a kind of casuistry is further developed in "Political Decision-Making and Political Education," pp. 169-171.

the paucity of decided cases in contrast to domestic law. Morality has the advantage in this respect because it is based on the judgments of a much larger community of judges those "men and women who are not lawyers but simply citizens. . . ."[20] In morality, as opposed to law, "we are all judges. . . . There may be no case law, no authoritative decisions, but there is a long history of thinking about cases. In the course of that history, we have developed in everyday moral life a vocabulary and an arsenal of arguments. . . ."[21] Those who are moved to reflect on the morality of international relations and war can draw upon an inherited body of "norms, customs, professional codes, legal precepts, religious and philosophical principles, and reciprocal arrangements"[22] that together compose the resources of moral tradition more general than any of the particular traditions from which it is derived. To employ these varied resources in thinking about international relations and war is, as Walzer puts it, to inhabit "the moral world."[23] It is a world constituted by arguments, concepts, and judgments that, although not without ambiguity, yield a structure of principles giving it a certain unity. It is a world in which argument is possible because its inhabitants employ the same moral language (although there are many local dialects), even when, as is often the case, they want to say different things.

I shall have something to say in a later chapter about Walzer's account of the morality of war. For the moment I want to focus on his theory of morality—his account of the nature of international morality—because it constitutes a particularly clear and persuasive statement of the conception of morality and moral conduct that I have tried to explicate and defend in these pages. It is, first, a conception of morality as concerned with limits rather than ends. International morality is a set of authoritative considerations governing the pursuit of

[20] *Just and Unjust Wars*, p. xiii.
[21] "Law, Morality, and the War in Vietnam," p. 16.
[22] *Just and Unjust Wars*, p. 44.
[23] Ibid., p. xiii.

self-chosen ends by individuals and associations of individuals (political communities). It is not the task of morality to determine the content of these ends, but rather to specify how the pursuits of different individuals and communities are to be reconciled with one another, even in war. Moral considerations are authoritative in the sense that they generally override other sorts of considerations.[24] For Walzer, the limits that morality imposes on international conduct are ultimately those derived from a conception of "human rights."[25] Whatever the adequacy of this derivation, it clearly reflects a characteristically moral concern with personal autonomy or liberty, understood as the freedom to pursue one's own self-determined ends subject only to the constraints arising from the equal liberty of others to pursue ends of their own.

A second notable feature of Walzer's account of morality is his stress on moral language. A morality is to be found in the judgments that people make about conduct, not in conduct itself. Thus, we cannot get at the substance of the international morality by studying the actual conduct of statesmen, soldiers, or ordinary citizens in their relations with foreign countries and their inhabitants.[26] Moral principles are revealed in what people say, in the expectations, complaints, even hypocrisies to which they give expression when they criticize, persuade, justify, blame, or excuse themselves or others. Their judgments enter the realm of public discourse only by being expressed in words, words that must be understood by others if they are to serve the purpose of affecting their judgments. Therefore the beginning of moral inquiry is

[24] The concept of moral authority is not something that Walzer analyzes very closely, but it is certainly presupposed by his treatment of particular issues, such as whether rights should be understood as ends to be maximized or, as Walzer holds, as authoritative constraints to be respected. ("Moral Standing of States," pp. 222-228.) Elsewhere Walzer attacks the views of those who are skeptical of moral authority while assuming the authority of positive international law. (*Just and Unjust Wars*, p. 288, and "Law, Morality, and the War in Vietnam," pp. 91-92.)

[25] *Just and Unjust Wars*, pp. xvi, 53-54, 133-137.

[26] Ibid., p. 44.

to study the common vocabulary of moral discourse. "My starting point," Walzer writes, "is the fact that we do argue, often to different purposes, to be sure, but in a mutually comprehensible fashion: else there would be no point in *arguing*."[27] Indeed, to a significant extent, a morality is a common vocabulary, a common language within which the rights and wrongs of conduct can be argued among people whose judgments are not necessarily in agreement.[28]

The cases and arguments that Walzer draws from a fairly wide range of historical situations illustrate, although of course they do not prove, the persistence of certain fundamental moral concepts and arguments concerning warfare. Acts of war, he suggests, are repeatedly condemned as aggressions, interventions, or atrocities, justified as acts of self-defense, self-determination, or lawful reprisal, and excused by appeal to notions like military necessity and superior orders. Thus the most obvious objection to the view that there exists a common moral vocabulary—namely that no such vocabulary can be shown to exist—is effectively rebutted by the recurrence of similar distinctions and arguments in response to similar situations, from Thucydides on down. If this were not the case we would be at a loss to account for the frequency with which the arguments of the past are deployed in the moral controversies of our own time.

A deeper objection to the conception of international morality as a common vocabulary is that, even if such agreement exists, it is empty. "It is true," argues one of Walzer's critics, "that all statesmen use the same moral language. . . . Unfortunately, from the viewpoint of moral harmony, this is meaningless. A community of vocabulary is not the same thing as a community of values. . . . Behind the common grammar

---

[27] Ibid., p. xiii.
[28] Compare Oakeshott, *On Human Conduct*, p. 63: "The conditions which compose a moral practice" do not "compose anything so specific as a 'shared system of values'; they compose a vernacular language of colloquial intercourse." Oakeshott recurs often to the metaphor of morality as a language; see, e.g., pp. 59, 62-66, 78-81, and 120.

there are competing ideological logics."[29] But it does not follow that because there is ideological disagreement that the common vocabulary is empty or meaningless. A common moral vocabulary leaves room for disagreement, even fundamental disagreement, and indeed provides the means of exploring the extent of such disagreement. It is certainly true that the common language of moral discourse can be abused, even debased, when people with very different values use it to defend those values. This is not a problem limited to the discourse of statesmen, for it also occurs within a political community. The persistence of a common moral tradition suggests that moral discourse can recover from such debasement and that the tradition with which Walzer is concerned is to a significant degree self-correcting.

Walzer's point is that we use moral language not only to express agreement but also to express disagreement in a way that we hope will be both intelligible and persuasive. If the moral vocabulary were truly empty there would be no point in using it. Once we begin to use this vocabulary, moreover, we are committed to a structure of distinctions and arguments that limit the conclusions we can reasonably draw. A common vocabulary does not completely determine our judgments but it does constrain and influence them. Moral talk is, as Walzer says, "coercive."[30] To characterize an act as unjust, aggressive, or criminal is not merely to condemn it but to do so for particular reasons and to make claims that require particular kinds of evidence for their substantiation. Moral concepts are descriptive as well as evaluative; there are rules for their use that put constraints on the kinds of arguments that they can be used to frame. It is because moral concepts and arguments possess a definite structure that terms like "self-defense" and "military necessity" are not infinitely elastic: they can be stretched, but only so far. It is because moral terms do express a core of common meaning that the mistakes and lies

[29] Hoffmann, *Duties Beyond Borders*, p. 20.
[30] *Just and Unjust Wars*, p. 12.

of moral discourse can be exposed, gradually and with the help of disinterested judges, for what they are.

This tendency for moral error and hypocrisy to be corrected over time points to a third dimension of Walzer's conception of international morality: its historical and therefore general character. Moral judgments are shaped by action and by passionate self-justification, as well as by a common vocabulary. But in the end "it is the words that are decisive" in shaping the standards by which military conduct is judged—"the 'judgment of history,' as it is called, which means the judgment of men and women arguing until some rough consensus is reached."[31] The common morality is based not on the judgments of any particular nation, church, profession, or political party but on the judgments of people in general, on "the opinions of mankind."[32] To identify the common morality with the kinds of distinctions and arguments that occur again and again in the judgments that people make in different situations is not to claim the existence of complete consensus on all matters; it is to claim a partial consensus on some matters, and, even more importantly, to describe the character and basis of such consensus as can be shown to exist. It is certainly not to claim that the common morality, even as a common language and way of thinking rather than a unified doctrine, is universally accepted; there are certainly inhabitants of the world, perhaps many, who are not inhabitants of "the moral world." Nor is it to advance an irrefutable claim for the validity of its principles; the accumulated judgments of this inclusive moral tradition are not free from ambiguity, prejudice, fashion, or the possibility of serious error. It is, however, to claim for the common morality a high degree of generality and authority and to claim for the judgments based upon it a character that is not "idiosyncratic and private"[33] but objective and public. Not everyone is commit-

[31] Ibid., p. 44.
[32] Ibid., p. 15.
[33] Ibid., p. 45.

ted to a pluralist world, but everyone must live in one. The common morality reflects an appreciation of that fact.

The common morality of war explored by Walzer is an instance of what I have been calling "moralities of accommodation." Like all such moralities, it is a way of thinking and speaking in which judgments of conduct are made on the basis of authoritative rather than instrumental considerations. It presupposes the coexistence of individuals pursuing a diversity of ends, and is concerned to define the terms of association among such individuals in the absence of agreement on ends. Such a morality prescribes limits, not ends. Its standards consist not of unambiguous and exceptionless rules prescribing a single correct course for every contingency but rather a structured pattern of ideas, distinctions, principles, and arguments to be taken into account in reaching decisions and making judgments.

Although there is a sense in which the idea of a common international morality includes that of customary international law, both ordinary usage and analytic clarity require that we continue to refer to each by its familiar name. But the resemblance between the two should not be overlooked. Each is concerned with the conduct of states as well as that of individuals, although the nature and emphasis of this concern differs. Both are "practical," that is, concerned with prescribing limits rather than ends. And both are customary in the sense that they are not the outcome of deliberate acts of will but rather the residue of innumerable particular acts and judgments repeated with a consistency sufficient to allow a pattern or practice to be discerned. To a significant extent they share a common vocabulary and point of view. But the differences between them are equally significant. Customary international law is shaped by the judgments of a particular community of specialists and experts and supports an elaborate superstructure of positive law by which it is in turn greatly influenced. Because international morality and international law are founded on the practices and judgments of different judges they inevitably differ in many details even if their outlook is broadly similar. One might say that they constitute parallel but not identical ways of conceiving and judging international conduct.

LEGAL AND MORAL OBLIGATION

Human activity, I have argued, takes place within a matrix of practices; customs, traditions, arts, techniques, laws, directions, rituals, and other guides to conduct. Some of these practices are instrumental to the achievement of particular substantive purposes; others are authoritative, that is, to be attended to regardless of one's purposes. Because there are always many different practices that have relevance for any particular human activity, there is always the possibility that considerations arising from different practices may pull in different directions. To act is therefore often to choose among competing considerations. Where the conflict is between considerations derived from different instrumental practices, one chooses to be guided by those that appear most conducive to the end in view: one weighs the alternatives, and does the best thing "all things considered." Where considerations derived from an instrumental practice appear to be incompatible with those of an authoritative practice, however, such a resolution is not so easily reached. Authoritative considerations are in some sense superior to merely instrumental ones, and are ordinarily supposed to override them; that is what it means to say that they are authoritative. Hence the problem of how to act when faced with an apparent conflict of instrumental and authoritative considerations is more acute than when authoritative considerations are not involved. Most acute of all are problems that arise from a conflict of different *authoritative* practices. If in the first case one must deal with conflicts of desire and in the second with a conflict between desire and duty, in the third one is confronted with a conflict of duties. Conflicts between considerations of law and those of morality, where both are regarded as authoritative practices, are therefore conflicts, or apparent conflicts, of duty or obligation.

Our attention so far has been focused largely on conflicts between international practices that are authoritative, on the one hand, and those that are instrumental to the pursuit of particular substantive purposes, on the other. But to argue that instrumental considerations must give way to authoritative ones, and therefore that in the society of states considerations of international law must override those of both national and international advantage, still leaves the question of how an apparent conflict of authoritative considerations is to be resolved. Even if one accepts the conclusion that instrumental considerations cannot be allowed to override those derived from an authoritative practice, one must still come to terms with the possibility that conduct in some situations may be governed by more than one authoritative practice, and that these practices may contain contradictory principles of conduct.

The character of the problem can be brought out by noticing that, where a course of action is opposed by considerations derived from an authoritative practice, one would be wrong to adopt it whatever the reasons for doing so might be. The "exclusionary reasons" provided by an authoritative rule override other kinds of reasons.[34] When authoritative considerations are in conflict with nonauthoritative ones, the former are to prevail over the latter. So much follows logically from the concepts of authority and obligation. But these concepts do not provide us with a way to resolve conflicts between two or more authoritative practices. Is there any general solution to the problem of what it is right to do when two reasons, each authoritative within a particular practice, exclude each other? It would seem that there is not. Within a particular authoritative practice, the considerations of another such practice may be treated as subordinate: morally speaking, one should take account of the law, but it is considerations of

[34] See the discussion of authoritative practices in Chapter 1, above.

251

morality rather than of law that constitute the ultimate standard of conduct, whereas from the point of view of the law it
is legal considerations that are decisive. What one ought to
do, one's obligations, cannot be determined apart from some
particular authoritative practice. There exists no Olympian
standpoint from which the diverse principles of obligation of
different practices can be rationalized *sub specie aeternitatis*.

This conclusion is often denied. Moralists commonly attempt to define just such a standpoint. The view that the task
of moral inquiry is to articulate the principles of right conduct, all things considered, may conveniently be labeled the
"moral supremacy thesis." According to this thesis, moral
considerations are not on the same plane as other sorts of
considerations and cannot be overridden by them. Moral considerations are always supreme. Such a view is most plausible
when moral considerations appear to contradict those of mere
desire and interest. As one defender of the moral supremacy
thesis puts it, "the principles of morality are not one among
a number of competing interests and . . . cannot be subordinated to other interests. They are, rather, the principles
that govern the pursuit of all interests."[35] But obeying the
law is subscribing to an authoritative practice, not the "pursuit of an interest." The moral supremacy thesis requires that
considerations of other forms of authoritative practice besides
those of interest give way to moral considerations.

Despite its plausibility, the moral supremacy thesis is either
false or tautological, according to how it is interpreted. If it
is interpreted as stating that, as the world goes, moral considerations do in fact override considerations of prudence, interest, or positive law, it is false. If, on the other hand, the
thesis is that moral considerations ought to override such other
considerations, then it is a tautology, at least if "ought" is
understood as a moral ought. For it then says no more than
that moral considerations ought morally speaking to override

[35] Cohen, "Morality and the Laws of War," p. 88.

nonmoral considerations.[36] Instead of a judgment from out-side morality concerning the proper place of moral consider-ations in relation to conduct, we have only a restatement of the moral point of view, a reassertion from within the au-thoritative practice of morality that the considerations of this practice are authoritative. Judgments of obligation and right conduct can only be made from within some body of author-itative practice, and therefore the resolution of conflicts be-tween different bodies of authoritative practice can only be made from within one or another of them. If one is faced with a conflict between morality and law, one has a choice be-tween conduct that is lawful but morally wrong and conduct that is morally right but unlawful. I can do the thing that is legally right or the thing that is morally right, but I cannot do that which is simply right without qualification. It is le-gally right to act legally and morally right to act morally. Where different authoritative practices govern conduct in the same situation and cannot be reconciled, there is no criterion in-dependent of those practices to tell us what to do. The idea of a single coherent scheme of principles according to which all conflicts of principle can be reconciled is a Chimera.

Practices emerge from conduct and tend to accommodate themselves to it and to each other. The law bends to equity, and the moral Christian is advised to render Caesar his due. Morality does not require the existence of particular institu-tions—contract, family, property, civil society—but where they exist it allows for them and seeks to regulate them. Legal systems, too, support institutions by providing for the rec-ognition and enforcement of contracts and the rules of private associations. No authoritative practice is indifferent to cir-cumstances. Moreover, the existence of competing authori-tative practices is certainly a circumstance to which the mem-bers of any community cannot avoid responding, and their responses will be reflected in their principles of conduct. By providing the resources for justifying or excusing departures

---

[36] Quinton, "Bounds of Morality," p. 136.

from its rules, a morality or legal system manifests its acknowledgment of the claims of other practices, as well as of interest, need, and human weakness. A practice that cannot acknowledge such claims is in danger of rendering itself irrelevant to experience through rigidity, just as one that is too ready to give way may become irrelevant through flaccidity. By allowing weight to be given to considerations arising from other practices, and often by adopting such considerations as their own, moralities and legal systems work toward a modus vivendi based on the reconciliation of competing demands.

CHAPTER 10

International Justice

THE DISAGREEMENTS concerning the character of international society, law, and morality with which I have been concerned are reproduced in the controversy that has been going on for most of the present century about the meaning of "justice" in international affairs. The argument has not of course been primarily about a word, but rather about what sort of international order would count as just and about what sort of international conduct a just order would require of states and individuals. At the beginning of the century those who spoke of international justice were largely concerned with strengthening international institutions and with the international rule of law. The strongest expressions of this concern are to be found in the two Hague Conferences and in the founding of the League of Nations and the Permanent Court of International Justice. Since the Second World War the belief that international law and international justice are closely related seems to have weakened, although it persists in the human rights movement and in the movement to codify customary international law.

The arguments about the injustice of the Versailles settlement advanced after the First World War mark the beginning of a shift toward a conception of international justice as a matter of substantive benefits rather than of legality, as having to do above all with the distribution of wealth, power, and other goods among states. In this respect international thinking merely reflected a tendency already well advanced in discussions of justice within the state. Today, as in the 1930s, those who speak of international justice are likely to speak of international inequality, particularly that represented by the gap

255

between the haves and the have-nots, and of the redistributive measures required to rectify what is thought to be the
injustice of this gap. In the thirties, like today, international
law was depreciated, and for similar reasons: it was argued
on behalf of the have-nots of the day, Germany and Italy,
that the international legal system protected the interests of
the ascendant powers, Britain and France, at their expense—
just as in recent decades it has been argued on behalf of the
disadvantaged states of Latin America, Asia, and Africa that
the present system is one that guarantees disproportionate
benefits to the economically developed societies of the West.[1]
Revolutionary claims are once again being advanced in favor
of a new order that would rectify the injustices of existing
arrangements, and in defense of "just" but legally questionable acts such as the forcible seizure of contested territories or
the nationalization of foreign-owned economic enterprises. At
the same time other, and not always compatible, claims on
behalf of the liberty and welfare of the individual are being
made in the language of human rights. It is now argued that
justice requires new rules of international law aimed at redistributing wealth on a global scale directly among individuals
as well as among states.

These disagreements about international justice focus our
attention on two questions. The first is whether a just international order is one in which the conduct of states conforms
to the common rules of international society, or one in which
wealth and power are more evenly distributed. The second
is how the claims of states and individuals are to be balanced.
Neither of these questions can be discussed fruitfully without
paying attention to ambiguities in the concept of justice itself
and making clear the implications of particular uses of the
term "justice."

---

[1] On the redistributive arguments of the thirties, see Carr, *Twenty Years'
Crisis*; for those of the seventies, see Erb and Kallab, *Beyond Dependency*,
and Bedjaoui, *Towards a New International Economic Order*.

JUSTICE AS A MORAL CONCEPT

Conduct that disregards moral or legal limits is open to the charge of being unjust. Such criticism invites in response an attempt to defend the questioned conduct as just, according to what are claimed to be the appropriate moral or legal standards—in other words, to justify it. Arguing about justice forces one to articulate and clarify the standards on which one's judgments are based. The result is a form of discourse in which the subtleties of an authoritative practice are resolved into the more sharply defined configuration of explicitly formulated rules, rights, entitlements, duties, obligations, exceptions, and excuses.

Arguments about justice therefore tend toward the forensic, even when the standards appealed to are moral rather than strictly legal ones. As its Latin origin suggests, the word "justice" (*iustitia*) stands for what is essentially a juridical concept—one of a family of ideas concerned with authoritative rules and rights (*ius*) and with the duties derived from them.[2] The world "justice" is therefore most at home in discourse concerning rules of morality and law that arise out of the practices of a community and prescribe forms and limits to be observed by individuals in their transactions and cooperative engagements. Just conduct is conduct responsive to the considerations comprising an authoritative moral or legal practice—that is, conduct that is lawful or right.

The idea of justice, so understood, has both a positive and a critical aspect. Just conduct is, first of all, conduct that is lawful or right in the sense that it conforms to the standards of a particular legal or moral practice. But because there are many such practices, acts deemed just according to one set of standards may appear unjust according to another. And because there exist different standards of justice, authoritative practices are themselves open to criticism. It is possible to argue about the justice of practices and institutions as well

---

[2] On the meaning of *ius* see Tuck, *Natural Rights Theories*, ch. 1, and Finnis, *Natural Law and Natural Rights*, pp. 206-209, 228.

257

as of conduct. Justice is therefore in the first instance what might be called the "formal justice" of a rule-governed community: a condition in which the authoritative rules of the community are consistently or impartially applied in making judgments about conduct. A condition of this kind might, however, permit the impartial application of arbitrary and discriminatory rules, such as those creating rights and privileges on the grounds of race or caste or authorizing arbitrary arrest, enslavement, or genocide. The concept of justice therefore also has a critical aspect; it allows for the criticism of laws and institutions according to other standards. Among these are the standards of morality understood as the principles of association among the members of a community of intelligent and free beings—persons or individuals. Morally speaking, laws and institutions that violate the principle of impartiality among persons and their ends are themselves unjust.

Justice as a moral concept thus involves the idea of impartial rules as well as that of the impartial application of rules. Just conduct, on this view, is conduct that is impartial or nondiscriminatory in the sense that the practices and rules to which it conforms are those of a community of juridical or moral equals. Thus the concept of justice is not limited to legal justice in the narrow sense of the impartial application of positive laws, including those depriving some persons of their status as equal members of the community. Although it is possible that the impartial application of discriminatory laws might meet the requirements of legal justice, it would unquestionably violate the justice of what I have been calling practical association: that is, the application of rules according to which the members of a community of formal equals are related to one another in the pursuit of their own self-chosen ends. Justice as a moral concept, in other words, means the impartial application of rules of conduct that are themselves impartial in the sense that they do not discriminate arbitrarily against particular persons or ends.

Such an account of justice will strike many as too narrow.

It is certainly true that the word "justice" as it is now ordinarily used refers to a wider range of ideas than that of conformity to authoritative rules, even to those of a community of formal equals. The idea of justice has been stretched and altered under the impact of instrumentalist conceptions of law and morality, with the result that it has come to be identified with the creation of a state of affairs regarded as good rather than with conformity to the rules of an authoritative practice. For the instrumentalist, justice is a condition to be achieved as a result of action, and just conduct is conduct aimed at or resulting in the achievement of such a condition. The justice of an act is therefore judged according to the ends it serves: a just act is one that serves good ends. Justice as a moral concept, in contrast, is identified with the observance of certain constraints in the pursuit of ends; to act justly or morally is to respect these constraints in acting, whatever one's ends.

The distinction can be brought out more clearly by noticing that justice as a moral concept is not concerned to prescribe ends but only to govern their pursuit. Justice in this sense is not itself an end, but rather a value internal to the practices of morality and law, one that is realized in respect for the limits or constraints specified by these practices. These constraints may restrict or even rule out altogether the pursuit of certain ends regarded as good, but if so it is not because such ends will have been shown to be bad in themselves but because to pursue them is incompatible with the requirements of a common morality.

The manner in which the word "justice" is ordinarily used would therefore appear to refer to two distinct ideas. The first is the idea of justice as conformity to the considerations of an authoritative practice, or "formal" justice; the second is justice as the pursuit of good ends, an idea that might be labeled "substantive" or "purposive" justice. Each of these conceptions of justice covers a range of alternative interpretations. Justice as a moral concept, for example, is one interpretation of the idea of formal justice: it refers to conformity to rules of a certain sort, namely those regulating the relations of the members of a community of formal equals. The idea of purposive justice is also open to a variety of interpretations, depending upon which substantive ends are defined as good and upon the criteria according to which the substantive goods thus identified are to be distributed. Utilitarian conceptions of justice, for example, typically identify the good with pleasure or happiness, and adopt some principle of maximization as the criterion of justice. Other conceptions give particular weight to the reduction of suffering or the provision for basic human needs. Some purposive conceptions of justice are radically egalitarian; others understand justice to require no more than that degree of equality represented by a minimum level of benefits for the most unfortunate members of society. Because of its importance in debates about international justice, I want to consider more closely the idea of justice as concerned with the distribution of substantive goods or benefits among the members of a community. This form of justice is commonly referred to as "distributive" or "social" justice.

Most of the discussion of international distributive justice has focused on the question of the criteria according to which such goods as wealth and power should be distributed in international society. In doing so it has tended to ignore the question of the relationship between international distributive justice and the older idea of international justice as conformity to the common rules of international society. This question is clearly a particular version of the more general question of the relationship between distributive and formal justice. Three points concerning this relationship are of particular importance for evaluating how much weight should be given to formal and to distributive considerations in thinking about international justice.

The first is that, strictly speaking, distributive considerations have no place in the concept of formal justice. Formal and distributive justice are distinguished not by differences regarding the criteria according to which substantive goods should be distributed but by their different responses to the more fundamental question of whether justice has anything to do with distribution at all. The concept of distributive justice is tied to a purposive conception of society and government and has no place in discourse concerning practical association.[3] Where distributive considerations enter the province of formal justice, they do so indirectly. That is, considerations of *formal* justice may require the adoption of policies designed to benefit a portion of the community not because the welfare of this portion is an end in itself but because that portion is in a condition (for example, of indigence or ignorance) that bars their participation even as formal equals in the community. Therefore, justice as a moral concept may require government to pursue social and economic welfare policies as a means for securing formal justice, for example by providing free legal services for the poor, or to realize or protect the conditions for the existence and survival of a society based on the principles of formal justice and the rule of law. Public education has often been justified in this way, on the assumption that the existence of a literate and civically educated populace is a condition for the success of constitutional democracy.

Secondly, the expressions "distributive justice" and "social justice" are often used in ways that obscure the distinction between rule-based association and association for the pursuit of shared purposes. This obscurity is not an inevitable result of the concept of distributive justice. It does not arise, for example, when the goods whose distribution is considered are substantive goods such as land and income and do not

[3] Oakeshott's remarks on the place of distributive justice in political association of a purely practical kind—"civil association"—are brief: "There is . . . no place in civil association for so-called 'distributive' justice; that is, the distribution of desirable goods. Such a 'distribution' of substantive benefits or advantages requires a rule of distribution and a distributor in possession of what is to be distributed; but a rule of civil association cannot be a rule of distribution of this sort, and civil rulers have nothing to distribute." (*On Human Conduct*, p. 153.) Actual states, of course, are not pure civil associations; their governments may indeed have substantive benefits to distribute; and questions of distributive justice may therefore arise.

include the "moral goods" of liberty and formal equality.[4] Because the happiness of a community depends upon the extent to which civil rights and liberties are protected within it, as well as on the kind of material wealth its members enjoy, the distinction between these two very different kinds of goods is blurred when both are regarded as purposes to be promoted by collective action. Thus, if distributive justice is understood as referring to the distribution of whatever is conducive to happiness and welfare, it is easy to slide into speaking of the distribution of liberties and rights as well as of substantive goods, and then into confusing distributive considerations with those of formal justice.

Even Rawls, who deliberately sets out to devise an account of justice that encompasses, while carefully distinguishing, principles of formal justice and those pertaining to the distribution of substantive goods, seems at times to run the two together. It is true that his account of justice is stated in the form of two principles, one pertaining to restrictions on liberty and the second to the distribution of substantive goods, and that exchanges between the sorts of benefits defined by each are specifically ruled out (that is, the denial of civil liberties cannot be compensated by material advantages). But Rawls also identifies the sort of justice with which he is concerned—"justice as fairness" or "social justice"—with "the way

---

[4] Aristotle distinguishes a form of justice that arises "in the distribution of honor, money, or other such possessions of the state as can be divided among its citizens." (*Nichomachean Ethics*, 1130b-30.) This assumes that the state is in possession of substantive goods to be distributed, which suggests that in discussing distributive justice Aristotle is thinking of the state in purposive and not purely in practical terms. According to W. D. Ross, the citizen of a Greek state was regarded as, among other things, a shareholder in the state understood as a kind of enterprise: "public property, e.g., the land of a new colony, was not infrequently divided among them, while public assistance to the needy was also recognized." (*Aristotle*, p. 205.) Although Aristotle's way of speaking about distributive justice is thus ambiguous on the question of the character of the state as a mode of human association, it is clear that the goods to be allocated according to the principles of distributive justice are substantive, not moral, goods.

in which the major political institutions *distribute* fundamental rights and duties and determine the division of advantages from social cooperation."[5] The premise of this way of conceiving justice is that liberty and rights are benefits to be produced and distributed by collective action, rather than constraints upon it.

More is at stake here than the possibly casual use of the term "distributive." The conception of justice as having to do with the distribution of desired goods tends to undermine the distinction Rawls sets out to defend because he writes throughout as if the state were an association of individuals united in the pursuit of a shared end—an association whose rules are instrumental to that pursuit, and are binding on the associates only to the extent that their individual interests are served. Rawls understands not only political institutions but society itself to be a "scheme of social cooperation" among individuals, whose rules are authoritative only to the extent that they derive "fair shares" from participating in it.[6] "In justice as fairness," Rawls suggests, "society is interpreted as a cooperative venture for mutual advantage." It is based upon "a public system of rules defining a scheme of activities that leads men to act together so as to produce a greater sum of benefits and assigns to each a certain recognized claim to a share in the proceeds."[7] The principles of social justice underlie the rules according to which the benefits of this venture are to be distributed. Society, in other words, is conceived by Rawls in purposive terms as an association of individuals united in the pursuit of a shared end, the production and distribution of benefits of various kinds.

Thirdly, the purposive conception of society that underlies the idea of distributive justice is incompatible with the idea of justice as conformity to the rules of an authoritative prac-

---

[5] *Theory of Justice*, p. 7, emphasis added. Later on the "assignment of fundamental rights and duties," as well as of economic benefits, is identified by Rawls as a "distributive problem" (p. 84).

[6] Ibid., p. 4.

[7] Ibid., p. 84.

tice. It is an essential characteristic of such a practice that its rules are binding on those associated in terms of the practice, regardless of the particular substantive ends to which they are devoted. But where society is understood in purposive terms, its rules cannot be authoritative unless they meet certain distributive criteria. Thus, again to take Rawls as an example, a person is obligated to conform to the rules of an organization only if the organization is substantially just according to the two principles of justice as fairness, the second of which is a principle governing the distribution of substantive goods. "Obligatory ties presuppose just institutions,"[8] and therefore there is no moral obligation to comply with rules that are (substantially) unjust, as measured against the principles Rawls proposes. This is true even where there is general acceptance of the rule in question. For Rawls, "acquiescence in, or even consent to, clearly unjust institutions does not give rise to obligations" because "unjust social arrangements are themselves a kind of extortion, even violence, and consent to them does not bind."[9]

The difficulty with all such accounts of obligation is that they confuse the authority of a body of common rules with its desirability. To acknowledge the authority of a rule is not the same thing as to approve it. The obligation to conform to a body of rules where those rules are the basis of association is not contingent upon approval of them, either by the persons whose conduct they regulate or by philosophers. In rule-based association the authority of the common rules is distinguished from judgments concerning their desirability. The associates acknowledge as authoritative both the rules in terms of which they are related and the decisions of those authorized to interpret them. For if in their disputes the members of a community were to ignore the rules and the decisions of adjudicators that did not, in the judgment of each, represent a desirable resolution of the dispute, they could not be said to

8 Ibid., p. 112.
9 Ibid., p. 343.

be governed by any common rules at all, but only by temporary agreements. It is certainly open to anyone to judge the common rules as desirable or undesirable according to some external criterion, such as whether they reflect or promote a fair distribution of substantive goods or advantages, but the authority of the common rules and the duty to respond to the considerations embodied in them are not thereby brought into question. On the contrary, evaluation of the common rules from the standpoint of their desirability presupposes acknowledgment of their authority, for without this there are no rules whose desirability can be debated.

To identify justice with the pursuit of substantive purposes is, in short, to call into question the authority of the common rules insofar as they are not shaped to the realization of those purposes. But to make the authority of the common rules conditional on approval of the purposes they are thought to serve is to violate one of the premises of association on the basis of common rules: acknowledgment of the authority of the common rules regardless of one's purposes. Therefore, in a community based on respect for the limits defined by authoritative common rules the demand for justice is restricted to the demand for impartiality—that is, for the impartial application of rules that are themselves impartial in the sense that they reflect the liberty and formal equality of the members of the community. It does not include the demand that the state promote *as such* the purposes of its members.

The objection that a formal conception of justice prevents any effective criticism of an authoritative practice is unfounded. Nothing I have said bars criticism of a practice from the perspective of particular interests, beliefs, or ethical ideals, as well as from the perspective of other authoritative practices. Certainly, one can engage in the criticism of law without embracing the view that the authority of law, and therefore the obligation to obey it, must depend upon the values in terms of which it is criticized. Furthermore, one can also criticize a moral or legal practice in terms of its own premises, for often these are violated by the practice itself.

It is this kind of immanent criticism that is at the heart of constitutional argument and that is often most effective in reforming a body of laws, while also maintaining their integrity. An authoritative practice based on the premise of individual liberty and formal equality provides its own grounds for self-criticism when it violates these principles. Justice as a moral concept makes fundamental criticism of moral and legal practices possible, without making the authority of such practices dependent upon the particular substantive ideals and purposes of those whose disparate pursuits they seek to regulate.

The diversity of things for which the word "justice" has been made to stand arises from the temptation to make use of it in advancing claims that might be expressed more precisely in other terms. Among the issues raised in debates about justice is therefore the question of the integrity of the concept itself.[10] When the concept of justice is adapted to a variety of different uses, it no longer stands for a distinct and particular way of judging human conduct. Every act must be under-

[10] An example of social criticism that resists the temptation to appropriate the concept of justice is provided by Marx's critique of capitalism. For Marx, the arrangements of capitalist society are to be judged from the standpoint of human nature, that is, according to how well they serve human needs. To make this judgment one must abandon those critical concepts that are part of the very way of life that is being criticized—concepts like "legal," "right," "obligatory," and "just." Because these concepts are derived from traditional political, legal, moral, and religious practices, to use them is to criticize a society in terms of its own principles. (Wood, "Marxian Critique of Justice," pp. 255-260, 267-272.) For a worker to demand his "rights," to demand "justice," is therefore (except perhaps a matter of tactics) conservative rather than revolutionary. In place of a criticism of capitalist society made in terms of the capitalist concept of justice, Marx proposes an alternative critique based on a scientific theory of what is good for man as a "species-being" rather than as a member of this or that historical community. The concept of justice has no place in such a theory. The consequence of Marx's rejection of the concept of justice and related juridical and moral ideas is thus in effect to preserve rather than to undermine their integrity. The controversy generated by this interpretation of Marx's views on justice may be followed in Cohen et al., *Marx, Justice, and History*, part 1, and Wood, *Karl Marx*, chs. 9 and 10.

stood as having both a purposive and a formal aspect—that is, as being at the same time action directed toward some substantive good and action relative to certain rules. Justice as a moral concept represents one way of looking at conduct, one that focuses on it in relation to rules, and in particular in relation to rules of a certain sort: those of an authoritative moral or legal practice. This concern needs to be distinguished clearly from a concern with what might be called the "economy" of an act,[11] which has to do with the relation between an act and its ends. Where expressions like "moral" and "just" are used indiscriminately to refer both to the rule-oriented and the end-oriented aspects of conduct, this essential distinction is obscured and we are forced to invent some new way of making it. No doubt any effort to limit the word "justice" in such a way as to exclude the pursuit of substantive ends would constitute a futile attempt at linguistic legislation. But one can at least hope for greater clarity concerning the precise sense in which the word is being used in a particular context.

JUSTICE IN THE SOCIETY OF STATES

Justice among states has traditionally been understood as requiring conduct according to the rules of the society of states reflected in international law and international morality. Conspicuously missing from the perennial debates concerning the character of this society and the adequacy of its rules was the issue of whether the institutions of the states system should be responsible for the social and economic well-being of its member states and their inhabitants. It is only in the present century, as the states system has become increasingly organized, that the idea of international society as an arrangement for furthering the particular substantive ends of providing social and economic benefits and redistributing global wealth has become significant. Before these developments the issue

[11] Collingwood, *Autobiography*, p. 149.

267

of distributive justice in international relations scarcely existed. Justice, in the classical system, meant conformity to "the law of nations" understood broadly as encompassing both international custom and natural law. Today, the discussion of international justice is dominated by redistributive demands and attacks on international law, in part because the states system has been transformed from a European into a worldwide society of states whose many new members possess in various international organizations a forum for the expression of their views. International justice has come to be identified with reforms aimed at securing a more equal distribution of wealth rather than with conduct according to the common rules of international society.

It is important to understand, in assessing the implications of this shift that the demand for distributive justice in the society of states is not limited to transfers of wealth from the developed states of the West to the less developed states of the Third World. It also involves changes in the rules and institutions of the society of states, especially, but not exclusively, those most directly concerned with economic matters. One can find in the arguments of those favoring redistribution some extreme rhetoric, although it is not always clear how seriously it is intended. There is, for example, the charge that the current regime of international law constitutes an exploitative order of rules created by the Western states during the colonial period—a charge that continues to be made after decades of participation by the new states in the international practice upon which customary international law is based, as well as in the renegotiation and codification of many important areas of international law, including the law of treaties, diplomatic representation, armed conflict, human rights, and the law of the sea. There is also the assertion that those who are disadvantaged by international law as it exists have no legal or moral duty to observe the limits it imposes, that unjust rules cannot create binding obligations.

To some extent these charges and claims are well founded, for to some extent it is accurate to characterize the institutions of the society of states as enterprises for the promotion of the interests of the rich and powerful. It is therefore understandable and reasonable that the disadvantaged should wish to use these institutions for their own purposes. Nor is it surprising or unreasonable that in these circumstances they should adopt an instrumentalist approach to the question of obligation. The attractions of instrumentalism grow when expressions like "civility" and "the rule of law" are invoked hypocritically to justify the pursuit of self-serving policies. Insofar as international institutions are indeed enterprises for the pursuit of particular purposes, judgments of their desirability and of the authority of their rules will appropriately depend upon instrumentalist considerations. The rationale of participation in a purposive association lies in the advantages to be derived from it.

But, as I have tried to show, it is a mistake to regard international society itself as an association of this kind. Although states may decide how they will interact with each other *within* it (by making treaties or becoming members of international organizations), they are members of the society of states as such whether they choose to be or not. A state may withdraw from the International Labor Organization, but not from international society. A state may seek to minimize its transactions with other countries, but no state can participate in international society entirely on its own terms. The idea of society is the idea of certain shared understandings, practices, and standards of conduct. Even the most isolated states cannot escape the rules defining statehood, sovereignty, and territorial jurisdiction, and it is hard to imagine any state succeeding for long in ignorning the rules governing treaties and diplomatic representation. A state, like an individual, may be impatient with the rules and duties of social existence, but it cannot escape them so long as there remains any regular contact with others.

There are certain principles of customary international law that are so basic that it makes sense to say that they reflect the requirements of society in the circumstances of international relations. These principles include the independence and legal equality of states, the right of self-defense, the duty of nonintervention, the obligation to observe treaties, and restrictions on the conduct of war.[12] Although one may make the authority of a purposive arrangement, such as that of a treaty or international organization, contingent on whether or not it is successful in serving its assigned purpose, the authority of those rules that are constitutive of international society itself is independent of any such consideration. If there exists an international society, in the sense of a universal association of states within a common framework of rules, it follows that individual states are not at liberty to accept or reject these rules at will, or to insist on their own private understanding of what the rules require in particular situations. And this is so regardless of whether or not these rules are advantageous, fair, or otherwise desirable. To require that all states benefit from a rule as a condition of acknowledging its authority is to demand the unattainable and to make life according to rules impossible.

Deference to the limits defined by a common set of rules means more than abandoning the proposition that the pursuit of particular substantive goals, such as economic development and redistribution, should override even the most fundamental and morally significant principles of international association. It also means that, even if the desirability of these rules is carefully distinguished from the question of their authority and ideals of distributive justice brought forward only as a standard for the criticism and reform of international law and institutions, any proposed alteration must itself be evaluated according to the constitutional principles embodied in international law and morality. Foreign policy in the world as it is cannot ignore distributive considerations, for the states system rests in part upon purposive arrangements that are

---

[12] This list of basic principles resembles closely that defended by Rawls in *Theory of Justice*, pp. 378-379. It is noteworthy that Rawls's account of international justice does not include principles governing the distribution of substantive goods, although such principles do apply within the state.

open to criticism in purposive terms. Furthermore, redistributive policies might indeed strengthen the foundations of a rule-based international order. But that a particular redistributive proposal violates acknowledged moral limits is a consideration that should tell decisively against it. A just world is a world in which distributive considerations are subordinated to moral ones, not the reverse.

Despite their occasionally extreme rhetoric, this seems to be generally understood by the advocates of international redistribution. The demand for a "new international economic order" is basically a demand that certain rules of international law regulating international economic relations be altered to advance the development and increase the autonomy of the non-Western nations. It is essentially a set of proposals for reform, and like all such proposals it presupposes the existence and continued viability of the institutions within which the desired changes are to be implemented. The demand, for example, that the new states have a significant voice in an International Seabed Authority assumes an effective authority whose legal powers will be generally recognized. The demand for trade preferences requires a legally binding structure of trade rules into which preferential tariffs can be incorporated. Even the demand for exemptions from the requirements of international law, which is often made by representatives of the new states in treaty negotiations, presupposes rules from which exemptions can be granted and which others are required to observe. None of the changes sought by the less developed states as part of a "planetary bargain" with the developed states can be realized except on the basis of an authoritative body of common rules. While it is usual to demand that international law serve as the instrument of some higher purpose such as economic development and redistribution and that the only rules anyone has a duty to observe are those that serve to further these ends, the actual conduct of states suggests widespread recognition that such a doctrine is in fact subversive of a common moral order.

COSMOPOLITAN JUSTICE AND INDIVIDUAL RIGHTS

In attempting to make explicit one dimension of the controversy concerning the meaning of international justice, I have ignored another: the extent to which international justice concerns the liberty or welfare of individuals. Although, as I argued in the preceding chapter, international law as traditionally understood included a characteristically moral concern for individual liberty, this concern was reflected for the most part only indirectly in that law. Until the present century the individual possessed virtually no status and no rights under international law. International society was a society of states, and this meant that only states were regarded as members of that society and as subjects of international law. International justice, in other words, meant justice among states. A good illustration of the way in which international law avoided the problem of regulating individual conduct is provided by its principles of responsibility. If the citizens or officials of one state injured someone who was a national of another, it was the first state and not its citizens or officials that incurred international responsibility, and it was the state of the injured party that was considered to have suffered a wrong and to have a right to seek redress. Similarly, while a state might appear as a litigant before an international tribunal, an individual could not. If a person wished to press a legal claim against a foreign government, his only recourse, other than bringing an action against it in its own courts, was to have his claim adopted by his government as its own. Only in exceptional circumstances could an individual advance claims or be held responsible directly on the basis of international law.

During the present century the idea that international law regulates only the conduct of states has come to be challenged. The principle of indivdual responsibility under international law for a variety of acts is now well established, as is the idea that the definition and protection of individual rights is something with which international law may properly concern itself. The view that states have a duty to respect individual rights has received even more support outside positive international law, where a new cosmopolitan ethic based on the moral unity of the human community seems to have established itself. Weight is once again being given to the idea of a universal human community and to the belief that it is unjust to discriminate among members of this community according to whether or not they are members of the more restricted local communities to which we ourselves belong. For some the plausibility of this view is bolstered by the idea that international interdependence is rendering the division of mankind into states increasingly irrelevant to judgments about what is just in world affairs. In its more utopian versions cosmopolitanism regards the state system as an obsolete institution that must be transcended and envisions a world order in which states would cease to exercise sovereign powers and would become little more than administrative units within an inclusive world polity. A single moral and legal order would have replaced the plural order of the states system.[13]

[13] A cosmopolitan ethic based on Rawlsian principles is defended by Beitz, *Political Theory and International Relations*. For an example of "utopian cosmopolitanism," see Falk, "Anarchism and World Order." The degree to which cosmopolitanism is accepted in Western countries is unclear; outside the West its appeal would appear to be small. The proposals for a "new international economic order" contained in the Declaration on the Establishment of a New International Economic Order (United Nations General Assembly Resolution 3201, S-VI, May 1974) and the Charter of Economic Rights and Duties of States (Resolution 3281, XXIX, December 1974) are addressed to the problem of achieving global justice through the redistribution of wealth and power from the rich to the poor states. They are not concerned with inequalities among individuals within the poor states, or with measures aimed at internal redistribution. Thus, as Robert W. Tucker in *Inequality of Nations*, pp. 61-65, 155-156, 178-179, and others have argued, it is not the state-centric assumptions of the existing international order that are challenged but rather the distribution of wealth and power within it. The proposals, moreover, do not seek to strengthen respect for individual rights. On the contrary, they seek to increase the discretion of the governments of the less developed states by relaxing the constraints imposed on them by international law to respect individual rights.

Despite their recurrent appeal, the utopian versions of cosmopolitanism are neither representative of, nor essential to, a cosmopolitan morality. Indeed, in their preoccupation with the notion of a future world order they distract our attention from what is perhaps the most significant element of cosmopolitanism: that the members of the society of states have duties toward individuals as well as toward other states. The idea of cosmopolitan justice does not require the disappearance of the state as a form of human association any more than it requires that we abandon the family, municipality, or private association. But it does require that the rights of individuals be respected by governments. The essential element of cosmopolitan justice in the circumstances of the states system is the idea of an international minimum standard to be observed by states in their treatment of individuals, regardless of whether these are their own nationals or those of another country. The most significant task of cosmopolitan thinking is to provide a basis for criticism of the principles governing the conduct of states toward individuals.

International law has for some time included such principles and sought to provide for their application. One of the most important of them is the principle of state responsibility for injuries to aliens, according to which states are to be held accountable for conduct toward the nationals of other states that falls below a certain minimum standard that is embodied in customary international law and enforcible by an appropriate tribunal. But the definition and even the existence of such a standard has always been controversial, as has the identity of the appropriate tribunal. More recently, principles of cosmopolitan justice have tended to be expressed in terms of the idea of internationally protected human rights. The idea of human rights follows directly from the ideal of a universal human community, for human rights are rights persons have as members of such a community—that is, as human beings—and not as citizens of a particular state. But nothing in the idea of human rights rules out the possibility that the postulated universal community might organize itself as a society

274

of states. And if it is organized in this manner, the idea of human rights requires that these rights be acknowledged and respected by states. This, in turn, is most likely to occur if human rights are given a foundation in the common rules of conduct governing the society of states, that is, in international law. The tendency of efforts to strengthen respect for human rights is thus toward the creation of rules and institutions that would require states to treat all persons, and especially their own inhabitants, according to certain internationally recognized standards and that would make states accountable in an international forum for failing to do so.

There is, therefore, no reason why the regime of international rules conferring rights on individuals might not be greatly augmented within the framework of the society of states and international law as we know it. This is sometimes denied, on the grounds that the idea of human rights is incompatible with the premises of the states system and classical international law. But this is a mistake. Strengthening the international regime of human rights would, it is true, require changing many particular international practices and rules. Among the more noticeable of such changes would be a reduction in the weight allowed to the principle of domestic jurisdiction and therefore some alteration in the definition and scope of intervention. Those changes would in turn involve further restrictions on the traditional sovereign powers of states. But state sovereignty would not necessarily vanish, nor would the principle of nonintervention become irrelevant. International law in general and the international minimum standard in particular would continue to be based on the practices and agreements of states.

International justice, then, does not exclude a concern for individual rights. But neither does it follow that everything that has been claimed under the label of human rights is something that falls properly within the scope of international morality and international law. In practical association the ideas of justice and rights are intimately connected. Each reflects, from a slightly different angle, the constraints of a common body of practices and rules. To speak of rights is to invoke the considerations of a moral or legal practice in such a way as to emphasize the point of view of those toward whom one has a duty or obligation. To fail in that duty or obligation would be an injustice *to them.*[14] It is the most basic and general of these duties, such as the duty to avoid interfering arbitrarily with the liberty of individuals to live, think, worship, and associate as they choose, that we point to when we speak of human rights. To insist on respect for human rights is to demand that the policies and laws of a community reflect the principles of impartiality with respect to persons and their ends inherent in the idea of practical association. It is to judge these policies and laws not according to their relation to the achievement of particular substantive purposes or goods but in terms of their relation to the common good of the community. And this common good is not an aggregate of substantive benefits to be distributed but simply the totality of those conditions, embodied in the common rules of the community, for the pursuit by its members of their own self-chosen ends.

Debates about the content of human rights are therefore best understood as debates about the common good. Some human rights, such as the right not to be tortured or enslaved, or subjected to arbitrary arrest, detention, or exile, are unquestionably part of the common good. They are rights that are implicit in the idea of persons as members of a community governed according to the principles of impartiality, individual freedom, formal equality, and the rule of law. They reflect what it means to be an associate of such a community. Other human rights, such as the right to vote, are less fundamental because they pertain to the contingent arrangements of certain forms of political community. As such they constitute part of the common good of some, but not all, com-

[14] "The modern vocabulary and grammar of rights . . . provides a way of talking about 'what is just' from . . . the viewpoint of the 'other(s)' to whom something . . . is owed or due, and who would be wronged if denied that something." (Finnis, *Natural Law and Natural Rights*, p. 205.)

munities. Finally, there are those human rights that have to do not with the premises of practical association itself, nor with the particular forms it might assume under various circumstances, but with the pursuit and distribution of substantive goods bearing only a contingent relation to the existence of practical association. Like the idea of social justice, this last and necessarily open-ended class of rights—usually labeled "social and economic human rights"—reflects a purposive conception of society and raises similar issues. Although such rights constitute part of the common good, they are nevertheless a subordinate part: substantive or external goods whose pursuit is subject to the constraints of impartiality, noninterference, and mutual accommodation that constitute the core of the common good in any community of formal equals. Practical association disappears when respect for these constraints is reduced to the level of one set of social goals among others and the common good subordinated to the pursuit of other goods.

CHAPTER 11

Justice in War

THE IDEA of justice in war follows from the existence of a
common good even for societies whose members are at war
with one another, as is often the case in the society of states.
The content of this common good is, moreover, reasonably
clear. It consists of constraints on the initiation of war and on
the conduct of hostilities once war has begun: constraints such
as the avoidance of aggression, a willingness to make peace
on reasonable terms, insistence on military discipline, and
respect for the rights of civilians, the wounded, and prisoners
of war. Thus, in war as well as peace, the content of the
common good it to be found in the common rules of international society—that is, in the standards embodied in the
authoritative practices of international law and international
morality. It is to these rules and standards that one turns both
in seeking to act justly and in judging the justice of past actions. Although the criteria of justice in war have traditionally
allowed the pursuit of certain ends as a lawful ground for
using force, it is a misconception to think that force is justified if it is used for a good end. An act of war, like any other
act, is just or unjust in relation to the considerations of a
moral practice, not in relation to its instrumental utility for
the realization of desired ends. The expression "just war,"
like "justice" itself, is not a general term of approbation, but
one specific to discourse concerning the relation between
conduct and rules.

Many of the perplexities raised by the idea of justice in
international wars have to do with the character of war itself
rather than with the specific forms it may assume in the circumstances of the society of states. The idea of the just war

278

is much older than that of the society of states, and it continues to have relevance for wars that, like civil wars, take place outside the framework of interstate relations. Therefore a comprehensive discussion of justice in war cannot be limited to the topic of war among states. My concern here, however, is not with war in general but with the place of war in international society, and in particular with the implications of the ideas about international law and morality explored in the preceding pages for understanding the rights and wrongs of war among states.

THE RIGHT TO MAKE WAR

The right of a state to make war presupposes the existence of rules from which that right can be derived. It rests, in other words, on the premise that states comprise a society constituted by authoritative common practices and rules. But the right to make war also assumes that the rules governing the use of force significantly circumscribe the liberty of states to make war, for if the rules permit sovereigns to attack whom they please the resort to war by states cannot be said to be regulated. An unrestricted right of self-help places the initiation of war by states beyond the reach of legal and moral judgment. Any war that a sovereign chooses to wage becomes a just war.

As this last is a view of justice in war that has existed throughout the modern period, its origin and rationale are worth considering. The ancient idea that a war cannot be just unless it has been declared by a duly constituted authority appears to have acquired increasing importance in the fourteenth century as a consequence of two developments. One was the need arising from the anarchy and turbulence of the Hundred Years' War to control the depredations of freebooters. The other was the increasing authority of certain powerful lords who claimed, as princes, to possess rights superior to those of other nobles. One of these rights was the right to declare war. The use of force in self-defense was recognized as lawful for private persons, but it did not create a legal state of war and private persons could not lawfully resort to arms except in self-defense. Only "public war" initiated by the authority of a prince was lawful or just.[1] But this solution, which answered the question of how the justice of wars within the state might authoritatively be judged, only exacerbated the problem of determining the justice of wars among states. Each prince was "sovereign": a ruler without secular superior, so far as the government of his realm was concerned. The subjects of a prince were legally constrained to use force within limits imposed by a superior, but the prince himself acted under no such constraint.

This history should cause us to rethink our assumptions concerning the relation between war and peace, which we are accustomed to regard as alternatives. Organized warfare against foreigners is very different from the violence that disrupts a political community itself. In the late Middle Ages, before the invention of the modern state, civil peace was rare and unreliable. This was especially the case during the latter part of the fourteenth century. In a society permeated by violence, the gradual consolidation of the right to make war in the hands of a few recognized sovereigns, who were increasingly the only powers capable of enforcing it, was thus a victory for internal peace and order. At the same time the definition of a just war as one authorized by a sovereign imposed no limit on wars between sovereign states. It is true that authorization by a sovereign was not the only recognized criterion for judging whether a war was just or unjust, for, as Augustine, Aquinas, and others had argued, the justice of a war also depends upon the ends for which, and the means by which, it is fought. But the tendency throughout the late medieval and early modern period was toward assimilation of the criterion of ends under the category of authorization by the sovereign power. Only the requirement that war, once under way, be conducted so as to spare clerics, prisoners of war,

---

[1] Keen, *Laws of War in the Late Middle Ages*, pp. 66-70.

farmers, and other noncombatants continued to impose significant limits on the conduct of war among sovereign states. Although theologians and moralists argued that there existed restrictions on the right of sovereigns to make war, the idea of the just war in Europe between the seventeenth and twentieth centuries was often scarcely distinguishable from the idea of reason of state, which would appear to be its opposite.[2]

In the present century this state of affairs has increasingly come to be regarded as intolerable, not only because of the evident urgency of the need to limit war but also because the failure of international law to limit the initiation of war is now seen as undermining the reality of international law itself. As J. L. Brierly argued in 1944, the absence of such limitations is inconsistent with the idea of a rule-governed international order. While professing to be a system of law, the international legal system was in his view "incapable of making the most elementary of all legal distinctions, that between the lawful and the unlawful use of physical force." This was not merely a weakness, it was an absurdity: "To hold at one and the same time that states are legally bound to respect each other's independence and other rights, and yet are free to attack each other at will, is a logical impossibility."[3] Revival of the distinction between just and unjust wars within the framework of international law had come by the end of the Second World War to be seen as an indispensable element of the international rule of law.

This shift in an attitude toward the right of states to make war that had prevailed in Europe for several centuries appears to have begun during the Great War of 1914-1918. To-

[2] On the transformation of just war principles into the doctrines of *raison d'état* and *compétence de guerre*, see Sturzo, *International Community and the Right of War*, pp. 181-182; Midgley, *Natural Law Tradition and the Theory of International Relations*, chs. 2-6; and Johnson, *Just War Tradition and the Restraint of War*, pp. 170-178. The importance during the Middle Ages of legitimate authority as a criterion of just war is considered by Johnson at pp. 123, 150-165, 166, and 168-170.

[3] *Outlook for International Law*, p. 21.

ward the end of the war the idea emerged that Germany was the aggressor against whom Britian and France, with American help, were defending themselves. Punitive provisions reflecting this understanding of the origins of the war were written into the Treaty of Versailles, and an abortive attempt was made to prosecute the Kaiser for war crimes. Scholarly interest in the idea of the just war flourished.[4] The next world war reinforced the increasingly accepted view that just wars were defensive. Among the crimes for which German and Japanese leaders were held accountable at the war crimes trials following the war were those characterized at Nuremberg as "crimes against peace," defined as the "planning, preparation, initiation, or waging of aggression."[5] A just war, by implication, is one waged to resist aggression—a war of self-defense. This identification of injustice with aggression and justice with self-defense is reflected in the Charter of the United Nations, which explicitly rules out the threat or use of force against the political independence or territorial integrity of any state, while allowing the use of force in self-defense.[6] But if the sole justified ground for resorting to armed force is to repel aggression, much will depend on how "aggression" is defined and on the degree to which a common definition is recognized throughout the international community.

The division of all acts of war into two classes, those that are aggressive and those that are defensive, suggests that aggression is a breach of peace and self-defense a response to that breach. Yet to identify aggression with the violation of a condition of peace is simply to push the argument back a step, from debate concerning the meaning of "aggression" to that concerning the meaning of "peace." Two distinct conceptions of aggression as a breach of peace are reflected in the Charter. According to one conception, an act of aggression is

[4] On the revival of just war thinking after the First World War, see Bull, "Grotian Conception of International Society."

[5] *Judgment of the International Military Tribunal at Nuremberg*, p. 3.

[6] Art. 2(4) and Art. 51.

an armed attack by one state against another, regardless of the circumstances and justifications attending it. The other, taking account of these circumstances and justifications, identifies aggression with the use or threat of force by one state against another in a manner that violates international law. Aggression, according to the first definition, is a fact; according to the second, which defines it in relation to standards of conduct, it is a wrong.[7] In the first case, the peace that is disrupted by war is a condition defined by the absence of fighting; in the second, it is a condition in which disputes are settled on the basis of common rules.

If peace is no more than the absence of fighting, then any state that resorts to armed force commits an act of aggression. But can peace plausibly be defined in this way? Even Hobbes's definition of war identifies it not only with fighting but also with "the known disposition thereto during all the time there is no assurance to the contrary."[8] To say, as he does, that "all other time is peace" is to define peace in terms of the existence of such assurances. Peace is not merely the absence of war but a social state in which war need not be feared because peace is guaranteed by a pact creating political institutions to define and enforce its terms. (It is because there is no state within which sovereigns are themselves united that international relations remains, for Hobbes, a condition of war.) Kant's view is similar. "A state of peace among men living together is not the same as a state of nature, which is rather a state of war. For even if it does not involve active hostilities, it involves a constant threat of their breaking out. Thus the state of peace must be *formally instituted*, for a suspension of hostilities is not in itself a guarantee of peace."[9] Peace, on

---

[7] The implications of this distinction for the conception of the just war embodied in the United Nations Charter are explored by Johnson, "Toward Reconstructing the Jus Ad Bellum," pp. 469-475. On the genesis and interpretation of the Charter's crucial Article 2, Paragraph 4, see Goodrich et al., *Charter of the United Nations*, pp. 43-55.

[8] *Leviathan*, ch. 13.

[9] *Political Writings*, p. 98.

this view, is a juridical rather than a natural condition. It is not a condition to be enjoyed whenever the fighting has ceased but one that can only be realized and preserved through political artifice and on the basis of law.

That this conception of peace is not limited to the theories of a handful of philosophers is suggested by the etymological link between the words "peace" and "pact." The former, together with the French *paix*, is descended from the Latin *pax*, which is itself thought to have been derived from the hypothetical Indo-European *pak*, meaning "to fasten." Other Latin descendants from this root include *pangere*, "to fasten," and *pacisci*, "to confirm an agreement." And from this cluster of Latin words we have the English "pact" as well as "peace." The ideas of peace and compact are also closely related. A peace is a compact or agreement, typically a most solemn legal agreement, not to fight. The medieval *paces* and *Frieden*, for example, were initially legal agreements establishing certain immunities for ecclesiastical bodies in the Gothic kingdoms, subsequently enlarged to provide legal security for other limited spheres of life such as the home, the popular assembly, and the highways. As time went on such peaces multiplied, became more inclusive, and began to overlap in jurisdiction, resulting in the development of increasingly general and permanent systems of law.[10] Peace is disrupted, according to the juridical view, only when force is used in violation of the common law.

When peace is understood in this way, it is not the use of armed force that constitutes aggression but rather the use of force in a way that violates the rights established by a juridical or moral order. Aggression is a disruption not of "peace," understood as the mere absence of fighting, but of "peace-with-rights."[11] Aggression, which disrupts the peace within which members of the society of states enjoy the rights of political sovereignty and territorial integrity, is not a mere

[10] Bozeman, *Future of Law in a Multicultural World*, pp. 43-44; Wright, "Peace," p. 490.
[11] Walzer, *Just and Unjust Wars*, p. 51.

fact but a wrong. The use of force to meet this disruption is justified because it is a way of deterring and punishing a wrong. The resort to war is therefore never a matter wholly within the discretion of the state, in the sense that it is unregulated by international standards. In complete contrast to the view of nineteenth-century positivist international lawyers that the decision to go to war is immune from judgment on the basis of international law, just war thinking regards war as always either a crime or a remedy.[12]

The premise of the idea of the just war, insofar as it pertains to war within the society of states, is that the states comprising this society are related to one another in the same way that citizens are related within the civil order of a political community: as associates united by their acknowledgment of the authority of a common body of rules. In the same way that the civil order of the state is founded on the juridical equality, liberty, and personal security of its citizens, international legal and moral order rests on the formal equality, liberty, and security of the independent political communities comprising the society of states. The equality and liberty of states are embodied in the idea of sovereignty, their security in the idea of territorial integrity. Therefore states must respect each other's political sovereignty and territorial integrity, unless by its conduct a state forfeits its right to this respect. A state that commits aggression exposes itself to the just efforts of other states to defend their rights. An aggressor state that suffers attack by those whom it has wrongly injured is not itself a victim of aggression, provided the response of those whose rights have been violated respects the standards of morality and international law. The use of force is "unjust" when it violates these standards of international association, "just" when it is relied upon to uphold them.

It follows that the just use of armed force is not limited to self-defense, unless "defense" is interpreted very broadly. A

---

[12] According to the idea of the just war, war is, in Kelsen's terminology, either a "delict" or a "sanction." (*Principles of International Law*, p. 29.)

state defending its rights as a member of international society does more than defend itself against armed attack, for those rights may be violated in many ways. In the mainstream of just war thinking—that running through Vitoria, Suarez, Grotius, Locke, and Vattel, each of whom was concerned with the problem of how to reconcile divergent wills within a common moral order—every sovereign has a duty to uphold the law of nations. As Walzer, summarizing the collective judgment of these thinkers, suggests, "the rights of the member states must be vindicated, for it is only by virtue of those rights that there is a society at all. If they cannot be upheld (at least sometimes), international society collapses into a state of war or is transformed into a universal tyranny."[13] A state may seek vindication of its rights through self-help because there is no superior power upon whom it can rely. Furthermore, because aggression is both an attack against a particular state and a crime against international society itself, resistance to aggression is an act of law enforcement as well as of self-defense. A state that goes to war to resist aggression is not merely defending its interests and security. Indeed, in some situations these ends may be better served by capitulation. By defending its rights it is upholding the common rules of the society of states. It defends the international community by acting on those principles that make it a community.[14]

[13] *Just and Unjust Wars*, p. 59.

[14] A just war, so understood, must be distinguished from a "holy war" undertaken to propagate a religious faith. Such a war—a crusade or *jihad*—may indeed be "holy" in terms of the religious ends it is intended to serve, but it is not on that account "just." "In the notion of the Just War, the premise is that all parties *have* their due rights, and war is a means of penalizing violation of right and ensuring restoration and restitution. It is a juridical conception, of war as the instrument of law. In the notion of the Holy War, the premise is that the true believers *are* right, and that infidels are to be converted or exterminated. . . . It is a religious conception, of war as the instrument of God's will, or of history." (Wight, *Systems of States*, pp. 34-35.) The view of war as an act of justice when undertaken in defense of law or for the punishment of criminal acts has been a part of Christian thought

The dissociation of the right to make war from self-defense has another implication as well, and this is that a state may in some circumstances use force to vindicate the rights of other states and their inhabitants. The defense of rights is not limited to "self-" defense. Therefore a state may in certain circumstances come to the aid of those who are the victims of aggression, even if it has not itself been directly injured. A state that commits aggression invites the concern and possibly the intervention of the other members of the society of states, each of whom has a legitimate interest in seeing that the rules upon which that society rests are upheld. Furthermore, aggression against other states is not the only ground for a response by other states. A state may become liable to intervention by other states—and in extreme cases, to armed intervention—because of its domestic as well as its foreign policies. The rights of political sovereignty and territorial integrity are not absolute, and therefore the ban on intervention is not absolute either. The limits of sovereignty on the one hand and of intervention on the other are determined by the standards of international law and morality, and these include an international minimum standard of conduct according to which the relation between a government and its own subjects may be judged.[15]

JUSTICE AND THE CONDUCT OF WAR

If the idea of international society requires that the discretion of states to make war be limited by common standards, it equally requires common standards for the conduct of hostilities once war has begun. Yet the idea of fighting according

at least since Augustine and was first adapted to the relations among sovereigns in the writings of certain early modern thinkers working within the scholastic tradition. See, for example, Suarez, *On the Three Theological Virtues*, D. XIII, s.iv.

[15] The moral content of this international minimum standard is considered in connection with the topics of sovereignty, intervention, and individual rights, in Chapters 9 and 10, above, and more fully in the reference cited there.

to rules strikes many people as paradoxical. We commonly think of rules as part of the order of a society at peace and of war as a breakdown of rules and of order: a condition in which the normal order of life is turned on its head. "War," says Herodotus, is "a state in which instead of sons burying their fathers, fathers bury their sons."[16] But it does not follow from the fact that in war the normal order of society is disrupted that the state of war is one without order. The alternative to life according to one set of rules is not necessarily life without any rules at all, but rather life according to different rules. Only exceptionally does war approach the anarchy of ubiquitous and indiscriminate violence. On the contrary, war is an institution with its own characteristic practices and rules. It is, as Rousseau suggests, "a permanent state that presupposes constant relations,"[17] by which he means, I think, that it is a normal and regular activity for which provision is made in the internal as well as the international arrangements of states. That war is a disorder of the states system does not mean that it is itself without order. And that order rests in part on the customs and laws of warfare. Only on the view—one that has, indeed, often been put forward—that war represents the total destruction of international society does the idea that war is necessarily without restraint, that all war is total war, even begin to appear plausible.

The basic premise underlying the idea of just conduct in war is the same as that underlying the idea of international society itself: that international conduct, including the military conduct of statesmen and soldiers, falls under the jurisdiction of authoritative and not merely prudential rules. This does not mean that the rules are always observed, or that the authoritative considerations upon which legal and moral judgments of military conduct are based must always be understood as abstract and determinate rules. The idea of international society means that in war no less than in peace

[16] *Histories*, I, 87.
[17] *Oeuvres complètes*, 3:602.

international conduct is to be directed and judged with reference to recognized standards. But the specific constraints
imposed on military conduct by these standards depend on
circumstances. Ideas and principles are affected by experience. The meaning of ideas such as "military necessity," "military objective," and "incidental damage," for example, is altered by changes in military technique, and these changes
lead in turn to differences in the scope and application of
principles, such as the principle of noncombatant immunity,
that are expressed in terms of these ideas. Underlying the
historical, cultural, and circumstantial diversity of institutionalized warfare, however, is the core notion that military conduct, like all conduct, falls under the jurisdiction of moral and
legal constraints, as well as considerable agreement concerning the content of those constraints.

Conduct prohibited by the rules of war has traditionally
been regarded as falling into two classes, the first defined by
restrictions on weapons and methods of warfare, the second
by restrictions on permissible targets. Restrictions on the use
of poison gas, expanding bullets, biological weapons, or tar-
get-area bombing illustrate constraints of the first kind, while
the latter are manifested in prohibitions of attacks on hospi-
tals, dams, historic monuments, children, or prisoners of war.
In practice the two kinds of constraints often overlap, but
from the moral point of view it is the latter that are fundamental. Such limits embody the basic principle of war understood as an activity within the society of states: that war "is
not a relation among men, but among states," and that in war
"individuals are enemies only by chance, not as men, nor
even as citizens, but as soldiers; not as members of their
country, but as its defenders."[18] From this principle follows
another, that of noncombatant immunity, according to which
it is forbidden to attack those who are not directly engaged
in the military struggle: soldiers who are wounded or who
have been taken prisoner, for example, or civilians engaged

[18] Ibid., p. 357.

in military activity. Those who do not participate in military activities are "innocent," in the traditional vocabulary of moral theology, and it is wrong to attack them on purpose, although they may without injustice be harmed incidentally in the course of attacks on permitted targets.

The rationale for such limitations on military conduct is certainly in part that the conduct to be limited is often inexpedient. Why kill a captured knight whose value in ransom might be considerable, or visit upon an enemy atrocities likely to be returned in kind? From about the middle of the seventeenth century, civilian lives and property were protected from destruction largely because the economic advantages of preserving them outweighed the military advantages of wanton violence. Pillage and devastation, while on occasion deliberately adopted as a means of warfare, were increasingly restricted. The ever larger armies of the European monarchs, which lived by requisition off the land and therefore had an interest in preserving the source of their supplies, were thus provided with a strong incentive to maintain the local agricultural economy. The recklessness and brutality so often brought on by war were recognized as dangers to be repressed, or at least controlled, by prudent sovereigns and commanders, for they not only threatened the discipline and military effectiveness of the armies under their command but also tended to unleash forces attacking the foundations of established power. Relations between the armed forces of states at war were also improved by the traditions of military professionalism decended from the medieval institution of the calling to arms. Chivalry, however, was never an attitude directly relevant to the treatment of civilians, for its norms applied largely to the conduct of men of rank toward one another and were compatible with the grossest brutality toward common people.

As the laws of war evolved, considerations of expediency were formalized in the concepts of "military necessity" and "proportionality." The result was a calculus of advantage in which practices were condemned that did not further, or were an obstacle to, the realization of military purposes. *Gratuitous* violence and *excessive* damage were ruled out. But no practice was absolutely barred, for any practice might under some circumstances turn out to be necessary—that is, expedient. It was not until the middle of the nineteenth century that the idea began to take hold that certain military practices should be prohibited, regardless of their utility, because they were inhumane. The founding of the International Committee of the Red Cross to look after the welfare of soldiers wounded, sick, shipwrecked, or in the hands of the enemy reflects a growing humanitarianism, which historians have linked to the increasingly middle class and commercial character of European societies during the industial revolution.[19] As the laws of war continued to evolve during this period and were increasingly codified in national military law and in international treaties, such as the successive Geneva and Hague Conventions, humanitarian considerations took their place beside those of expediency. The result was an uncomfortable tension: when military and humanitarian considerations pulled in opposite directions, which came first? Too often it was expediency—or that which was mistakenly believed to be expedient—that carried the day. As a basis for standards of conduct in war, humanitarian principles are perpetually subject to corruption by the rude pressures of necessity on the one hand, and the seductive lure of a higher humanitarianism on the other. Whereas the first tempts us to waive the prohibitions of the rules of war for the sake of momentary advantage, the latter invites us to inflate the worth of the ends for which we are fighting, identifying the victory of our own side, for example, with the liberty, welfare, and sometimes even the survival of humanity as a whole (as Secretary of State Dean Rusk argued in the case of the Vietnam War, which he defended before Congress as necessary to prevent a third world war). In either case, the appeal to humanitarian ends is used

[19] The history of the laws of war from the eighteenth century is examined from a humanitarian rather than a moral perspective by Best, *Humanity in Warfare*.

to justify conduct that violates the common rules, which appear as an obstacle to their realization.

Therefore to the extent that limitations on the conduct of war are grounded on humanitarian considerations they do not represent a departure from an essentially purposive conception of warfare as a means to some putatively good end. On the contrary, the principle that the use of military force must be limited to what is necessary to accomplish the purposes of war and the principle that in the use of military force weight is to be given to humanitarian considerations are in fact two ways of expressing a single underlying idea. The principle of military necessity does not justify gratuitous or excessive injury. And the principle that one should fight as humanely as possible does not rule out all uses of force that cause suffering and other injury. It is only unnecessary damage that is prohibited. So the increasing emphasis on humanitarian considerations represents no more than an alteration of the weight to be given, in estimating the costs of victory, to the welfare of those affected by the struggle.

The view that military conduct is subject to constraints derived from the existence of certain fundamental human rights constitutes a more radical challenge to the idea that military conduct is limited only by the demands of necessity and proportionality.[20] Humanitarianism, or a concern with human welfare, always operates within bounds defined by expediency, for the duty to avoid harm is always a duty to avoid unnecessary or disproportionate harm. But a morality of war

[20] The view that human rights are fundamental to the laws of war has gained in acceptance among diplomats, lawyers, and moralists since the Vietnam War. Revision of the laws of war was for several years after 1968 an annual item on the agenda of the United Nations General Assembly under the title "The Protection of Human Rights in Armed Conflicts." That the regime of human rights law derived from the Charter and other treaties is the most significant present source of moral restraints on the conduct of war is argued by Draper, "Ethical and Juridical Status of Constraints in War," pp. 177, 179, 184. The morality of war expounded by Walzer is presented as a morality of human rights. (*Just and Unjust Wars*, pp. xv-xvi, 53-54, 134-135.)

founded on human rights prescribes a more exacting standard. If military conduct that violates human rights is wrong,
then a limit has been placed on considerations of expediency.
Bringing in the idea of human rights does more than simply
make it harder to justify such things as killing prisoners of
war or bombing cities; it brings in considerations of a different order. If there are human rights, then there are limits to
military conduct beyond which utilitarian calculations are not
permitted to carry one. Some ways of fighting are ruled out,
even if to refrain from them is to forgo military advantages
that may be important, even "necessary," for achieving one's
ends.

International law gives support to the view that considerations of military expediency operate within the bounds of more
or less absolute prohibitions of the sort that follow from the
idea of human rights. Consider, for example, the rules appended to the Fourth Hague Convention of 1907, rules that
have been incorporated into the military codes of many states
and are generally acknowledged to have acquired the status
of customary international law.[21] According to the Hague
Convention it is prohibited without exception to "kill or wound
any enemy who, having laid down his arms, or having no
longer means of defense, has surrendered at discretion,"[22] or
to engage in "the attack or bombardment, by whatever means,
of towns, villages, dwellings, or buildings which are unde-
fended."[23] According to other provisions of the Convention,
it is always wrong to allow troops to pillage and rape, to make
hostages of civilians, and deceptively to display a flag or other
sight of truce. These rules are absolute in the sense that they
may not be overriden by considerations of military necessity.
If a measure is forbidden by international law, it cannot be
justified by appeal to the principle of military necessity. Such

---

[21] A convenient and reliable source for the Hague Conventions and other
treaties pertaining to the conduct of war is Schindler and Toman, *Law of
Armed Conflicts*.

[22] Art. 23c.

[23] Art. 25.

absolute prohibitions might conceivably be defended in terms of long-range utility: all states, it might be argued, would be better off in the long run if they were to accept the short-run military disadvantages that acceptance of such restraints might produce in particular circumstances.[24] The human rights argument, however, seeks to justify these prohibitions without relying on such considerations.

Respect for human rights does not necessarily rule out all utilitarian calculations, but it does circumscribe the scope of these calculations within a set of moral constraints that are not themselves the outcome of utilitarian calculation. The argument for such constraints, however, could be made—and possibly made better—without relying on the idea of human rights. Moral rules may be thought of as giving rise to rights, just as they give rise to duties. But it is the rules, not the rights, that are fundamental. The view that the rules of war are founded ultimately on human rights is forced simply to postulate the existence of certain rights, for there is—by hypothesis—no more fundamental body of rules from which such rights can be derived. Unlike the moral and legal rights defined by the practices and rules of particular communities, human rights are mysterious entities. An account of rights and duties in war that begins with the concept of morality as a certain kind of authoritative practice avoids the difficulties of trying to defend a theory of rights apart from a theory of moral rules. The idea of human rights reflects the moral point of view, but it does not explain it.

WAR AND THE BOUNDS OF MORAL CONDUCT

The idea of moral conduct in the waging of war has always inspired doubts and misgivings. There is, on the one hand, the fear that in accepting the idea of regulated warfare one may be approving conduct that is evil. Warfare, even when it is confined within limits prescribed by the rules of war, is

[24] Brandt, "Utilitarianism and the Rules of War," p. 30.

always to some degree horrible. So it is not surprising that
the question whether it is really possible to fight wars morally
should arise again and again. But people do fight, and so there
are standards for judging when and how they should fight.
The real question, then, is whether those rules of war that
have developed within particular legal and moral traditions
are morally sound. Moral reflection and criticism of the rules
of war often leads to demands for stricter limits on military
conduct. But it can also lead to criticism of those rules as
unrealistically stringent. This suggests a second kind of mis-
giving concerning the idea of regulated warfare: a fear not
that the rules are too permissive but that they may not be
permissive enough because they forbid absolutely certain kinds
of military conduct, such as direct attacks on noncombatants,
even to avoid worse evils. If we take the position that the
innocent may not be made the object of attack no matter what
consequences may follow from adhering to such a constraint,
then we must have an answer for the obvious next question:
suppose those consequences are very bad? Is it not unreasonable to obey a rule when the consequences of doing so are
likely to be catastrophic?

It is at this point that defenders of a morality of common
rules are most apt to falter. For to defend such a morality as
a guide to conduct in extreme situations, situations of looming
catastrophe, is to adopt a position that appears to be rendered
untenable by its own rigidity. Inflexibility and irrationality
are implied by the very name often given to it—"moral absolutism"—with its suggestion that we are blindly to follow
the moral rules regardless of circumstances and against our
measured judgment. The problem is one that is hardly confined to the morality of war; it is, on the contrary, one of the
most fundamental sources of perplexity in moral reflection.
But the question of whether the moral constraints on military
action should always be observed raises it in a particularly
compelling form, for war is an activity in which one's ultimate
values may be at stake. Yet to adopt measures such as killing
the innocent to defend those values attacks one of the most

basic of moral principles, and therefore the presumption against it is very strong. For many people the most reasonable position seems to be one in which a morality of rules is supplemented by a qualifying provision to the effect that an act that is ordinarily impermissible may be performed if failing to perform it would have truly catastrophic consequences. The result is a morality of rules with a utilitarian escape clause, a hybrid morality that relies on authoritative rules for ordinary situations but allows instrumental or utilitarian calculation in certain extraordinary or extreme situations.[25]

Arguments for a "utilitarianism of extremity," like those for utilitarianism in general, commonly rest upon cases in which observing a moral rule appears to lead to unacceptable results. Often these are hypothetical cases in which it is assumed, for purposes of argument, that terrible consequences will follow unless a lie is told, an innocent murdered, a child tortured. Would it not be right for the members of a trapped or marooned party to kill one of their number if by doing so they could save themselves? Must one refuse the invitation of a tyrant to kill one of twenty innocent hostages who are about to be executed, if the remaining nineteen will be released as a consequence of doing so? Suppose that through torture one can obtain information that would lead to the saving of thousands of lives? Such thought-experiments may pro-

---

[25] In considering the alleged defects of moral absolutism, it is important to keep in mind that the "rules" upon which moral judgment relies are typically general, complex, and qualified. They may be far more subtle than our attempts at verbal formulation suggest. Rules that appear inadequate as stated often turn out to have been inadequately stated. The moral injunction not to kill, for example, presupposes a highly circumscribed and qualified definition of the kind of killing that is forbidden. A morality based on the rule "thou shalt not kill" without further qualification would indeed require an escape clause. But the rule does not, in fact, forbid killing: it forbids homicide, the intentional and unjustified killing of human beings. The more completely and correctly formulated the rule, the fewer the required exceptions. On rules and exceptions, see Baier, *Moral Point of View*, pp. 96-100; Feinberg, *Social Philosophy*, pp. 79-83, 85-88, and 94-97; and Twining and Miers, *How to Do Things With Rules*, pp. 55-57, 127-128.

vide the challenge of a puzzle, and perhaps they are even helpful in exploring the theoretical limits of moral principles, but their relevance for moral judgment and conduct is slight. These are not the sorts of situations in which actual moral decisions are made, not only because people are hardly ever faced with such choices but more importantly because the usual assumption that the chooser is faced with a limited number of clearly defined alternative courses of action, the consequences of which are reliably known in advance, is one that will almost never hold in real life. It is not a serious defect in a morality that its precepts might lead one astray in artificially constructed circumstances that one is unlikely ever to encounter. The common morality whose implications for international conduct we have been exploring is one that has developed in and is appropriate to a real, not an imaginary, world.[26]

The other kind of case against which moral rules are sometimes tested is one arising from or based upon actual historical events. There are difficulties here as well, however, for the most we can know about such events is what actually happened, not what would have happened if another course of action had been chosen. Nevertheless, if principles are to be tested against cases, it is better that these should be cases involving decisions of the sort that people might actually have to make—complex decisions, made in circumstances rich in possibilities for an imaginative or unanticipated response, but also made with imperfect information and therefore in partial ignorance of both the short- and, especially, the long-run consequences of alternative choices. It is the method of testing moral principles against historical cases that Michael Walzer appears to adopt in his discussion of whether the rules of war

---

[26] The tendency of utilitarian arguments against a morality of common rules to rely on hypothetical cases is criticized by Donagan, *Theory of Morality*, pp. 206-209. Cf. Bennett, " 'Whatever the Consequences,' " pp. 89-90. My formulation of the issues raised by "the utilitarianism of extremity" owes much to Donagan's discussion, as well as to Anscombe, "Modern Moral Philosophy."

must be observed in situations of "supreme emergency" in which a political community is in imminent danger of destruction. Such, Walzer argues, was the situation in which Britain found itself in 1940 when, in the face of the imminent prospect of being overrun by Nazi Germany, the decision was made to bomb German cities. Given the possibility of such a calamity—one that did, in fact, befall other European nations—to hold that the rules of war must be regarded as categorical and exceptionless prohibitions is, Walzer argues, "a hard line to take, and especially so in the modern age, when aggression has assumed such frightening forms."[27] How, more generally, can the principles of a rule-governed social order plausibly be invoked against resistance to such aggression when the very survival of that order is at stake? "If what is being defended is the state itself and the political community it protects and the lives and liberties of the members of that community. . . . *Fiat justicia ruat coelum*, do justice even if the heavens fall, is not for most people a plausible moral doctrine."[28] Walzer goes on to defend a morality of rules with an escape clause, one that concedes that "in certain very special cases, though never as a matter of course even in just wars, the only restraints upon military action are those of usefulness

[27] *Just and Unjust Wars*, p. 230. I say that Walzer "appears" to test his principles against actual cases because in at least some instances he relies on hypothetical variations. A careful reading of his discussion of the British decision suggests that his argument for suspending the principle of civilian immunity is not really based on the historical situation in 1940 but on a hypothetical reconstruction of it. After correctly observing that those who made the decision could not know that unless German cities were bombed Britain would be defeated, Walzer invites the reader to engage in a "a morally important fantasy" in which a German defeat would be the consequence, or probable consequence, of attacking civilians. "Here," says Walzer, "was a supreme emergency, where one might well be required to override the rights of innocent people and shatter the war convention." (*Just and Unjust Wars*, p. 259.) But the "here" is located in an imaginary world in which we know the long-run consequences of our actions and which, however much it may resemble the actual world, is not identical with it.

[28] *Just and Unjust Wars*, p. 230.

and proportionality."[29] Moral considerations, including considerations based upon the common rules of international law and international morality, must in the face of an imminent calamity for a political community give way to considerations of expediency.

Despite the attractions of Walzer's argument, I doubt that it is sufficient to warrant modification of the traditional prohibition against shedding innocent blood by direct attacks on noncombatants. There are several grounds for entertaining such doubts. Some have to do with the character of moral judgment and moral discourse. Others challenge the utilitarian assumption that the consequences of adopting a morality of rules with a utilitarian escape clause can be shown to be better than sticking with the traditionally acknowledged principle of noncombatant immunity. I want to argue against the view that a morality of rules without an escape clause is necessarily defective. My claim is that such a view is itself defective, both because it confuses moral and nonmoral considerations and because it makes certain assumptions concerning what is good that are hard to defend even on utilitarian grounds.

To accept the necessity for an escape clause is, in the first place, to adopt the view that the common morality is necessarily inconsistent: that it cannot be other than a bifurcated morality, with considerations of utility excluded in some situations and rule-based considerations excluded in others.[30] Far from being necessary, however, this conclusion is the product of a confusion between moral or practical and nonmoral or purposive considerations. What one is morally required to do—what is right or just—is determined by considerations constituting a moral practice. These considerations will, of course, reflect a very complex conception of the good, one that gives weight to substantive or (as they are sometimes called) "nonmoral" goods like happiness or the absence of suf-

[29] Ibid., p. 231.
[30] Cameron, "Morality and War," p. 13.

fering. But that an act is intended or is likely to result in the realization of a nonmoral good of some kind, even so important a good as survival, does not by itself make the act *right*. What makes an act right or just is that it is supported by moral considerations, not that it has good consequences. Strictly speaking, "good" (in the nonmoral sense) and "right" are different concepts and pertain to different kinds of discourse. This is in a way acknowledged by Walzer when he formulates his version of the escape clause for the morality of war as the proposition that we are to "do justice unless the heavens are (really) about to fall."[31] If what we do to avoid catastrophe violates the moral rules, it is *by definition* unjust, however good the consequences of doing it may be. An exception to a moral rule, therefore, is never strictly speaking "justified," unless it is derived from another moral rule. "Justice" and "justification" pertain to rules, not ends.

The escape clause argument is thus one that takes us outside the proper realm of moral discourse and judgment. Still, the question of whether it would be better to suspend the constraint against directly attacking noncombatants is one that can be considered on its own terms. In considering it, I leave aside those issues that are in some sense empirical, even though they may have moral implications, such as whether it is conceivable that British leaders in 1940 could have refused to use one of the few means available to them for striking out against their enemy. The escape clause argument is not concerned with helping us to escape from responsibility; on the contrary, it is proposed as a way of defending the responsibility we assume when we break the moral rules for the sake of a higher good. Here we are on the utilitarian's chosen ground, and so it is appropriate to raise the question of whether the consequences of supplementing the common morality with a utilitarian escape clause can be defended even on utilitarian grounds. Looked at in this way, it is not at all clear that the consequences of the bombing of cities that the British initi-

[31] *Just and Unjust Wars*, p. 231.

ated were on the whole good, either for them or for anyone else. The policy is one that not only invited retaliation upon the British people but also set in motion a train of events that led to the continued bombing of German cities long after the threat of a Nazi conquest had receded, to the devastation of Japanese cities, and to the use of nuclear weapons. These observations, furthermore, are not wholly the product of hindsight, for the bombing was condemned on consequentialist as well as on moral grounds while the war was going on. "There is no *certainty* that . . . shortening the war will result," wrote Vera Brittain in 1944, and she went on to argue that nothing less than certainty entitles a government to use "these dreadful expedients."[32] "The evil wrought by obliteration," wrote another wartime critic, "is certain injury and death, here and now, to hundreds of thousands, and an incalculable destruction of their property. The ultimate good which is supposed to compensate for this evil is of a very speculative character."[33] And he pointed out that we must certainly consider the future consequences of this means of warfare becoming generally legitimate.[34] Those who argue against the utilitarianism of extremity cannot prove that the consequences of adopting it will be bad, but neither can its defenders prove that they will be good. Surely the burden of proof rests with those who argue that the constraints of morality should be overridden for the sake of ends that will, it is asserted, thereby be realized.

The particular version of the utilitarianism of extremity defended by Walzer is open to another kind of objection as well. I will put it in the form of a question: If the violation of the

[32] *Seeds of Chaos*, p. 8.

[33] Ford, "Morality of Obliteration Bombing," pp. 35-36.

[34] Ibid., p. 39. It is likely that the bombing of German cities would have been protested right from the start had the British government not sought to conceal the true character of the raids by claiming that they were aimed at military targets. Arguments against the anticipated bombing of cities were also made before the war: see, e.g., Spaight, *Air Power and the Cities*, and Ryan, *Modern War and Basic Ethics*.

rules of war is to be judged by its consequences, is it sufficient to argue that these consequences are good for the state
in whose interest the rules are violated? Walzer's answer is
"yes." If the state is truly threatened, if the danger it con-
fronts is both "imminent" and "of an unusual and horrifying
kind,"[35] then its conduct should be judged by a lower standard, one that tolerates the violation of rights, though never
of the principles of necessity and proportionality. "Utilitarian
calculation can force us to violate the rules of war only when
we are face to face not merely with defeat but with a defeat
likely to bring disaster to a political community."[36]

Like the doctrine of reason of state, of which it is clearly a
variant, Walzer's argument is that the moral law may be violated for the good of the state. His version of reason of state
is, to be sure, a rather restricted one: it would allow the moral
rules to be overridden only for the preservation, and not merely
for the aggrandizement, of the state, and it understands by
"state" not the government of a political community but that
community itself. But these refinements do not challenge the
central premise of reason of state, which is that moral precepts cannot be observed where the fate of the community is
at stake. Political leaders, whose office is to protect society
and its laws, cannot be bound by the laws that govern the
conduct of ordinary citizens. By acting in ways that are ordinarily regarded as criminal, they are ensuring the very existence of association on the basis of law by securing the survival
of the state. It follows that they may violate the rules of war
if it is reasonable to think that doing so is necessary to avoid
the destruction of the community. "Political leaders can hardly
help but choose the utilitarian side of the dilemma. That is
what they are there for. They must opt for collective survival
and override those rights that have suddenly loomed as obstacles to survival."[37] But if leaders are "there" for anyone's
good, it cannot be solely for the good of the members of their
own community. No doubt leaders have a special responsi-

[35] *Just and Unjust Wars*, p. 253.
[36] Ibid., p. 268.
[37] Ibid., p. 326.

bility to their own people, but the prospect of being con-
quered cannot by itself justify measures of defense that make
others the victims of injustice. Walzer implies the relevance
of the good of a community more inclusive than that of a
single state when he suggests that it was not merely the British who were threatened by Nazi aggression but all of Europe; that Nazism constituted a threat to civilized values, and
that if Britain fell a German conquest of the whole of Europe
would in all probability have followed.[38] But his argument
does not depend on the likelihood of this outcome: the British
bombing of Germany would have been justified, Walzer argues, even if it had been Britain alone whose fate had depended on it.[39] The argument for discounting the common
good—the good of the society of states and of mankind as a
whole—in the calculation of utilities remains to be made.

There is, finally, the question of whether the kinds of judgment required by the utilitarianism of extremity can in fact
be made in what is, by hypothesis, a situation of impending
disaster. Moral rules exist to simplify calculations and to ease
the burden of making rational decisions even in mundane situations. The danger to be guarded against is not that people
in situations of crisis will act irrationally by allowing their
judgment to be guided by moral rules but rather the likelihood that in such situations they will regularly confuse the
unpleasant consequences of acting morally with catastrophe,
defeat with annihilation, the victory of their enemies with the
triumph of evil. Walzer's argument, in effect, is that the rules
are suitable for ordinary moments, when there is time for
deliberation and second thoughts, but that they must be
abandoned in favor of a more direct reliance on reason in
extreme situations, which are by definition situations of crisis
in which imperfect knowledge and errors of reasoning are
more likely than in calmer moments. To insist on using one's
reason in situations in which it is apt to be unreliable is not
necessarily to be rational. The rules of morality are needed

[38] Ibid., pp. 253-254.
[39] Ibid., p. 254.

303

most of all in those emergencies in which there is little time for dispassionate analysis and careful deliberation. The assumption of the escape clause argument, that it is clear what is and what is not an extreme situation and that this clarity will persist in the course of events that are likely to appear "unusual and horrifying" to those living through them, is highly questionable.[40] However attractive the idea of an escape clause may appear in principle, its practical utility is certain to be small.

The issue, says Walzer, "takes this form: should I wager this determinate crime (the killing of innocent people) against that immeasurable evil (a Nazi triumph)?"[41] In accepting this wager, one is betting that the judgment one is making in the present emergency is wiser than the judgment one would make if one were to respect the moral rules that the experience of a civilization, itself encompassing the responses of countless individuals to innumerable greater and lesser emergencies, has contributed to shaping. Every war produces new circumstances and new temptations to violate the traditional restraints. Although it is always possible that the circumstances of the present are truly novel and therefore that to follow the old rules really would be foolish or evil, it is far more likely that these rules, which reflect the experience of a long history of warfare, including warfare for the survival of political communities, embody more wisdom than the judgments of the moment.

[40] As James Turner Johnson suggests, Walzer's characterization of Nazism as an ultimate evil ("an ultimate threat to everything decent . . . immeasurably awful") resembles the identification in holy war doctrines of the enemy as an agent of Antichrist or Satan to be resisted by ordinarily prohibited means. The problem, Johnson correctly points out, is whether ultimate threats can be perceived historically—how we can know, as Walzer puts it, that the heavens are *really* about to fall. "It is one thing to argue in the abstract that in particular circumstances military necessity may require that moral or legal restraints on war be abrogated; it is another matter to identify a moment in history in which this justifiable overturning of just limits can take place or has done so." (*Just War Tradition and the Restraint of War*, p. 25.)

[41] *Just and Unjust Wars*, p. 259.

CHAPTER 12

Morality, Law, and Coexistence

INTERNATIONAL MORALITY and international law each demands, in its own way, the subjection of substantive purposes
to formal constraints. Both are authoritative practices linking
those who are members of different political communities,
regardless of the existence or absence of other ties, including
those of shared belief and common purpose. Even those who
are linked by few such ties remain within the jurisdiction of
these practices, and it is this fact that explains their importance in international society. For international morality and
international law provide the basis—often the only basis—on
which those who are engaged in pursuing different ends can
associate with one another. Shared beliefs, values, and purposes can provide the basis of association only where they
exist. International morality and international law have arisen
in response to the question, posed again and again in the
relations of states, how association is possible among those
who lack these shared commitments.
The two are alike in being systems of mutual accommodation among formal equals. But they are distinct systems, dif-
fering both in content and in origin. The constraints of international law are largely, though not exclusively, those governing
the international conduct of states and their official respresen-
tatives—statesmen, legislators, judges, administrators, diplomats, and soldiers. And these constraints are derived largely
from the customs and agreements of states as interpreted by
international lawyers. International morality, on the other hand,
pertains above all to the conduct of individuals, and then by
extension to the conduct of collectivities. Its principles grow
out of a dialogue among various moral traditions insofar as

they are concerned with international conduct. Unlike international law, the common international morality has no specially designated interpreters. The moral conversation, that is to say, is one in which everyone has a voice. But although they have different jurisdictions and are derived for the most part from different sources, international morality and international law reflect to a significant degree a common concern with the impartial reconciliation of competing demands and depend upon similar principles and concepts.

It is worth noticing, moreover, that international morality and international law are contingently as well as conceptually related. Few, I think, would deny that international law has from its origins been parasitic on moral ideas and that it continues to be so. That moral ideas exert a continuing influence on international law is therefore perhaps not in need of a general defense, although one would like to know more about the way in which this influence manifests itself. But the reverse proposition, that international morality is strongly influenced by international law, may appear less plausible. Can it be shown that the moral world of international affairs is significantly affected by, and indeed to some extent even dependent upon, the existence of international law?

It is often argued that international law is uncertain and inconsistent, because the states system lacks institutionalized procedures for securing agreement on the meaning of terms and therefore on the interpretation of rules, both of which are required for the uniform application of rules to cases. I have already considered a number of such arguments, and have tried to show that the defect to which they point, though a real one, is also one for which the international legal system has evolved its own distinctive remedies.[1] Uniformity, certainty, and consistency are in any case a matter of degree. The concepts and rules of international law would probably be more precise if there existed a more highly developed international judicial system rendering authoritative judgments. But these concepts and rules would be even less pre-

---

[1] See Chapter 7, above.

cise than they are were it not for the customs and procedures maintained by the community of international lawyers—those judges, attorneys, legal advisers, commentators, and scholars whose ideas and judgments give international law much of the certainty and uniformity that it does in fact display. Like international morality, international law is the product of a conversation, but it is one with fewer speakers, who address each other more directly in virtue of the smaller training and experience they have undergone. That this conversation of professionals, with the customs and procedures that sustain it, constitutes an ongoing institution of critical importance for the creation and perpetuation of common standards can be appreciated by reflecting on what the international legal system would be like without it.

The moral world also has its experts, yet it would be odd to claim that there exists a distinct and self-conscious community of moralists who regard themselves as the particular custodians of the common international morality. There are, to be sure, particular moral traditions that are relatively institutionalized—those, for example, that have been significantly shaped by the teachings of a church—but the common morality of international conduct that has evolved out of these various traditions is certainly far less institutionalized than international law. Furthermore, there is a strong tendency within at least some moral traditions toward individual reasoning, judgment, and choice. Law, in contrast, places more emphasis on collective judgments that are at least in principle subject to authoritative determination unlike those of individual conscience. In recognizing certain standards as having the status of law we acknowledge the authority of common rules even in situations in which reason demands different conclusions in the minds of different individuals. Public acknowledgment of the authority of a common body of international law interpreted according to recognized canons and procedures by specialists whose disagreements, while substantial, are usually confined within certain understood bounds serves to provide at least a common point of departure for individual moral judgment concerning international affairs. The moral concepts and principles upon which we depend in thinking about the rights and wrongs of international conduct—like "self-defense," "intervention," and "human rights"—owe much of their precision and utility to the manner in which they have been shaped in legal argument.

Because every state participates in and helps to shape its practices, the international legal system is the single most important institution through which *common* standards of international conduct are defined and perpetuated and through which the idea of a rule-governed international society is upheld. As such it is a vehicle not only of legal but also of moral conduct in international relations—a vehicle, that is, of "lawfulness" in a comprehensive sense of that term. That international law is often invoked to justify morally questionable acts does not undermine this conclusion; on the contrary, it shows that the authority of common standards has already been acknowledged. The incorporation of moral standards into international law provides a basis for applying them in particular disputes, bolsters recognition that conformity with these standards is a matter of common concern, and shifts the focus of debate from the mere existence of such standards to questions of interpretation and application. To a significant extent, then, the prospects for moral conduct in international affairs are bound to those of international law.

International law can only perform this function, however, to the extent that it is understood in practical rather than instrumental terms. Therefore it may be useful to restate some of the distinctive characteristics of the practical conception of international society and international law that we have been engaged in investigating. According to the practical conception, international law is best understood as a body of common rules, rooted in the customary practices of the society of states, on the basis of which independent political communities pursuing diverse and often incompatible ends are related to one another, and which itself defines the terms of their coexistence. International law cannot be understood simply as an instrument for furthering the shared purposes of states, nor as an outcome of the transactions arising from the pursuit of shared purposes. More fundamentally, it is a condition of the pursuit of all purposes, and exists only where common procedures for undertaking particular transactions are acknowledged. This acknowledgment need not be conscious and explicit. It certainly need not amount to acceptance in the sense that the common procedures in question are thought to be desirable. But the authority of these procedures must be at least implicitly acknowledged in the conduct of states, in much the same may as the authority of linguistic rules is implicitly acknowledged by the users of a language.

It was one of the great achievements of eighteenth-century European thought on international relations that it was able to articulate the idea that international society is defined by the deference of states, despite various differences, to the authority of a common body of practices and rules. We have considered how this idea came to be distinguished both from the idea of a universal society of individuals governed by natural law and from the idea of an association of states inspired by commonality of ends and an intention to pursue those ends in concert. Thinkers from Montesquieu and Voltaire to Burke, Martens, and Kant were able with increasing clarity to recognize the society of states as a distinct, historical institution, one not to be confused with the great society of mankind. They saw that the definitive mark of this society lay not in the shared purposes of its member states (for since the Reformation such shared purposes had often been strikingly absent) but in their acknowledgment of formal rules of mutual accommodation. By the end of the eighteenth century the idea had emerged that the states system constitutes a society of states only to the extent that its members observe limits on their freedom of action in pursuing their own interests and acknowledge the authority of these limits—that is, recognize them as law.

This conception of international society implies rejection of a competing conception according to which that society is understood to be an association of states for the pursuit of shared purposes and international law an instrument of that pursuit. Although this instrumental or purposive conception

309

does explain the character of certain kinds of international association, it cannot account for international society as such—that is, for the association of states in terms of those most fundamental practices and procedures, embodied in customary international law, that are presupposed by the particular transactions through which states bind themselves jointly to pursue certain shared purposes. Any account of international society as the outcome either of a single transaction (an "original contract") or of many separate transactions is necessarily defective because it cannot explain how in the absence of preexisting rules—that is, apart from the practices of a preexisting, more fundamental society—such transactions could have taken place. Particular arrangements—treaties, alliances, international organizations—may be regarded as associations for the pursuit of shared purposes, but international society itself cannot coherently be so regarded. International society cannot be defined in terms of shared beliefs and interests. These things may be *contingently* related to the existence and importance of international society. But it is the existence of general participation in and deference to a common body of authoritative practices and rules that is the *criterion* of that society.

Judged in the light of the practical conception of international society, law, and morality, the attitudes both of those realists for whom the common rules are only to be recognized as authoritative when they serve the national interest and of those idealists who insist that the only authoritative rules are those that serve the common interests of states, or of mankind, are equally misconceived. Both amount to a withdrawal from the idea of common standards of international conduct, standards without which neither national nor international interests can be pursued. It is a withdrawal rendered plausible by the mistaken notion that the authority of common rules presupposes agreement on the substantive ends to be served by them—which means that no claim to authority is ever likely to succeed—and by the failure to realize that subscription to authoritative practices makes most sense when agreement on ends is lacking.

All this may be granted and yet the significance of the thesis that practical association is prior to purposive association disputed on the grounds that the kind of relationship postulated by the former is simply not possible unless those involved share at least some common beliefs, values, and ends. Purposive or ideological agreement, it may be argued, is the condition of all inclusive, durable human association, all social solidarity, and such agreement therefore underlies practical as well as purposive association. What holds for society in general, furthermore, is supposed to hold for international society. It follows that the kind of solidarity represented by international law can exist only to the extent that such agreement exists. International society, like all society, rests ultimately on shared beliefs and values.

This argument, in one form or another, has been advanced again and again by sociologists and political theorists. The argument appears to have gotten its start with certain nineteenth-century French critics of the Revolution for whom social order meant restoration of the authority of traditional religious beliefs and political principles. Joseph de Maistre, for example, argued that no durable human association could be formed except on the basis of authoritative shared beliefs— literally, prejudices, opinions adopted without examination— and he defended the superiority of traditional, and specifically Catholic, religion over arrogant but fallible human reason.[2] Auguste Comte conceived of sociology itself as provid-

---

[2] "Human reason left to its own resources is completely incapable *not only of creating but also of conserving any religious or political association*, because it can only give rise to disputes and because, to conduct himself well, man needs beliefs. . . . Without them, there can be neither religion, morality, nor government. There should be a state religion just as there is a state political system; or rather, religion and political dogmas, mingled and merged together, should together form a *general* or *national mind* sufficiently strong to repress the aberrations of the individual reason which is, of its nature, the mortal enemy of any association whatever because it gives birth only to divergent opinions." (*Works*, p. 108.)

ing a body of scientifically verified beliefs (a "positive religion") upon which European society, disrupted by revolution and the breakdown of religious unity, might be reconstituted and rendered stable.[3] Tocqueville, too, emphasized the importance of shared beliefs.[4] The argument linking social order with shared beliefs and values seems thereafter to have become a standard part of the sociological tradition, appearing in the writings of Durkheim, Parsons, and others.[5] Still another version of this view is argued by Richard Flathman,

[3] *System of Positive Polity*, IV, pp. 8-17, 36-37, 66-67, 618-644. Comte argued that unity of belief was equally necessary to domestic and international society. Regarding the latter, he wrote that realization of the common interest of all nations requires "the establishment of a social doctrine, common to the various nations, and, consequently, of a spiritual sovereignty fitted to uphold this doctrine. . . . Until this takes place European order will always stand on the verge of disturbance, notwithstanding the action, alike despotic and inadequate (although provisionally indispensable) exerted by the imperfect coalition of the ancient temporal powers, but which can present no solid guarantee for security, since by its very nature it is always on the point of dissolution" (pp. 642-643).

[4] *Democracy in America*, pp. 433-434. A recent version of the argument that society rests on shared beliefs and values can be found in Patrick Devlin, *Enforcement of Morals*. For criticism see Hart, "Social Solidarity and the Enforcement of Morality."

[5] According to Talcott Parsons, the stability of a society depends upon the integration provided by shared beliefs and values, for "without attachment to the constitutive common values the collectivity tends to dissolve. . . ." (*Social System*, p. 41.) For Durkheim, it is the existence of shared beliefs or "collective representations" that accounts for the submission of each individual, contrary to his own immediate interests and inclinations, to the demands of society—a submission without which social life would be impossible. (*Elementary Forms of the Religious Life*, p. 207.) Durkheim argues that diversity inherent in a world divided into separate societies makes a pacifically regulated international society impossible and that the aspiration for a peaceful world order will be satisfied "only when all men form one society, subject to the same laws." (*Division of Labor in Society*, p. 405.) "We must recognize that this ideal is not on the verge of being integrally realized for there are too many intellectual and moral diversities between different social types existing together on the earth to admit of fraternalization in the same society. But what is possible is that societies of the same type may come together, and it is, indeed, in this direction that evolution appears to move" (p. 405; also see pp. 280-282).

who links the possibility of legal and political authority to the existence of shared beliefs and criticizes Oakeshott and others for ignoring the ideological "setting" that makes possible the exercise of authority.[6]

In assessing these arguments several points should be kept in mind. First, these thinkers are largely concerned with the *empirical conditions* for the existence or flourishing of social solidarity within, and in a few cases among, societies. Therefore their conclusions do not necessarily contradict those derived from an analysis of the *ideas* of political and international society. I have not been concerned in this book with empirical conditions, except indirectly in the effort to distinguish these conditions from the essential or defining characteristics of practical international association. To carry out this analysis requires neither affirmation nor denial of any theory concerning the empirical conditions of such association.

Second, it should be noticed that the argument that shared beliefs and values are required for social order contains a number of ambiguities. Most versions of the argument are advanced at a rather high level of generality. Its adherents often fail to specify whether it is the stability, the persistence, the scope and significance, or the very existence of social order that depends upon ideological unity; the degree of ideological unity or agreement that is required; and whether such agreement is a necessary or merely contingent empirical condition of various kinds and degrees of social order, solidarity, or stability. What we have here is not a single argument but many, and sometimes quite different, arguments.

When the terms and relations embodied in particular versions of the thesis that shared beliefs and values are a condition for social order are closely examined, the gap between it and the view that social order requires agreement at the level of procedure is considerably narrowed. For many of the so-called shared beliefs and values upon which social solidarity is said to depend turn out upon examination to be of a pro-

6 *Practice of Political Authority*, ch. 4.

cedural rather than a substantive character. This particular ambiguity is well illustrated by Flathman's account of the conditions for the exercise of political and legal authority. Such authority, or authority over conduct, is said by Flathman to presuppose the existence of another kind of authority, the authority of certain shared values and beliefs among those whose conduct is regulated by authoritative rules.[7] And he goes on, rather tentatively, to propose two such values or beliefs. But the first, a common language,[8] would scarcely seem to count as a value or belief at all, and is certainly very different from the kind of shared values and beliefs represented by a common religion, moral outlook, or political creed. Nor is the existence of a common language at all plausible as a condition for the exercise of political authority, for linguistic heterogeneity is surely compatible with the existence of government and law.[9] If the claim that political authority rests on a common language means only that for law and government to exist those governed must be capable of understanding its rules, then we are left with an extremely weak version of the ideological unity argument. The second kind of shared belief or value Flathman proposes as a condition of political

[7] Ibid., pp. 6-7. "In order for there to be rules that carry and bestow *authority* . . . there must be values and beliefs that have authoritative standing among the preponderance of those persons who subscribe to the authority of the rules" (p. 6). It is "in terms of authoritative values and beliefs that both authority as such and a practice of authority with a particular shape are acceptable (or not) as features of a society or association. And it is by reference to authoritative values and beliefs that the most basic of the rules that carry and that bestow authority are formulated, mutually understood by subscribers, and interpreted and acted upon in the everchanging circumstances of social and political life" (p. 7).

[8] *Practice of Political Authority*, pp. 78-83.

[9] Flathman writes that "it is clear that the participants in a practice of authority must share a language" (p. 78), but this claim is immediately withdrawn in a footnote: "Not all participants need share the same language, but it must be possible, through translation among the languages of the society or association, for all or nearly all participants to understand the concept of authority and to understand the rules, commands, and so forth of which the practice consists" (p. 256).

authority is a belief among those whose conduct is regulated by authoritative rules that such regulation is desirable or acceptable.[10] But this too is very far from what is ordinarily meant by "shared beliefs and values."

Stronger versions of the ideological unity argument are even less adequate as accounts of social order in general than the weak version defended by Flathman. A stable social order is possible where there exists great diversity of basic beliefs and values, even if religious, ethnic, and other differences are often associated with conflict and civil war. Certainly people are often inclined to quarrel with those whose religious, ethnic, and cultural traditions are different from their own. It is the existence within a society of a habit of deference to common rules of mutual accommodation that helps to keep such differences from leading to civil war or other kinds of social dissolution. It is not differences of language, religion, or nationality alone that lead to civil war, but their existence along with doctrines that hold that such differences are intolerable. Conversely, a pluralist social order is most likely to prevail where the ideas of toleration and mutual accommodation have emerged and become rooted in custom, morality, and law. The shared beliefs and values needed for the existence and flourishing of a pluralist order are of a very different character from those shared purposes postulated by purposive conceptions of social solidarity.

Theorists of international relations have been on the whole rather cautious about claiming that international order is possible only on the basis of shared beliefs and values, perhaps because it is evident that an international order of sorts does exist even though the international system is culturally and ideologically heterogeneous. Thus Martin Wight, while suggesting that "a states-system will not come into being without a degree of cultural unity among its members," is by no means sure that the kind of unity required is religious or ideological, and he implies that it may consist of nothing more than "a

[10] *Practice of Political Authority*, ch. 4.

common morality and a common code, leading to agreed rules about warfare, hostages, diplomatic immunity, the right of asylum, and so on."[11] Stanley Hoffmann suggests as one of the "ideal conditions" for a stable states system the existence of "a common outlook among the leaders of the major states, provided by either similar regimes or a common attitude to religion or similar beliefs about the purposes of the state."[12] But to argue, as he does, that a states system might be destroyed by "an ideological explosion set off by a disparity of regimes or beliefs" is not to argue that international order is impossible where such disparity exists. And although Evan Luard argues that social order in international society depends upon consensus, he has in mind a procedural consensus concerning certain minimum constraints on international conduct and not a consensus on substantive ends and values.[13]

I have already considered a version of the argument that ideological heterogeneity is incompatible with the international order that emerged after the French Revolution and animated the conservative statesmanship of Metternich and others who sought to preserve a homogeneous system of monarchical states.[14] New versions of the argument have been proposed in the wake of the communist and anticolonial revolutions of the present century. In the light of these developments it may be argued that whatever relevance the practical conception may have had to eighteenth-century European international relations is disappearing because of the profoundly different character of the emerging global system, a system divided by ideological and cultural differences so fun-

[11] *Systems of States*, pp. 33 and 34.
[12] *State of War*, p. 95.
[13] *Types of International Society*, p. 378. "A worldwide commitment to abide in a general way with the traditions and rules of the society might be held to be a condition of social existence among states. But the theory of *value* consensus implies more than this: a commitment to specific values and ideas in common. And this is not essential in international societies any more than in domestic."
[14] See Chapter 5, above.

damental as to render association on the basis of common rules impossible. According to this version of the ideological unity argument, the absence of substantive agreement on ends is not an inevitable feature of the states system. Theorists who defend this view sometimes distinguish between "stable" and "revolutionary" international systems, the latter being defined as those in which the incompatibility of beliefs, values, and purposes makes it difficult or impossible to observe common rules.[15] International legal order grows and becomes more significant in the relations of states in periods characterized by substantive agreement and is weakened in times of fundamental disagreement. A common legal framework is undermined both by the purposive demands of revolutionary movements and states and by the desire of those with a large stake in the existing order to repudiate those demands.

This version of the ideological unity argument is compatible with my own argument that international legal order presupposes acknowledgment of the authority of certain constraints rather than agreement on ends, for it too suggests that a stable order requires the subordination of revolutionary demands to common rules of coexistence. Certainly this has happened in the case of the Soviet Union and China, each of which moved from an initial period of repudiating normal relations with bourgeois states to full participation in the diplomatic practices of international society. Each has produced its own version of a jurisprudence of international coexistence. Soviet international legal theory, for example, now distinguishes between the principles of "proletarian internationalism" that are supposed to govern the relations among socialist states and those of "peaceful coexistence" governing relations between socialist and bourgeois states. The latter are explicitly premised on ideological differences. Thus it is argued by Tunkin, the most prominent Soviet theorist of international law, that "the possibility of agreement of states of two op-

---

[15] Hoffmann, *State of War*, p. 93; Falk, "World Revolution and International Order," pp. 154-156.

posed social systems . . . does not preclude struggle between them but is born in such struggle. . . . The contrast of ideologies and uncompromising ideological struggle are not an insuperable obstacle to creating norms of international law. . . ."[16] Chinese doctrine and practice reflect a similar understanding of the possibility of legal order in an ideologically divided international system.[17]

It is worth remembering that the kind of legal order whose essential characteristics are reflected in the practical conception of international society first developed within European society during the early modern period, in the circumstances of a breakdown of ideological agreement. Unable to reconcile certain religious differences through agreement at the level of belief, this society was forced to deal with them at the level of conduct. It had, in effect, to work out principles of coexistence among individuals and groups committed to different conceptions of truth and of the good. The distinction between the public and private realms, the idea of toleration, and the gradual separation of natural and positive law are all aspects of this response to ideological conflict. Thus the kind of legal order that developed in Europe was shaped by the gradual discovery that, in the absence of agreement on ends, agreement on procedures is required if destructive conflict is to be avoided. This is exactly the predicament of modern international relations that the classical international law of the modern states system evolved to remedy. The international legal order that emerged during the more stable periods following the Protestant Reformation, the French Revolution, and the revolutions of the twentieth century is the outcome of a lesson learned and relearned in these struggles. The most im-

[16] *Theory of International Law*, p. 48.

[17] Evidence of the deference to traditional principles of international law on the part of the People's Republic of China is provided by Cohen, *China's Practice of International Law*, and Cohen and Chiu, *People's China and International Law*. The movement toward full Chinese participation in the international legal system has accelerated since the early 1970s, when these studies were compiled.

portant "shared purpose" underlying the rediscovery and reestablishment of legal order following these revolutionary
disturbances was that of avoiding mutual annihilation.

In the second half of the twentieth century the great expansion of the international system brought about by the
breakup of the European colonial empires has given renewed
plausibility to the proposition that international law must suf-
fer where shared beliefs and values are replaced by diversity.
The relations of societies with different cultural traditions
cannot effectively be regulated by a common body of international law, it is suggested, because international law rests
upon Western ideas and values not shared by the rest of the
world. If international society is to survive this epochal change
in its composition, it will have to be reconstituted on some
basis other than that of international law as it has been understood in the past: a basis more responsive to the "inner normative orders" of African and Asian societies.[18] The problem,
it is argued, is one that exists at two levels. There is a gap
between Western and non-Western ideas of morality and law,
because the former are inextricably linked to Christianity and
to the idea of the modern European state and are therefore
alien to the indigenous cultural traditions of non-Western societies. And there is a gap at the level of international relations, because classical international law represents an application of ideas drawn from the legal and political experience
of the West, which non-Western societies do not share and
cannot be expected to adopt.

Both parts of what might be labeled the "cultural gap hypothesis" may be doubted. The first, that the values and beliefs embodied in Western morality and law are not widely
shared and are therefore alien to non-Western societies, exaggerates the actual extent of moral and legal heterogeneity.
The widespread assumption that human societies are so diverse that no moral values and practices can be said to be

[18] Northrop, *Taming of Nations*, pp. 80-81, 267-277; Bozeman, *Future of
Law in a Multicultural World*, pp. 14-33, 44-49, 169-170, 180-186.

universal is false. It is true that there exists a very wide diversity of linguistic, aesthetic, religious, and other cultural forms. But the evidence accumulated through historical and anthropological study suggests the existence of certain striking moral similarities among otherwise dissimilar societies. All societies, for example, appear to manifest a value for human life by favoring procreation and by prohibiting homicide, while recognizing certain carefully specified exceptions (which typically include self-preservation, warfare, and the punishment of serious crimes). The bodies of the dead are everywhere treated in particular, often highly ritualistic, ways. All societies regulate sexual conduct, discouraging or carefully limiting incest, rape, and indiscriminate promiscuity. Friendship, cooperation, reciprocity, and fairness are valued in one way or another in all societies. Children are everywhere educated in these values and in the virtues of obedience, honesty, generosity, and truthfulness.[19] One explanation for these uniformities is that morality, like technology, is constrained by certain facts about human beings and their environment. The universal principles of morality are those that work under the recurrent circumstances of human existence and that have tended in consequence to be selected and perpetuated wherever there are permanent human communities. These common moral principles are also generally reflected in law, together with certain widespread though not universal procedures for the adjustment of differences, such as the settlement of disputes by third parties.[20]

[19] Surveys of the anthropological evidence from the point of view of moral philosophy that support the assertions made in the text include Edel and Edel, *Anthropology and Ethics*, and MacBeath, *Experiments in Living*. See Finnis, *Natural Law and Natural Rights*, pp. 81-85, for an attempt to formulate a list of universal moral values and practices on the basis of this evidence.

[20] Religious, aesthetic, and certain other cultural beliefs and values, on the other hand, are not constrained to the same degree by the requirements of social coexistence and therefore tend to display far greater variability. (Nowell-Smith, "Religion and Morality," p. 153.) The evolution of moral practices is considered by Singer, *Expanding Circle*. For an argument that cus-

The second part of the cultural gap hypothesis, that non-Western societies do not and cannot share the values embodied in international law and morality, is also doubtful. It underestimates the extent to which non-Western societies have become Westernized, especially with respect to the conduct of their foreign relations. International law may be largely Western in origin,[21] but it has come to be taught and practiced in all parts of the world. Many of its central ideas, such as those of statehood, national self-determination, and cooperation through international agencies, have been enthusiastically accepted outside the West. Many others, such as diplomatic immunity, the making of treaties, or the regulation of warfare, cannot be said to be wholly of Western provenance. Furthermore, the international practice of the newer states, despite their desire to alter international law in a way favorable to their interests and their espousal of the (Western) doctrine of consent as the basis of international legal obligation, reveals few cultural idiosyncrasies. The most momentous change lately in the international system has been that represented by decolonization—a movement aimed not at the secession of non-Western societies from the system of states but rather their incorporation within it as fully equal and independent associates. Decolonization has thus served to reaffirm rather than challenge the European concepts of statehood, sovereignty, and international society. And although many non-Western states have resisted such important international legal practices as arbitration and judicial settlement,

---

tomary international law has evolved "as if by a process of natural selection," see Allott, "Language, Method, and the Nature of International Law," pp. 129-130. "International law can be regarded as the natural law of international society, not in any religious sense but in a purely secular sense. It is the law by which international society prolongs its existence. . . ."

[21] Though even this is contested by some historians of international law, such as Alexandrowicz, *Introduction to the History of the Law of Nations in the East Indies*, who argues that European international law was influenced during its formative period by another body of international law indigenous to the Southeast Asian kingdoms with whom the Portugese and the Dutch began to have relations in the sixteenth and seventeenth centuries.

they are in no way distinguished by this from Western states (including those of Eastern Europe) whose overall record in this respect is equally bad. Being "Western" no more guarantees acceptance of the rule of law than being non-Western precludes it.

Often what appear to be conflicts rooted in ideological disagreement are in fact conflicts of interest in ideological guise, as those involved seek to rationalize or strengthen their respective bargaining positions. Many of the conflicts between Western and non-Western states concerning international law can be explained by the different situations and interests of each, without resorting to the idea of a cultural gap. No such gap is required to account for the division between the old and the new states on such issues as the control of deep-sea mining, the right of armed intervention, or the standards of compensation governing the expropriation of foreign-owned economic enterprises.[22] Nor is the present debate concerning international justice and human rights a "cultural" clash; it is, rather, a clash between two Western traditions concerning the relation between the state and economic welfare. In these and many other controversies the influence of cultural factors would appear to be secondary to that of the requirements of national interest.

This is not to deny the existence of cultural and ideological differences, or to suggest that different beliefs and values are never an obstacle to peaceful and rule-governed international association. But it is to reject all extreme claims that shared purposes are a necessary condition of international legal and moral order, and that such order is therefore impossible in a multicultural world. Not only are international law and morality possible in the face of ideological diversity, but they constitute practices peculiarly well adapted to helping states

[22] Characteristic non-Western attitudes and arguments concerning these and other issues are considered by Friedheim, " 'Satisfied' and 'Dissatisfied' States Negotiate International Law"; Friedmann, *Changing Structure of International Law*, chs. 18, 19, and 20; and Levi, *Law and Politics in the International Society*, ch. 8.

deal with the difficulties created by that diversity. International law especially can do this because it provides a widely acknowledged vocabulary and set of procedures in terms of which those with different beliefs, values, and ends can formulate their differences and negotiate with one another, and because it reflects a common concern with mitigating the worst consequences of this diversity without enforcing cultural and ideological homogeneity. International law, and especially customary international law, embodies the minimum principles of mutual accommodation required for the coexistence not only of separate states but of different *kinds* of states. Furthermore, it contributes to the creation of a diplomatic and legal culture within which these principles can be created and altered, their integrity preserved against a variety of self-serving and shortsighted challenges, and their perpetuation guaranteed. It is through the experience of international association defined and directed by this common law that an appropriate international culture bridging other cultural differences is created. The important point, then, is not that the practical conception of international law (which is, I have argued, thoroughly embedded in customary international law) reflects universally shared values, although to a degree this is in fact the case. It is rather that this conception embodies an understanding of international association that is conducive to a pluralist world—possibly the only understanding upon which a pluralist world order can be constructed.

The need for authoritative common rules constraining the pursuit of particular ends arises in inverse proportion to the degree to which such ends are shared by the members of a community. Where people hold common values and beliefs and thus tend to be united in their acceptance of shared purposes there are fewer divisions to be overcome. In a society united by common values and beliefs, the form and function of law is very different from what it is in a society characterized by a diversity of beliefs, values, purposes, and interests. Law understood as an instrument for the pursuit of shared purposes is clearly dependent upon the existence of such pur-

323

poses. But law understood as a framework of restraint and coexistence among those pursuing divergent purposes presupposes diversity and the toleration of this diversity. Given the existence in our world of significant differences of belief, value, and interest, the expectation of global unity on the basis of shared purposes is sure to be disappointed. The basis of international association lies in deference to practices that embody recognition of the fact that we must coexist on this planet with others with whom we sometimes share little beyond a common predicament. Such coexistence presupposes acknowledgment of certain common standards of conduct: that individuals and states are united on the basis of authoritative common rules and not merely by their possibly convergent desires. In the present circumstances of international society, it is through customary international law that this idea of practical association at the level of international relations receives its institutionalized expression.

Works Cited

Ago, Roberto. "Positive Law and International Law." *American Journal of International Law*, 51 (1957), 691-733.

Alexandrowicz, C. H. *An Introduction to the History of the Law of Nations in the East Indies*. Oxford: Clarendon Press, 1967.

Allott, Philip. "Language, Method and the Nature of International Law." *British Yearbook of International Law*, 45 (1971), 79-135.

Anscombe, G.E.M. "Modern Moral Philosophy." *Philosophy*, 33 (1958), 1-19.

Aquinas, Thomas. *On Kingship: To the King of Cyprus*. Trans. Gerald B. Phelan and I. I. Eschmann. Toronto: The Pontifical Institute of Medieval Studies, 1949.

————. *Summa Theologica*. Trans. Fathers of the English Dominican Province. 3 vols. New York: Benziger Brothers, 1947.

Aristotle. *Nichomachean Ethics*. Trans. W. D. Ross. *Introduction to Aristotle*. 2nd ed. Ed. Richard McKeon. Chicago: University of Chicago Press, 1973.

————. *Politics*. Trans. Ernest Barker. London: Oxford University Press, 1946.

Auspitz, Josiah Lee. "Individuality, Civility, and Theory: The Philosophical Imagination of Michael Oakeshott." *Political Theory*, 4 (1976), 261-294.

Austin, John. *The Province of Jurisprudence Determined*. Ed. H.L.A. Hart. London: Weidenfeld and Nicolson, 1955.

Baier, Kurt. *The Moral Point of View: A Rational Basis of Ethics*. Abridged ed. New York: Random House, 1965.

Barker, Ernest. *The Confederation of Nations*. Oxford: Clarendon Press, 1918.

Barkun, Michael. *Law without Sanctions*. New Haven: Yale University Press, 1968.

Bedjaoui, Mohammed. *Towards a New International Economic Order*. New York: Holmes and Meier, 1979.

Beitz, Charles R. *Political Theory and International Relations*. Princeton: Princeton University Press, 1979.

Bennett, Jonathan. " 'Whatever the Consequences,' " *Analysis*, 26 (1966), 83-102.

Bentham, Jeremy. *An Introduction to the Principles of Morals and Legislation*. Ed. J. H. Burns and H.L.A. Hart. The Collected Works of Jeremy Bentham. London: Athlone Press, 1970.

————. *Of Laws in General*. Ed. H.L.A. Hart. The Collected Works of Jeremy Bentham. London: Athlone Press, 1970.

————. *The Works of Jeremy Bentham*. Ed. John Bowring. New York: Russell and Russell, 1962.

Beres, Louis René, and Harry R. Targ. *Constructing Alternative World Futures: Reordering the Planet*. Cambridge, Mass.: Schenkman, 1977.

Best, Geoffrey. *Humanity in Warfare: The Modern History of the International Law of Armed Conflicts*. London: Weidenfeld and Nicolson, 1980.

Bokor-Szegó, Hanna. *New States and International Law*. Budapest: Akademiai Kiado, 1970.

Bozeman, Adda B. *The Future of Law in a Multicultural World*. Princeton: Princeton University Press, 1971.

Brandt, R. B. "Utilitarianism and the Rules of War." In Marshall Cohen, Thomas Nagel, and Thomas Scanlon, eds., *War and Moral Responsibility*, pp. 25-45. Princeton: Princeton University Press, 1974.

Brierly, J. L. "The Basis of Obligation in International Law." Chap. 1 of *The Basis of Obligation in International Law and Other Papers*, pp. 1-67. Ed. Hersh Lauterpacht and C.H.M. Waldock. Oxford: Clarendon Press, 1958.

————. *The Covenant and the Charter*. Cambridge: Cambridge University Press, 1947.

————. *The Law of Nations: An Introduction to the Law of Peace*. Ed. Humphrey Waldock. 6th ed. Oxford: Clarendon Press, 1963.

————. *The Outlook for International Law*. Oxford: Clarendon Press, 1944.

Brittain, Vera. *Seeds of Chaos*. London: New Vision, for the Bombing Restriction Committee, 1944.

Bull, Hedley. *The Anarchical Society: A Study of Order in World Politics*. London: Macmillan, 1977.

————. "The Grotian Conception of International Society." In Herbert Butterfield and Martin Wight, eds., *Diplomatic Investigations*, pp. 51-73. Cambridge, Mass.: Harvard University Press, 1968.

Burke, Edmund. *Works*. 8 vols. London: George Bell and Sons, 1899.

Butterfield, Herbert. *History and Human Relations*. New York: Macmillan, 1952.

————, and Martin Wight, eds. *Diplomatic Investigations: Essays in the Theory of International Politics*. Cambridge, Mass.: Harvard University Press, 1968.

Callières, François de. *On the Manner of Negotiating with Princes*. Trans. A. F. Whyte. Notre Dame, Ind.: University of Notre Dame Press, 1963.

Cameron, J. M. "Morality and War." *New York Review of Books*, 24, no. 20 (December 8, 1977), 8-15.

Carr, Edward Hallet. *The Twenty Years' Crisis, 1919-1939: An Introduction to the Study of International Relations*. 2nd ed. London: Macmillan, 1946.

Cicero, Marcus Tullius. *De Republica*. Trans. C. W. Keyes. The Loeb Classical Library. Cambridge, Mass.: Harvard University Press, 1928.

Cohen, Jerome A., ed. *China's Practice of International Law: Some Case Studies*. Cambridge, Mass.: Harvard University Press, 1972.

————, and Hungdah Chiu. *People's China and International Law: A Documentary Study*. 2 vols. Princeton: Princeton University Press, 1974.

Cohen, Marshall. "Morality and the Laws of War." In Virginia Held, Sidney Morgenbesser, and Thomas Nagel, eds. *Philosophy, Morality, and International Affairs*, pp. 71-88. New York: Oxford University Press, 1974.

————, Thomas Nagel, and Thomas Scanlon, eds. *Marx, Justice, and History*. Princeton: Princeton University Press, 1980.

Collingwood, R. G. *An Autobiography*. Oxford: Oxford University Press, 1939.

Comte, Auguste. *System of Positive Polity*. Trans. R. Congreve and H. Hutton. 4 vols. New York: Burt Franklin, 1973.

Coplin, William D. *The Functions of International Law*. Chicago: Rand McNally, 1968.

Corbett, Percy E. *Law and Society in the Relations of States*. New York: Harcourt, Brace, 1951.

Devlin, Patrick. *The Enforcement of Morals*. Oxford: Oxford University Press, 1965.

Donagan, Alan. *The Theory of Morality*. Chicago: University of Chicago Press, 1977.

Draper, G.I.A.D. "The Ethical and Juridical Status of Constraints in War." *Military Law Review*, 55 (1972), 169-186.

Durkheim, Emile, *The Division of Labor in Society*. Trans. George Simpson. New York: Macmillan, 1933.

————. *The Elementary Forms of the Religious Life: A Study in Religious Sociology*. Glencoe, Ill.: Free Press, 1947.

Dworkin, Ronald. "Comments on the Unity of Law Doctrine." In Howard E. Kiefer and Milton K. Munitz, eds., *Ethics and Social Justice*, pp. 200-206. Albany: State University of New York Press, 1970.

————. *Taking Rights Seriously*. Cambridge, Mass.: Harvard University Press, 1977.

Edel, May, and Abraham Edel. *Anthropology and Ethics: The Quest for Moral Understanding*. Rev. ed. Cleveland: Press of Case Western Reserve University, 1968.

Eppstein, John, ed. *The Catholic Tradition of the Law of Nations*. London: Burns Oates and Washburn, 1935.

Erb, Guy F., and Valeriana Kallab, eds. *Beyond Dependency: The Developing World Speaks Out*. Washington, D.C.: Overseas Development Council, 1975.

Falk, Richard A. "Anarchism and World Order." In J. Roland Pennock and John W. Chapman, eds., *Anarchism*, pp. 63-87. Nomos 19. New York: New York University Press, 1978.

———. "International Jurisdiction: Horizontal and Vertical Conceptions of Legal Order." *Temple Law Quarterly*, 32 (1959), 295-320.

———. *Legal Order in a Violent World*. Princeton: Princeton University Press, 1968.

———. *The Role of Domestic Courts in the International Legal Order*. Syracuse: Syracuse University Press, 1964.

———. *The Status of Law in International Society*. Princeton: Princeton University Press, 1970.

———. "World Revolution and International Order." In Carl J. Friedrich, ed., *Revolution*, pp. 154-177. Nomos 8. New York: Atherton Press, 1967.

Feinberg, Joel. *Society Philosophy*. Englewood Cliffs, N.J.: Prentice-Hall, 1973.

Fénelon, François de Salignac de la Mothe. *L'Examen de conscience sur les devoirs de la royauté. Oeuvres complètes*, vol. 7, pp. 85-102. 10 vols. Paris: J. Leroux and others, 1850-1852.

Finnis, John. *Natural Law and Natural Rights*. Oxford: Clarendon Press, 1980.

Fitzmaurice, Gerald G. "The General Principles of International Law Considered from the Standpoint of the Rule of Law." Hague Academy of International Law, *Recueil des cours*, 92 (1957), 1-227.

———. "Some Problems Regarding the Formal Sources of International Law." *Symbolae Verzijl*, pp. 153-174. The Hague: Martinus Nijhoff, 1958.

———. "Vae Victis, or Woe to the Negotiators! Your Treaty

or Our 'Interpretation' of It?" *American Journal of International Law*, 65 (1971), 358-373.

Flathman, Richard E. *The Practice of Political Authority: Authority and the Authoritative*. Chicago: University of Chicago Press, 1980.

Ford, John C. "The Morality of Obliteration Bombing." In Richard A. Wasserstrom, ed., *War and Morality*, pp. 15-41. Belmont, Cal.: Wadsworth, 1970. Originally published in *Theological Studies*, 5 (1944), 261-309.

Forsyth, Murray. "Thomas Hobbes and the External Relations of States." *British Journal of International Studies*, 5 (1979), 196-209.

————, H.M.A. Keens-Soper, and P. Savigear, eds. *The Theory of International Relations: Selected Texts from Gentili to Treitschke*. New York: Atherton Press, 1970.

Friedheim, Robert L. "The 'Satisfied' and 'Dissatisfied' States Negotiate International Law: A Case Study." *World Politics*, 18 (1965), 20-42.

Friedman, Richard B. "On the Concept of Authority in Political Philosophy." In Richard E. Flathman, ed., *Concepts in Social and Political Philosophy*, pp. 121-146. New York: Macmillan, 1973.

Friedmann, Wolfgang. *The Changing Structure of International Law*. New York: Columbia University Press, 1964.

Gentili, Alberico. *De Jure Belli Libri Tres*. Trans. John C. Rolfe. Oxford: Clarendon Press. 1933.

Gentz, Friedrich von. *Fragments upon the Balance of Power in Europe*. London: Peltier, 1806.

————. *On the State of Europe before and after the French Revolution: Being an Answer to L'Etat de la France à la fin de l'an VIII*. Trans. J. C. Herries. London: Hatchard, 1802. Reprinted New York: AMS Press, 1970.

————. *Schriften: Ein Denkmal*. Ed. Gustav Schlesier. 5 vols. Mannheim: Heinrich Hoff, 1838-1840.

Gibbon, Edward. *The Decline and Fall of the Roman Empire*. 6 vols. London: J. M. Dent and Sons, 1910.

Gierke, Otto. *Natural Law and the Theory of Society, 1500-*

1800. Trans. Ernest Barker. Cambridge: Cambridge University Press, 1950.

Gihl, Torsten. *International Legislation: An Essay on Changes in International Law and in International Legal Situations*. Trans. Sydney J. Charleston. London: Oxford University Press, 1937.

———. "The Legal Character and Sources of International Law." *Scandinavian Studies in Law*, 1 (1957), 51-92.

Goodrich, Leland M., Edvard Hambro, and Anne P. Simons. *Charter of the United Nations: Commentary and Documents*. 3rd. rev. ed. New York: Columbia University Press, 1969.

Gray, John Chipman. *The Nature and Sources of the Law*. New York: Columbia University Press, 1909.

Gross, Leo, ed. *The Future of the International Court of Justice*. 2 vols. Dobbs Ferry, N.Y.: Oceana, 1976.

———. "On the Justiciability of International Disputes." In K. Thompson and R. J. Myers, eds., *A Tribute to Hans Morgenthau*, pp. 203-219. Washington, D.C.: New Republic Books, 1977.

———. "The Peace of Westphalia, 1648-1948." *American Journal of International Law*, 53 (1959), 1-29.

Grotius, Hugo. *The Law of War and Peace*. Trans. Francis W. Kelsey. The Classics of International Law. Oxford: Clarendon Press, 1925.

Gulick, Edward Vose. *Europe's Classical Balance of Power: A Case History of the Theory and Practice of One of the Great Concepts of European Statecraft*. Ithaca: Cornell University Press, 1955.

Hackworth, Green W. *Digest of International Law*. 8 vols. Washington, D.C.: United States Government Printing Office, 1940-1944.

Hall, William Edward. *A Treatise on International Law*. 3rd ed. Oxford: Clarendon Press, 1890.

Hart. H.L.A. *The Concept of Law*. Oxford: Clarendon Press, 1961.

———. "Kelsen's Doctrine of the Unity of Law." In Howard

E. Kiefer and Milton K. Munitz, eds., *Ethics and Social Justice*, pp. 171-199. Albany: State University of New York Press, 1970.

―――. "Positivism and the Separation of Law and Morals." *Harvard Law Review*, 71 (1958), 593-629.

―――. "Social Solidarity and the Enforcement of Morality." *University of Chicago Law Review*, 35 (1967), 1-13.

Hayek, F. A. *Law, Liberty, and Legislation*. 3 vols. Chicago: University of Chicago Press, 1973-1979.

―――. *The Road to Serfdom*. Chicago: University of Chicago Press, 1944.

Hegel, G.W.F. *The Philosophy of Right*. Trans. T. M. Knox. Oxford: Clarendon Press, 1952.

Hehir, J. B. "The Ethics of Intervention: Two Normative Traditions." In Peter G. Brown and Douglas MacLean, eds., *Human Rights and U.S. Foreign Policy*, pp. 121-139. Lexington, Mass.: D. C. Heath, 1979.

Herodotus. *The Histories*. Trans. Aubrey de Sélincourt. The Penguin Classics. Baltimore: Penguin Books, 1954.

Herz, John H. *The Nation-State and the Crisis of World Politics: Essays on International Politics in the Twentieth Century*. New York: David McKay, 1976.

Hinsley, F. H. *Nationalism and the International System*. Twentieth Century Studies. London: Hodder and Stoughton, 1973.

―――. *Power and the Pursuit of Peace: Theory and Practice in the History of Relations Between States*. Cambridge: Cambridge University Press, 1963.

Hobbes, Thomas. *The Elements of Law Natural and Politic*. Ed. Ferdinand Tönnies. London: Simpkin, Marshall, and Co., 1889.

―――. *Leviathan; or, The Matter, Forme and Power of a Commonwealth, Ecclesiasticall and Civil*. Ed. Michael Oakeshott. Oxford: Basil Blackwell, 1946.

―――. *Philosophical Rudiments Concerning Government and Society*. Vol. 2, *The English Works of Thomas Hobbes of Malmesbury*. Ed. William Molesworth. 11 vols. London: Bohn, 1839-1845.

Hoffmann, Stanley. *Duties Beyond Borders: On the Limits and Possibilities of Ethical International Politics*. Syracuse: Syracuse University Press, 1981.

————. *The State of War: Essays on the Theory and Practice of International Politics*. New York: Praeger, 1965.

Holbraad, Carsten. *The Concert of Europe: A Study in German and British International Theory, 1815-1914*. London: Longman's, 1970.

Holland, Thomas Erskine. *The Elements of Jurisprudence*. 13th ed. Oxford: Clarendon Press, 1924.

Holmes, Oliver Wendell, Jr. *The Common Law*. Boston. Little, Brown, 1881.

Hurst, Michael, ed. *Key Treaties for the Great Powers, 1814-1914*. 2 vols. New York: St. Martin's Press, 1972.

Jenks, C. Wilfred. *The Prospects for International Adjudication*. London: Stevens, 1964.

Johnson, D.H.N. *The English Tradition in International Law*. Inaugural Lecture, London School of Economics. London: Bell, for the London School of Economics, 1962.

Johnson, James Turner. *Ideology, Reason, and the Limitation of War: Religious and Secular Concepts, 1200-1740*. Princeton: Princeton University Press, 1975.

————. *Just War Tradition and the Restraint of War: A Moral and Historical Inquiry*. Princeton: Princeton University Press, 1981.

————. "Toward Reconstructing the *Jus Ad Bellum*." *The Monist*, 57 (1973), 461-488.

Jouvenel, Bertrand de. "Pure Politics Revisited." *Government and Opposition*, 15 (1980), 427-434.

————. *Sovereignty: An Inquiry into the Political Good*. Trans. J. F. Huntington. Chicago: University of Chicago Press, 1957.

The Judgment of the International Military Tribunal at Nuremberg. Washington, D.C.: United States Government Printing Office, 1947.

Kant, Immanuel. *Foundations of the Metaphysics of Morals.* Trans. Lewis White Beck. The Library of Liberal Arts. Indianapolis: Bobbs-Merrill, 1959.

————. *Kant's Political Writings.* Ed. Hans Reiss, trans. H. B. Nisbet. Cambridge: Cambridge University Press, 1970.

Kaplan, Morton A., and Nicholas deB. Katzenbach. *The Political Foundations of International Law.* New York: John Wiley and Sons, 1961.

Kedourie, Elie. " 'Minorities.' " *The Chatham House Version and other Middle Eastern Studies*, pp. 286-316. New York: Praeger, 1970.

————. *Nationalism in Asia and Africa.* New York: New American Library, 1970.

Keen, M. H. *The Laws of War in the Late Middle Ages.* London: Routledge and Kegan Paul, 1965.

Keens-Soper, Maurice. "The Practice of a States-System." In Michael Donelan, ed., *The Reason of States*, pp. 25-44. London: George Allen and Unwin, 1978.

Kelsen, Hans. *General Theory of Law and State.* Cambridge, Mass.: Harvard University Press, 1945.

————. *The Law of the United Nations.* New York: Praeger, 1950.

————. *Principles of International Law.* 2nd ed. Rev. and ed. Robert W. Tucker. New York: Holt, Rinehart and Winston, 1966.

————. *The Pure Theory of Law.* Berkeley: University of California Press, 1967.

Klein, Robert A. *Sovereign Equality among States: The History of an Idea.* Toronto: University of Toronto Press, 1974.

Krieger, Leonard. *The Politics of Discretion: Pufendorf and the Acceptance of Natural Law.* Chicago: University of Chicago Press, 1965.

Lachs, Manfred. *The Teacher in International Law: Teachings and Teaching.* The Hague: Nijhoff, 1982.

Lauterpacht, Hersh. *The Function of Law in the International Community.* Oxford: Clarendon Press, 1933.

————. *International Law, Being the Collected Papers of Hersh Lauterpacht.* Ed. E. Lauterpacht. 4 vols. to date. Cambridge: Cambridge University Press, 1970–.

Leibniz, Gottfried Wilhelm. *Codex Juris Gentium (Prefatio).* In Patrick Riley, trans. and ed., *The Political Writings of Leibniz,* pp. 165-176. Cambridge: Cambridge University Press, 1971.

Levi, Werner. *Law and Politics in the International Society.* Vol. 32, Sage Library of Social Research. Beverly Hills: Sage Publications, 1976.

Llewellyn, Karl N. *The Bramble Bush: On Our Law and Its Study.* Dobbs Ferry, N.Y.: Oceana Publications, 1960.

Locke, John. *Second Treatise. Two Treatises of Government.* Ed. Peter Laslett. Rev. ed. New York: New American Library, 1965.

Lorimer, James. *The Institutes of the Law of Nations: A Treatise on the Jural Relations of Separate Political Communities.* 2 vols. Edinburgh: Blackwood and Sons, 1883-84.

Luard, Evan. *Types of International Society.* New York: Free Press, 1976.

Luban, David. "The Romance of the Nation State." *Philosophy and Public Affairs,* 9 (1980), 392-397.

Mably, Gabriel Bonnot de. *Le Droit public de l'Europe, fondé sur les traités.* The Hague: J. van Duren. 1746.

MacBeath, Alexander. *Experiments in Living: A Study of the Nature and Foundations of Ethics or Morals in the Light of Recent Work in Social Anthropology.* London: Macmillan, 1952.

Machiavelli, Niccolo. *The Art of War. The Chief Works and Others,* vol. 2, pp. 561-726. Trans. Alan Gilbert. 3 vols. Durham, N.C.: Duke University Press, 1965.

Maine, Henry Summer. *International Law.* New York: Henry Holt, 1888.

————. *Lectures on the Early History of Institutions.* 7th ed. Port Washington, N.Y.: Kennikat Press, 1966.

Maistre, Joseph de. *Works.* Trans. Jack Lively. London: Macmillan, 1965.

Manning, C. A. W. *The Nature of International Society.* London: Bell, 1962.

Martens, Georg Friedrich von. *The Law of Nations: Being the Science of National Law, Covenants, Power, Etc. Founded upon the Treaties and Customs of Modern Nations in Europe.* 4th ed. London: William Cobbett, 1829.

————. *Recueil des principaux traités d'alliance, de paix, de trêve conclus par les puissances de l'Europe depuis 1761 jusqu'à présent.* 10 vols. Göttingen: J. C. Dieterich, 1791-1801.

Mattingly, Garrett. *Renaissance Diplomacy.* Boston: Houghton Mifflin, 1956.

Mayall, James. "International Society and International Theory." In Michael Donelan, ed., *The Reason of States,* pp. 122-141. London: George Allen and Unwin, 1973.

McDougal, Myres S. "The Ethics of Applying Systems of Authority: The Balance of Opposites of a Legal System." In Harold D. Lasswell and Harlan Cleveland, eds., *The Ethics of Power: The Interplay of Religion, Philosophy, and Politics,* pp. 221-240. New York: Harper and Brothers, 1962.

————. "International Law, Power and Policy: A Contemporary Conception." Hague Academy of International Law, *Recueil des cours,* 82 (1953), 133-259.

————, and associates. *Studies in World Public Order.* New Haven: Yale University Press, 1960.

————, Harold D. Lasswell, and James C. Miller. *The Interpretation of Agreements and World Public Order: Principles of Content and Procedure.* New Haven: Yale University Press, 1967.

————, Harold D. Lasswell, and W. Michael Reisman. "The World Constitutive Process of Authoritative Decision." In Richard A. Falk and Cyril E. Black, eds., *The Future of the International Legal Order,* vol. 1, pp. 73-154. Princeton: Princeton University Press, 1969.

————, and W. Michael Reisman, eds. *International Law Essays: A Supplement to International Law in Contem-*

porary Perspective. Mineola, N.Y.: Foundation Press, 1981.

Mendlovitz, Saul H., ed. *On the Creation of a Just World Order: Preferred Worlds for the 1990's*. New York: Free Press, 1975.

Merrills, J. G. "Morality and the International Legal Order." *Modern Law Review*, 31 (1968), 520-534.

Midgley, E.B.F. *The Natural Law Tradition and the Theory of International Relations*. London: Paul Elek, 1975.

Mill, James. *Essays on Government, Jurisprudence, Liberty of the Press, and the Law of Nations*. London: J. Innes, 1825.

Mill, John Stuart. "A Few Words on Non-intervention." *Dissertations and Discussions, Political, Philosophical and Historical*, vol. 3, pp. 153-178. 3 vols. 2nd ed. London: Longmans, Green, Reader, and Dyer, 1867.

Miller, David Hunter. *The Drafting of the Covenant*. 2 vols. New York: G. P. Putnam's Sons, 1928.

Montesquieu, Charles Louis de Secondat, Baron de la Brede et de. *Considérations sur les causes de la grandeur des Romains et de leur décadence*. *Oeuvres complètes*. Ed. Roger Caillois. Vol. 2, pp. 62-209. 2 vols. Editions de la Pléiade. Paris: Librairie Gallimard, 1951.

———. *De l'Esprit des lois*. *Oeuvres complètes*, vol. 2, pp. 227-995.

———. *Réflexions sur la monarchie universelle en Europe*. *Oeuvres complètes*, vol. 2, pp. 19-38.

Moser, Johann Jakob. *Grundsätze des völkerrechts*. *Deutches Rechtsdenken*. Ed. E. Wolf. Vol. 16. Frankfurt am Main: V. Klostermann, 1959.

———. *Versuch des neuesten europäischen völkerrechts in friedens- und kriegszeiten*. 10 vols. Frankfurt am Main: Varrentrapp, 1777-1780.

Northrop, F.S.C. *The Taming of Nations: A Study of the Cultural Bases of International Policy*. New York: Macmillan, 1952.

Nowell-Smith, Patrick H. "Religion and Morality." In Paul

Edwards, ed., *Encyclopedia of Philosophy*, vol. 7, pp. 150-158. 8 vols. New York: Macmillan, 1967.

Nussbaum, Arthur. *A Concise History of the Law of Nations*. Rev. ed. New York: Macmillan, 1954.

Oakeshott, Michael. *On Human Conduct*. Oxford: Clarendon Press, 1975.

————. "The Rule of Law." *On History and Other Essays*. Oxford: Basil Blackwell, 1983.

————. "The Tower of Babel." *Rationalism in Politics and Other Essays*. New York: Basic Books, 1962.

O'Connell, D. P. *International Law*. 2 vols. 2nd ed. London: Stevens and Sons, 1970.

Oppenheim, Lassa F.L. *International Law: A Treatise*. 2 vols. London: Longmans, Green, and Co., 1905-1906.

Parry, Clive, ed. *Consolidated Treaty Series, 1648-1918*. 200 vols. Dobbs Ferry, N.Y.: Oceana Publications, 1969–.

Parsons, Talcott. *The Social System*. Glencoe, Ill.: Free Press, 1951.

Phillimore, Robert. *Commentaries upon International Law*. 4 vols. 3rd. ed. London: Butterworth, 1879.

Pound, Roscoe. *An Introduction to the Philosophy of Law*. Rev. ed. New Haven: Yale University Press, 1954.

Pufendorf, Samuel von. *The Duty of Man and Citizen*. Trans. F. G. Moore. The Classics of International Law. New York: Oxford University Press, 1927.

————. *The Law of Nature and of Nations*. Trans. C. H. and W. A. Oldfather. The Classics of International Law. Oxford: Clarendon Press, 1934.

Quinton, Anthony. "The Bounds of Morality." In Howard E. Kiefer and Milton K. Munitz, eds., *Ethics and Social Justice*, pp. 122-141. Albany: State University of New York Press, 1970.

Rachel, Samuel. *Dissertations on the Law of Nature and of Nations*. Ed. Ludwig von Bar, trans. John Pawley Bate. The Classics of International Law. Washington, D.C.: The Carnegie Institution, 1916.

Ranke, Leopold von. *History of the Latin and Teutonic Na-*

tions from 1494 to 1514. Trans. Philip A. Ashworth. London: George Bell and Sons, 1887.

Rawls, John. *A Theory of Justice.* Cambridge, Mass.: Harvard University Press, 1971.

Raz, Joseph. *The Authority of Law: Essays on Law and Morality.* Oxford: Clarendon Press, 1979.

————. *Practical Reason and Norms.* London: Hutchinson, 1975.

Reisman, W. Michael, and Burns H. Weston, eds. *Toward World Order and Human Dignity: Essays in Honor of Myres S. McDougal.* New York: Free Press, 1976.

Röling, B.V.A. *International Law in an Expanded World.* Amsterdam: Djambatan, 1960.

Ross, W. D. *Aristotle: A Complete Exposition of His Works and Thought.* New York: Meridian Books, 1959.

Rousseau, Jean Jacques. *Oeuvres complètes.* 4 vols. Editions de la Pléiade. Paris: Librairie Gallimard, 1959-1969.

Ryan, John K. *Modern War and Basic Ethics.* Milwaukee: Bruce, 1940.

Saint-Simon, Henri Comte de. "The Reorganization of the European Community." *Selected Writings,* pp. 28-68. Trans. Felix Markham. Oxford: Basil Blackwell, 1952.

Scelle, Georges. *Manuel de droit international public.* Paris: Domat-montchrestien, 1948.

————. "Le phénomène juridique du dédoublement fonctionnel." In Walter Schätzel and Hans-Jürgen Schlochauser, eds., *Rechtsfragen der internationalen organisation: Festschrift für Hans Wehberg,* pp. 324-342. Frankfurt am Main: V. Klostermann, 1956.

————. *Précis de droit des gens: principes et systématique.* 2 vols. Paris: Recueil Sirey, 1932-1934.

————. "Some Reflections on Juridical Personality in International Law." In George A. Lipsky, ed., *Law and Politics in the World Community,* pp. 49-58. Berkeley: University of California Press, 1953.

Schachter, Oscar. "The Invisible College of International

Lawyers." *Northwestern University Law Review*, 72 (1977), 217-226.

————. "Towards a Theory of International Obligation." In Stephen M. Schwebel, ed., *The Effectiveness of International Decisions*, pp. 9-31. Leyden: Sijthoff, 1971.

Schenk, H. G. *The Aftermath of the Napoleonic Wars: The Concert of Europe, An Experiment*. New York: Oxford University Press, 1948.

Schiffer, Walter. *The Legal Community of Mankind*. New York: Columbia University Press, 1954.

Schindler, Dietrich, and Jiri Toman, eds. *The Law of Armed Conflicts: A Collection of Conventions, Resolutions and Other Documents*. 2nd. ed. Alphen aan den Rijn: Sijthoff and Noordhoff, 1981.

Schrecker, Paul. "Leibniz's Principles of International Justice." *Journal of the History of Ideas*, 7 (1946), 484-498.

Simpson, A.W.B. "The Common Law and Legal Theory," *Oxford Essays in Jurisprudence*. 2nd Series. Ed. A.W.B. Simpson. Oxford: Clarendon Press, 1973.

Singer, Peter. *The Expanding Circle: Ethics and Sociobiology*. New York: Farrar, Straus and Giroux, 1981.

Skinner, Quentin. *The Foundations of Modern Political Thought*. 2 vols. Cambridge: Cambridge University Press, 1978.

Sørensen, Max. "Principes de droit international public." Hague Academy of International Law, *Recueil des cours*, 101 (1960), 1-254.

Spaight, J. M. *Air Power and the Cities*. London: Longmans, Green, 1930.

Stowell, Ellery C. *Intervention in International Law*. Washington, D.C.: Byrne, 1921.

Strauss, Leo. *Natural Right and History*. Chicago: University of Chicago Press, 1953.

Strawson, P. F. "Social Morality and Individual Ideal." In G. Wallace and A.D.M. Walker, eds., *The Definition of Morality*, pp. 98-118. London: Methuen, 1970.

Sturzo, Luigi. *The International Community and the Right of*

War. Trans. B. B. Carter. New York: Richard K. Smith, 1930.

Suarez, Francisco. *On the Three Theological Virtues, Faith, Hope, and Charity. Selections from Three Works by Francisco Suarez, S.J*. Trans. G. L. Williams and others. The Classics of International Law. Oxford: Clarendon Press, 1944.

Thomson, David. *Europe Since Napoleon*. 2nd ed. New York: Alfred A. Knopf, 1965.

Thucydides. *The Peloponnesian War*. Trans. Rex Warner. Harmondsworth: Penguin Books, 1972.

Tocqueville, Alexis de. *Democracy in America*. Trans. George Lawrence. Garden City, N.Y.: Doubleday, 1969.

Tönnies, Ferdinand. *Community and Society*. Trans. Charles P. Loomis. East Lansing: Michigan State University Press, 1957.

———. *On Sociology: Pure, Applied, and Empirical*. Selected Writings. Ed. Werner J. Cahnman and Rudolf Heberle. Chicago: University of Chicago Press, 1971.

Triepel, Hans. "Les Rapports entre le droit interne et le droit international." Hague Academy of International Law, *Recueil des cours*, 1 (1923), 77-119.

Tuck, Richard. *Natural Rights Theories: Their Origin and Development*. Cambridge: Cambridge University Press, 1979.

Tucker, Robert W. *The Inequality of Nations*. New York: Basic Books, 1977.

Tunkin, G. I. *Theory of International Law*. Trans. W. E. Butler. Cambridge, Mass.: Harvard University Press. 1974.

Twining, William, and David Miers. *How to Do Things with Rules: A Primer of Interpretation*. London: Weidenfeld and Nicolson, 1976.

Twiss, Travers. *The Law of Nations Considered as Independent Communities*. 2 vols. New ed. Oxford: Clarendon Press, 1884.

Vagts, Detlev F. "Are There No International Lawyers Anymore?" *American Jounral of International Law*, 75 (1981), 134-137.

Vattel, Emerich de. *Le Droit des gens; ou, principes de la loi naturelle appliqués à la conduite et aux affaires des nations et des souverains*. Trans. Charles G. Fenwick. The Classics of International Law. Washington, D.C.: The Carnegie Institution, 1916.

Vincent, R. J. *Nonintervention and International Order*. Princeton: Princeton University Press, 1974.

Vitoria, Franciscus de. *De Indis et de Jure Belli Relectiones*. Ed. Ernest Nys, trans. John Pawley Bate. The Classics of International Law. Washington, D.C.: The Carnegie Institution, 1917.

Voltaire, François Marie Arouet de. *Essai sur les moeurs et l'esprit des nations et sur les principaux faits de l'histoire depuis Charlemagne jusqu'à Louis XIII*. Ed. René Pomeau. 2 vols. Paris: Garnier Frères, 1963.

———. *Le Siècle de Louis XIV*. *Oeuvres complètes*, vols. 14-15. 52 vols. Paris: Garnier Frères, 1877-1885.

Walker, Mack. *Johann Jakob Moser and the Holy Roman Empire of the German Nation*. Chapel Hill: University of North Carolina Press, 1980.

Walters, Francis P. *A History of the League of Nations*. 2 vols. New York: Oxford University Press, 1952.

Walzer, Michael. *Just and Unjust Wars: A Moral Argument with Historical Illustrations*. New York: Basic Books, 1977.

———. "Law, Morality, and the War in Vietnam." Transcript of a talk given at a conference on "America in Vietnam: A Reappraisal," Department of Political Science, State University of New York at Buffalo, September 29, 1978.

———. "The Moral Standing of States: A Response to Four Critics." *Philosophy and Public Affairs*, 9 (1980), 209-229.

———. "Political Decision-Making and Political Education." In Melvin Richter, ed., *Political Theory and Political*

Education, pp. 159-176. Princeton: Princeton University Press, 1980.

Watson, Alan. *The Nature of Law*. Edinburgh: Edinburgh University Press, 1977.

Weber, Max. *Economy and Society: An Outline of Interpretive Sociology*. Ed. Guenther Roth and Claus Wittich. 2 vols. Berkeley: University of California Press, 1978.

——. *The Methodology of the Social Sciences*. Trans. Edward A. Shils and Henry A. Finch. Glencoe, Ill.: Free Press, 1949.

Webster, C. K. *The League of Nations in Theory and Practice*. Boston: Houghton Mifflin, 1933.

Westlake, John. *The Collected Papers of John Westlake on Public International Law*. Ed. Lassa Oppenheim. Cambridge: Cambridge University Press, 1914.

Wheaton, Henry. *Elements of International Law*. 6th. ed. Boston: Little, Brown, 1855.

Wicclair, Mark R. "Human Rights and Intervention." In Peter G. Brown and Douglas MacLean, eds., *Human Rights and U. S. Foreign Policy*, pp. 141-157. Lexington, Mass.: D. C. Heath, 1979.

Wight, Martin. *Power Politics*. Ed. Hedley Bull and Carsten Holbraad. Leicester: Leicester University Press with the Royal Institute of International Affairs, 1978.

——. *Systems of States*. Ed. Hedley Bull. Leicester: Leicester University Press with the London School of Economics and Political Science, 1977.

Wolff, Christian, *The Law of Nations Treated According to the Scientific Method*. Trans. Joseph H. Drake. The Classics of International Law. Oxford: Clarendon Press, 1934.

Wood, Allen W. *Karl Marx*. The Arguments of the Philosophers. London: Routledge and Kegan Paul, 1981.

——. "The Marxian Critique of Justice." *Philosophy and Public Affairs*, 1 (1972), 244-282.

Wright, Quincy. "Peace." In J. Gould and W. L. Kolb, eds.,

A Dictionary of the Social Sciences, pp. 489-490. New York: Free Press, 1964.

Zimmern, Alfred. *The League of Nations and The Rule of Law, 1918-1935*. New York: Macmillan, 1939.

Zouche, Richard. *An Exposition of Fecial Law and Procedure or of Law Between Nations*. Ed. Thomas Erskine Holland, trans. James Leslie Brierly. The Classics of International Law. Washington, D.C.: The Carnegie Endowment for International Peace, 1911.

Index

INDEX

Hegel, G.W.F., 16, 17n
Hinsley, F.H., 56n
Hobbes, Thomas: on idea of law,
71-72, 73, 78n, 122n, 154, 170n;
on law of nations, 41, 41n, 70n,
73, 120, 150n; on law of nature,
229-30, 230n; on relations of
states, 36, 38, 41, 41n, 283; on
the state, 16, 16-17n, 237-38
Hoffmann, Stanley, 46n, 246-47,
316
Holy Alliance, 22-23, 91-92
holy war, 286n
humanitarianism in war, 291-92
human rights, 104, 235, 239-40,
256, 274-77, 292-94, 322

impartiality, 179, 232, 258, 306
independence of states, 20, 22, 52-
53
individual in international society,
235, 236-37, 272-77. See also human rights
individualism, 229-30, 231-32n,
232, 258
instrumentalism, 95, 198-210, 259
instrumental practice, 8-9, 232,
250-51
internal perspective, 30, 30n, 31,
78n, 218
international association, 3-24, 146,
177, 184, 185-86, 216-17, 324.
See also international society
International Court of Justice, 136,
153, 164, 166, 175, 178, 178n,
181, 185
international government, 84-112
International Labor Organization,
108-9, 269
international law, 45, 118n, 149-86,
188-89, 241; as basis of international association, 20, 27, 56-68,
305, 308-9, 310-11, 322-24; China
and, 317-18, 318n; existence of,

137, 146-48; general, 151, 152,
153, 157, 165-66, 167-68, 175,
213; and international morality,
305-8; positive, 64-65, 69, 115-18;
requisites of, 119-21, 123-25,
129-32, 133, 146-48; Soviet view
of, 189, 199, 199n, 211-12, 317-
18; specific character of, 147-48,
149-50, 164-66, 186; United Nations Charter and, 105-7. See also
customary international law; law
of nations; treaties
international lawyer, 158, 173-77,
241, 305, 307
international legislation, 83, 123-25
international morality, 223-24, 233-
50, 305-8
international society, 5-6, 14-16, 18-
24, 27-48, 187. See also society of
states; world society
intervention, 287. See also nonintervention
ius, 257, 257n
ius feciale, 59n
ius gentium, 59, 59-60n
ius inter gentes, 59, 59n

Johnson, D.H.N., 173n
Johnson, James Turner, 281n,
283n, 304n
Jouvenel, Bertrand de, 10n
justice, 12-13, 14, 18, 257-67, 299-
300; distributive, 255-56, 260-65,
268-71; formal, 258, 259, 261,
265; international, 255-56, 267-
75, 322; United Nations Charter
and, 106; in war, 242, 278-304
just war, see justice in war

Kant, Immanuel, 75-76, 120, 185,
229, 231-32, 309; on international
relations, 22, 70, 74-75, 118, 283
Kelson, Hans, 16, 126, 129-30, 168-
69, 285n; on international law,

347

skepticism *(cont.)*
91, 195. *See also* rule-skepticism
society of states, 27, 43, 44-47, 49-
50, 60n, 84, 309; justice in, 267-
71. *See also* international society
sources of law, *see* validity
sovereignty, 52, 53, 54, 237-40,
280, 287
state, 4, 16-18, 21, 43, 45-46, 50-
51, 51n, 52, 183; legal order of,
146-47; as moral agent, 234-35
state of nature, 36, 38, 40, 70, 72
state practice, 7n, 60, 63-65, 167,
173
states system, 21-22, 29, 42, 49-68.
See also society of states
Strauss, Leo, 230n
Strawson, P.F., 227, 227n
Suarez, Francisco, 59-60n, 286,
287n

theory, international relations, x-xi,
29, 29-34, 76n, 118, 313. *See also*
empirical condition; essential
characteristic
Tocqueville, Alexis de, 312
toleration, 12, 18n, 226, 315, 318,
324; in international relations, 5,
50, 58. *See also* coexistence
Tönnies, Ferdinand, 13-14n
tradition, 7, 13n, 116, 250; moral,
223, 227-29, 241-43, 244
transnational relations, 47, 91, 158,
162, 163
treaties, 7-8, 15, 310; binding force
of, 152, 154, 212, 214-16; interpretation of, 71-72, 182, 208-9;
law-making, 124; Vattel on, 62
Tucker, Robert W., 273n
Tunkin, G.I., 317-18

uncertainty, 135, 138-39, 146, 193-
94; of international law, 166, 179,
181-82, 306; of treaties, 71-72

United Nations, 104-12, 124-25,
166, 175-76, 184; Charter of, 104,
105, 110-12, 282, 283n; purposive
conception of, 23, 105-8, 110,
112
utilitarianism, 293, 294, 296, 297n,
299-304

Vagts, Detlev F., 174n
validity, 126-27, 155-56, 157, 217-
19, 231; of international law, 157-
58, 165-66, 168-72, 174, 176,
215-16
values, shared: as basis of association, 14, 93-94, 203-4, 213-15,
311-22; international law as instrument of, 187-88, 201-4; and
international order, 311-23. *See
also* purposes, shared
Vattel, Emmerich de, 21, 62-63,
74, 286
vital interests, 37
Vitoria, Franciscus de, 52, 286
Voltaire, François Marie Arouet de,
61-62, 309
voluntarism, 95, 210-16

Walzer, Michael, 223n, 243-49,
286, 292n, 297-304
war, 38, 80, 99-100, 279-94; initiation of, 279-87; conduct of, 97,
287-94
Watson, Alan, 145n
Weber, Max, 13-14n, 34n
Wight, Martin, 3n, 37, 56n, 286n,
315-16
Wolff, Christian, 54, 60n
world order, 23, 23n
world society, 42-44, 46-47, 49, 59,
60n, 63, 273. *See also* international society

Zouche, Richard, 59n

Library of Congress Cataloging in Publication Data
Nardin, Terry, 1942–
Law, morality, and the relations of states.
Bibliography: p.   Includes index.
1. International law. 2. International relations—
Moral and ethical aspects. I. Title.
JX1255.N28   1984   341'.01   83-42570
ISBN 0-691-07663-4
ISBN 0-691-10155-8 (lim. pbk. ed.)